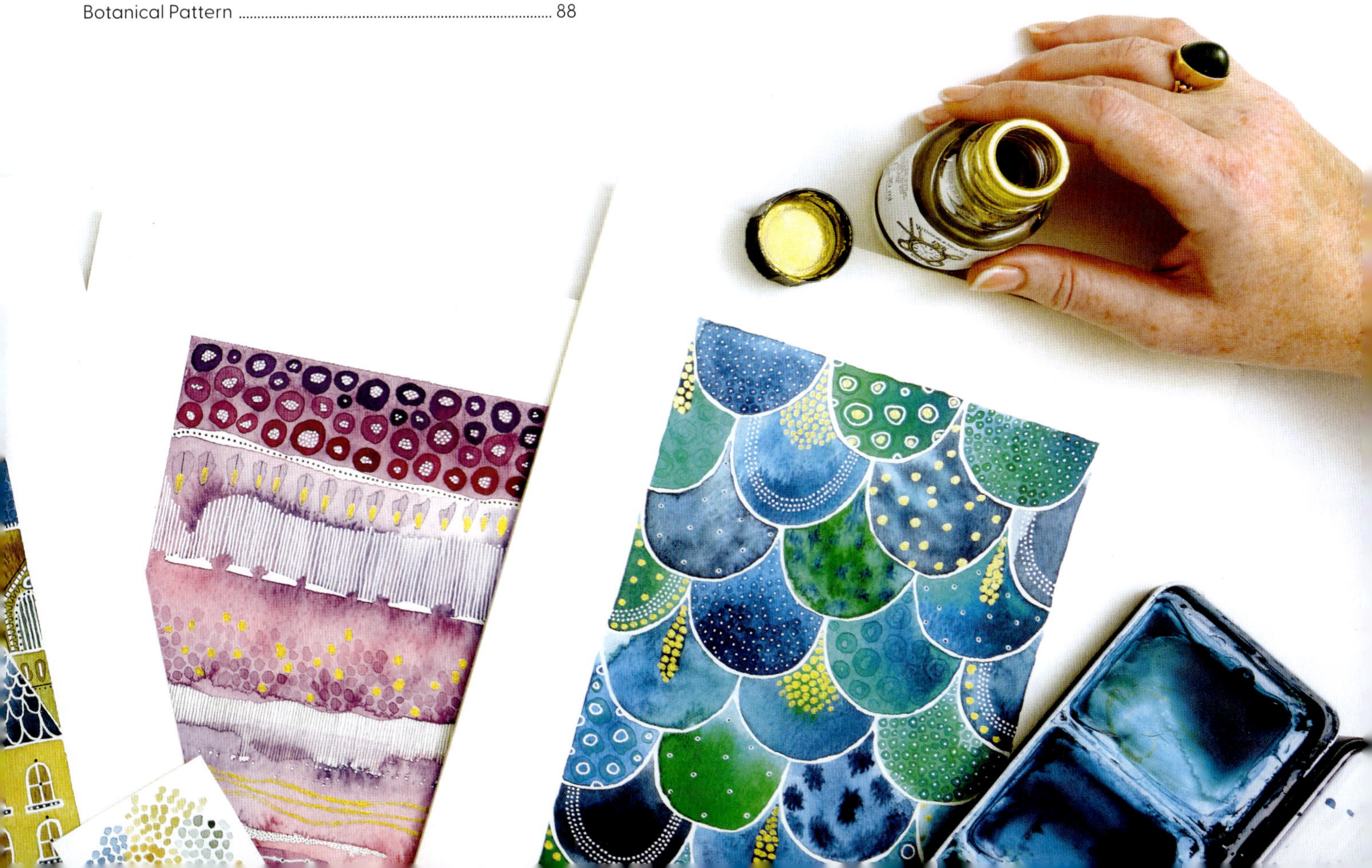

Introduction

I have always been a creative person, from extravagantly decorated cakes, to homemade gifts and crafts. I love to work with my hands, putting a little of myself into everything I do. Following an education in art, this was my only creative outlet for over twenty years, and then the great lockdown of 2020 hit!

To break up the monotony of weeks at home, and feeling a drive for creativity and purpose, I picked up a set of ancient watercolors bought many years before and left to grow dusty in a drawer. From the moment I began painting again, I felt a huge sense of calm and contentment (but finding my style and creating work I was proud of took a little longer!). As a creative person who nonetheless admits to having no skills in faithfully recreating people, objects, or landscapes, it left me with the quandary – what to paint? This question led to my journey of discovery through color, texture, and mark making – my love of abstract watercolors was born!

But why do I love watercolor, and why will *you*? To start with, I love to let the paint (and more importantly, the water) lead the way. Watercolor's charm is in its relaxed flow, which I like to get caught up in. Its fluid quality means the paint is not always easily controlled – happy accidents are bountiful. The result is the unexpected merging of color, textured "blooms" (more about those later), and other stunning effects too numerous to mention.

Watercolor has had a huge impact on my life and mental health. Some may choose meditation or yoga, but for me, the uncomplicated and freeing nature of abstract watercolor is a form of mindfulness. It allows me to switch off, unplug from the digital world, and unwind from the day-to-day pressures we all face.

In this book, you'll discover the best painting materials that I've found through *much* research, and even more trial and error. With a modest set of paints, a jam jar of water, a few brushes, and some paper, you will be all set to embark on your watercolor journey. There are simple techniques to help you create shapes and patterns, and step-by-step projects that let the paint lead the way. Discover new color palettes, mark-making and masking tricks as you create your art.

By writing this book, my aim is to share the simple skills required to create watercolor art fit to grace the finest of walls! Not only will it arm you with the skills to help you create, but also (hopefully!) the encouragement and inspiration to find your own style.

Happy painting!

Kate

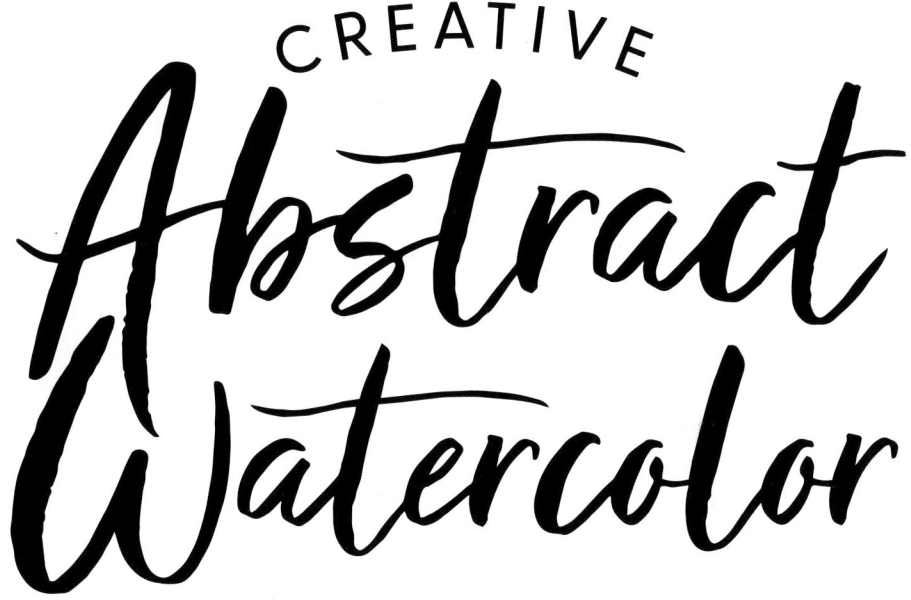

CREATIVE Abstract Watercolor

The beginner's guide to expressive and imaginative painting

KATE REBECCA LEACH

DAVID & CHARLES
—PUBLISHING—

www.davidandcharles.com

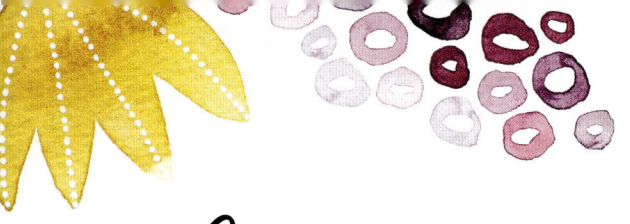

Contents

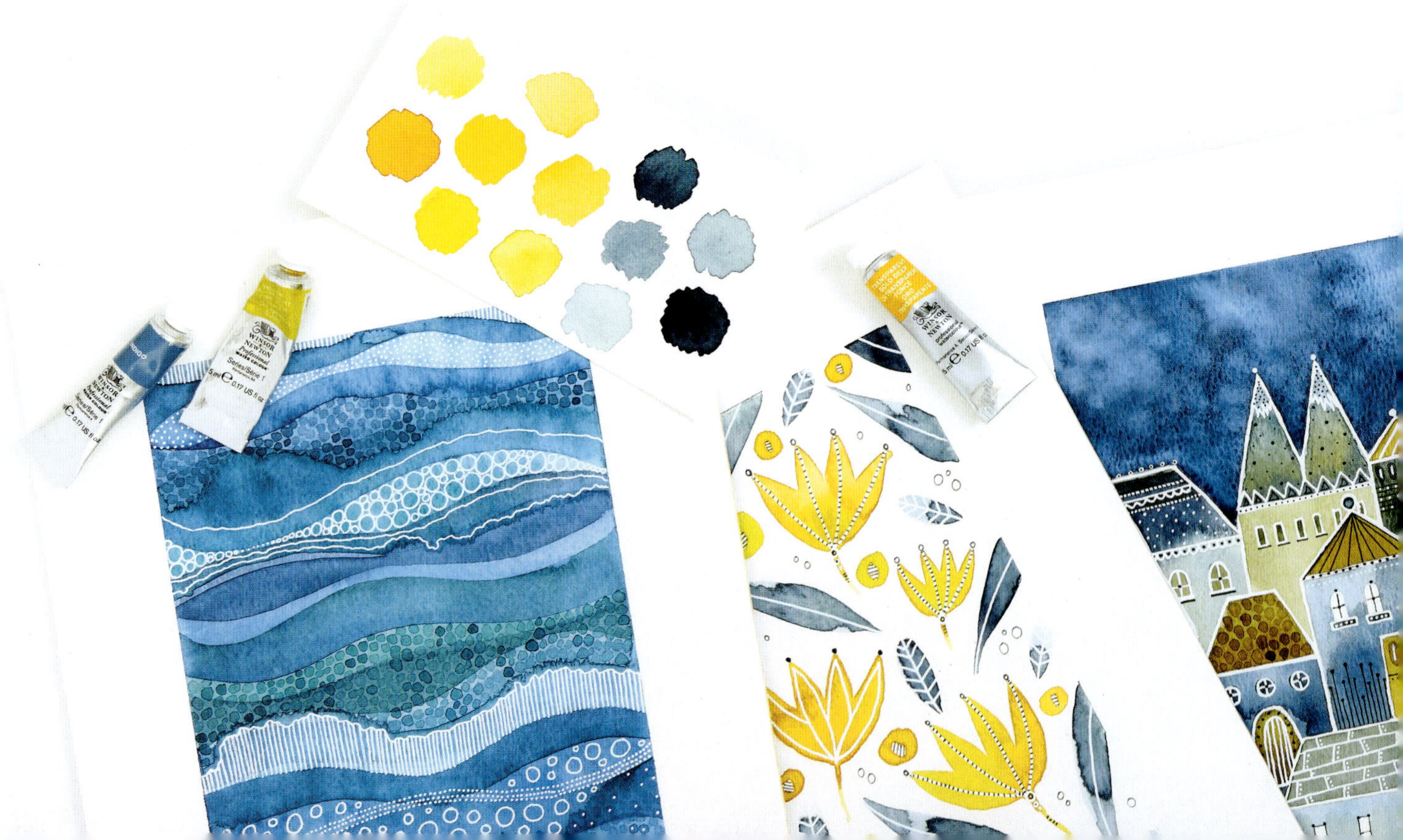

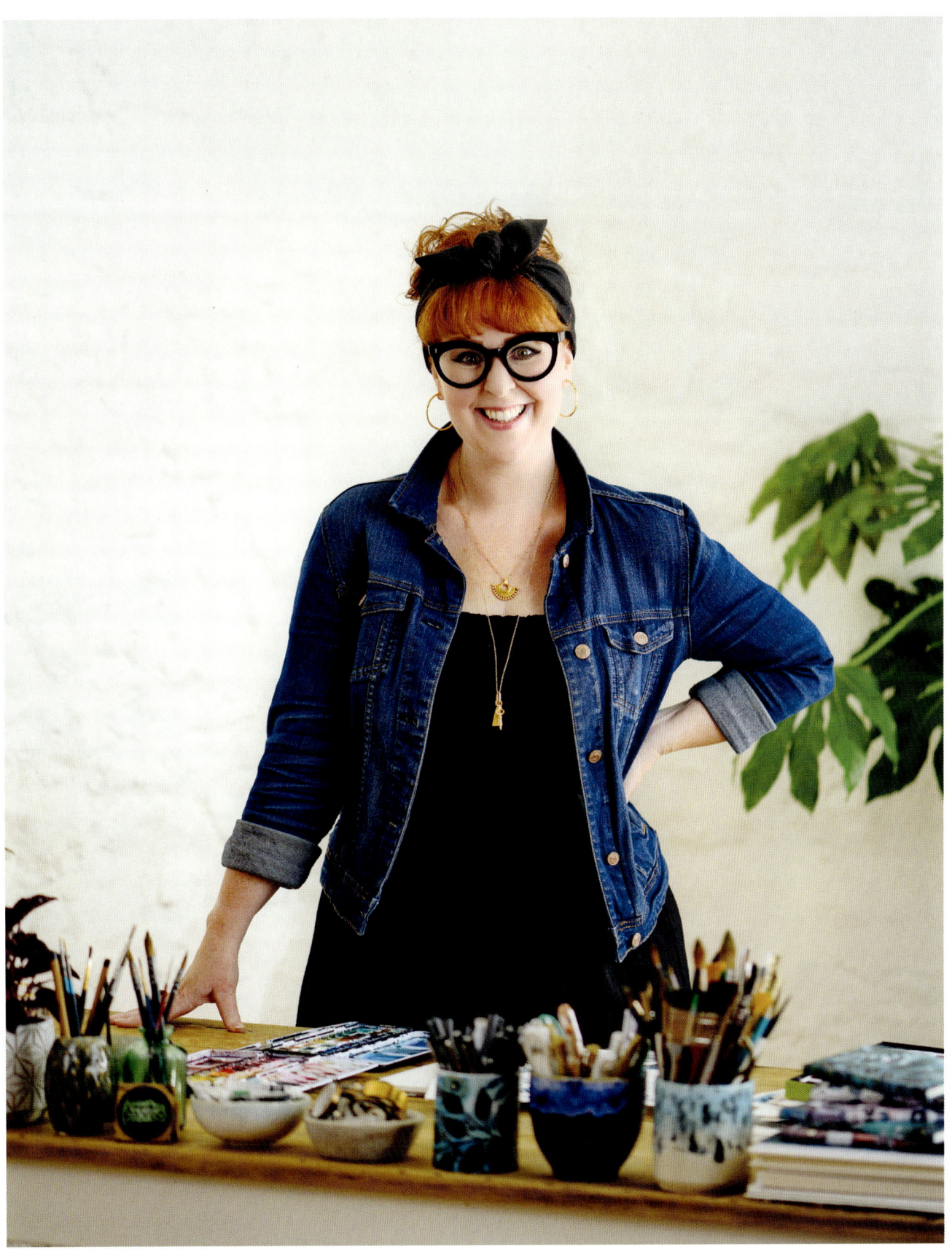

What is Abstract Art?

"Abstract art is art that does not attempt to represent an accurate depiction of a visual reality but instead use shapes, colors, forms and gestural marks to achieve its effect" **Tate Gallery**

This definition by one of my favorite galleries helps to sum up the answer. The general definition is subjective, but usually refers to art that is made from the imagination. Or put simply, not recreating in art something from the real world.

What abstract art means to me

For me, abstract art is a form of expression where I let simple shapes, colors, textures, and mark making do the talking! I'm not trying to recreate a human face, vase of flowers, or landmark, but simply use my paints to produce pleasing shapes, textures, and designs. These come from my imagination, or by letting "happy accidents" and the flow of the paint dictate the look. Some of my favorite paintings have started with a simple idea, then the way the watercolor paint has run, merged, and dried has led to the finished design.

Discovering abstract artists

To fully understand abstract art, I look at the work of artists throughout the movement. Not to recreate their styles, but to find inspiration in their use of color, shape, texture, and composition to create art outside our day-to-day reality. I imagine a scene behind their painting, creating a story from the art based on my own thoughts and feelings. I've spent many hours at galleries such as Tate Modern, London, sitting in awe as I experience the works of talented artists of the twentieth century and earlier. If you haven't already discovered the following abstract artists, check them out!

- Wassily Kandinsky
- Joan Miró
- Mark Rothko
- Paul Klee

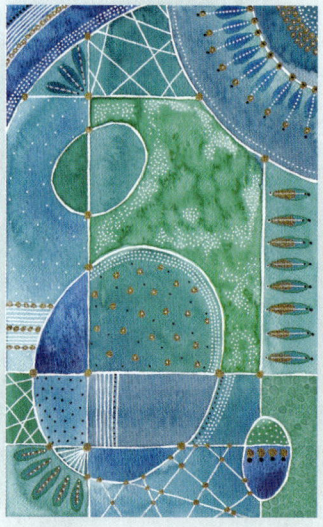

This painting is a great example of what "abstract art" means to me (see Abstract Shapes: Freestyle Abstract).

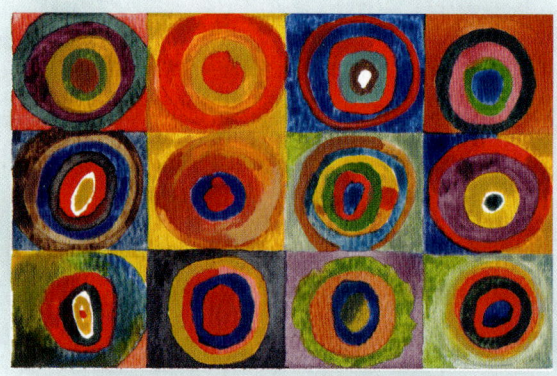

The famous work "Color Study. Squares with Concentric Circles" (1913) by Wassily Kandinsky, painted in my own style.

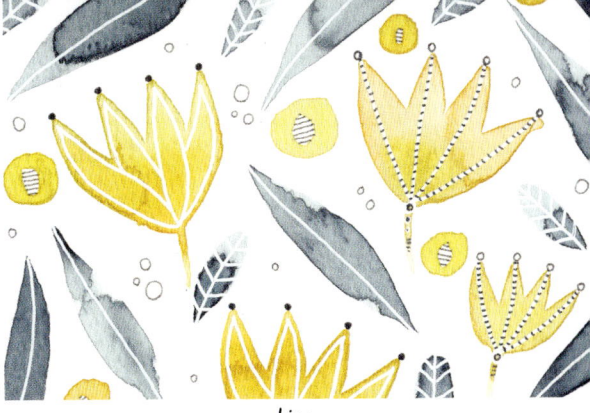

Line

SIX KEY ELEMENTS

To write this section of the book, I had to go "back to school" and revisit these key elements of abstract art. While these elements are useful to know about, don't get too hung up on sticking to these "rules". I prefer to go with the flow and simply do what feels right for each individual piece!

THE KEY ELEMENTS

Line   *Color*

Shape   *Value*

Form   *Texture*

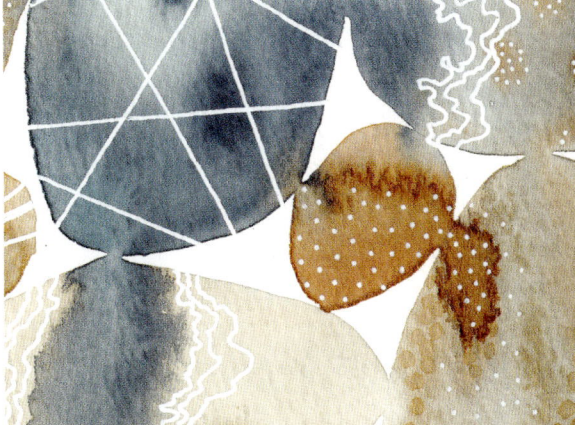

Shape and form

Line

For many artists, line is the most important facet of abstract art. These botanicals are simple outlines, but the additional white lines draw the viewer's eye up and through the composition. The lines also help to give form to the leaves (*see* Abstract Botanicals: Botanical Pattern).

Shape and form

Although they appear impossibly balanced, each ellipse in this design is believable as a pebble thanks to subtle shade and light, hinting at their three-dimensional form. Where they touch, each pebble "flows" into the next, guiding your eye over the canvas to create the overall form (*see* Abstract Shapes: Irregular Pebbles).

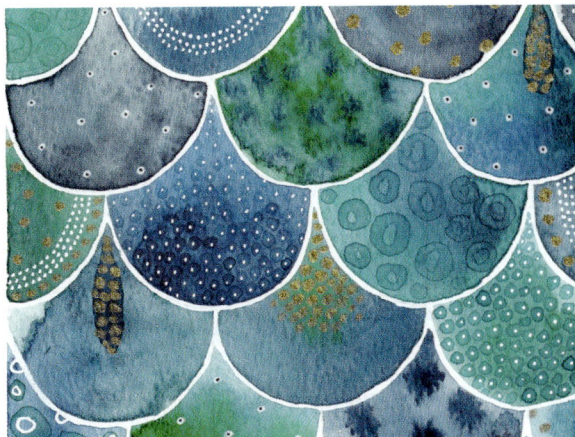

Color and value

Color and value

This simple scallop pattern paired with aquatic hues creates a strong color story. But playing with value (how light or dark the colors appear) also builds contrast. The pattern is transformed from flat shapes, to a form with depth. The dimensional, layered effect draws the eye into the canvas (*see* Abstract Shapes: Soothing Scallops).

Texture

Light-reflecting gold ink and white blooms recall a misty, moonlit night, while bright pinpoints of white add to the mysterious night sky. The clusters of gold dots evoke the moon's iconic bright and cratered surface (*see* Abstract Landscapes: Moonlight Seascape).

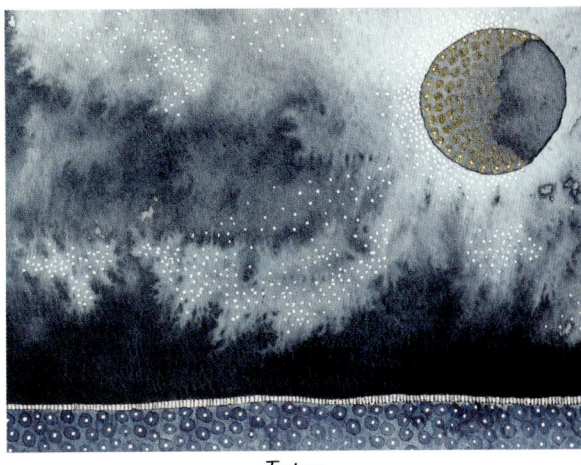

Texture

THE ELEMENTS IN MY OWN ART

It's true that the key elements of abstract art – color, texture, shape, line, value, and form – apply to most art forms. But it's fascinating to see how such fundamentals exist in even the most abstract painting. For example, darker values and smaller shapes still create depth and perspective. Colors such as bold red, serene green, or ethereal lilac can suggest mood or temperature. Lines – straight, curved, regimented, criss-crossing – add structure, movement, or form. You'll see in this book how texture is key in my own art, deliberately (or accidentally) creating shape and form. Maybe "happy accidents" work by organically suggesting one or more of these elements for you to develop further!

ABSTRACT SHAPES: BOLD BLOCKS

*Grouped thin **lines** create simple **texture** and structure.*

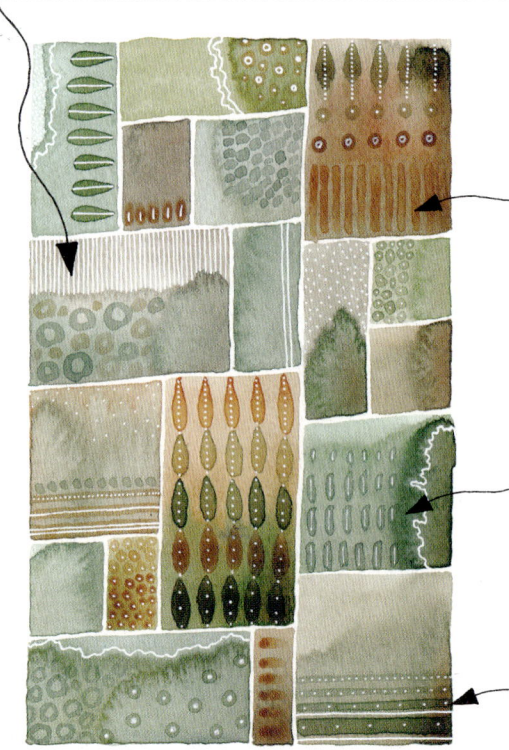

ABSTRACT LANDSCAPES: UNDERWATER WORLD

*Concentric circles add **form**, while detailed **texture** and darker **values** draw the eye into the distance.*

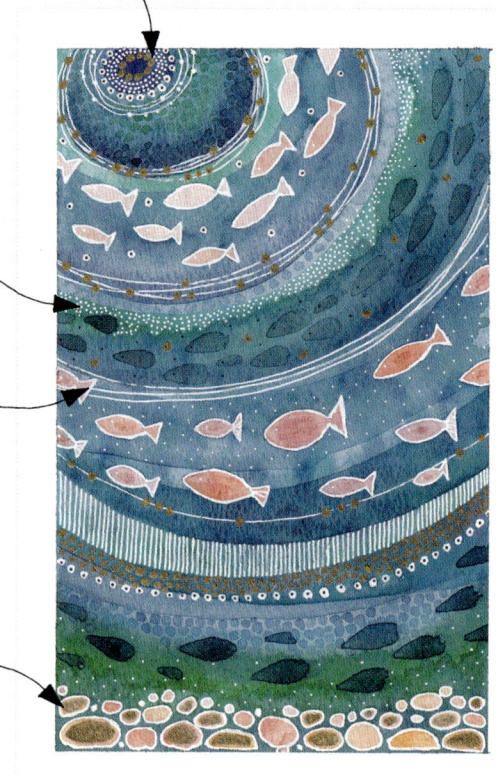

*Bright, cool **colors** suggest water and sunlight.*

***Lines** swirl to convey movement.*

*Warm colored pebbles add grounding with **shape** and **form**.*

*The **color** palette, **shapes** and **textures** evoke a rustic mood, but a different palette would transform the feeling.*

*Multiple **values** of the same color add depth and interest to each block, and the composition overall.*

*White embellishments add definition, and prevent the **color** palette from looking muddy.*

MY INSPIRATION

People often share with me how my art makes them feel, or what they believe inspired the piece. I love the fact that my work is subjective; much of the time their thoughts or ideas on the piece are very different to my own original inspiration.

Sitting down with a blank sheet of paper is daunting for many. But I love the excitement of a new piece – I'm never entirely sure how it will turn out, or which direction I'll take. I let the paint flow and go from there!

Nature, from flowers and greenery to gemstones and jewels, inspires me. I'm obsessed with embellishment (as my jewelry collection will attest!), so my work features a myriad of dots, decorations, and – most importantly – gold (although silver, pearl, copper, and gunmetal occasionally appear). I have items on my desk to inspire me – a beautiful leaf, a bejeweled vintage brooch, or a delicate shell. Even a simple postcard or magazine page can inspire with color, texture, or shape.

Finding your abstract mindset:

- Create a relaxing environment – even the smallest space is perfect for painting.

- Keep inspiration close by.

- Embrace the "happy accidents".

- Follow the flow of paint and water.

- Feed your obsession (in my case, embellishment!).

Top Tip: Pinterest is a useful resource. My aim is always to be original and never copy other artists, but it's a great place to find inspiration for color, shape and mark making.

When I sit down to paint, a calm, relaxed environment is as important as brushes and paper. I like to surround myself with my favorite objects, including various sources of inspiration and creative sparks. Then I'll pop on some music or an audio book, make a cup of tea, and settle down to see where the paint takes me...

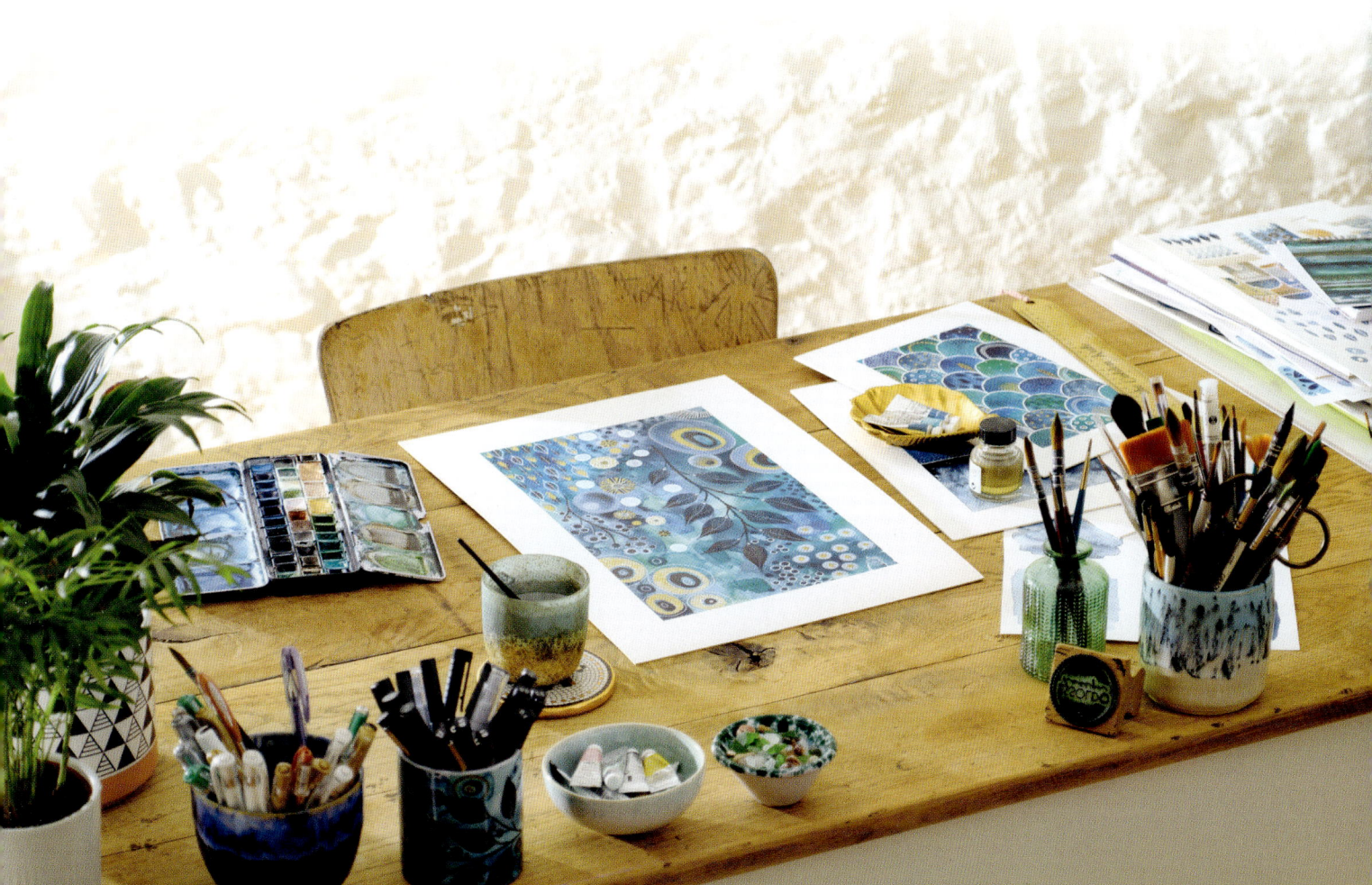

Materials

I found the subject of materials to be a minefield when starting out! The vast array of paints, papers, brushes, and more is incredibly hard to narrow down to a basic kit. Don't be daunted – it really is as simple as a small set of watercolors, a pad of paper, a brush or two, and a jam jar of water! This is how I started, and it stood me in good stead. Over the last three years of research, trial, and error, I've found my favorite materials, so here are my recommendations for your kit.

PAINT

Most paints can be bought in sets, which provides a useful collection of basic colors as you're learning. Paints can also be bought in individual colors, allowing you to buy an empty tin and create your own set.

FORMAT

Watercolor paint mainly comes in two formats – tubes of liquid paint, and small square or rectangular "pans" of dried paint. I prefer pans, as they're economical, portable, and easy to use. But I also have a variety of my favorite and most-used shades in tubes – I'll often mix a generous quantity of these in my palette before I even begin painting.

QUALITY

Many brands come in a choice of grade – either student or professional. Student paints are a great price, but contain far less pigment than their professional counterparts, so lack the same depth of color. I recommend buying the best paints you can afford – they last ages, especially pans! My first painting sessions started with an old set of Winsor & Newton's student range, Cotman. I quickly progressed to their professional watercolors, which I have used throughout this book.

TIPS FOR BUYING PAINT

- **Refill and reuse:** When using a set of pans, you may run out of one color more quickly than the rest. If so, buy that color in a tube and use this to refill the empty pan, letting it dry in the pan. Never throw away an empty pan – it can be filled and reused (as I'm self-taught, I didn't know this for my first year of painting!).

- **Shop around:** Many art shops and online suppliers offer great prices on basic sets, often saving up to fifty percent. Paint is the one material that I believe it's worth spending a little extra on – you'll get better results and will not regret it.

- **Experiment:** I use mainly Winsor & Newton professional watercolor pans and tubes, but I enjoy exploring other paints from time to time. For example, I've used Kuretake sets. These oversized pans are available in a fantastic array of colors. Their thicker paint can be used more like a gouache, which can give interesting results.

Top Tip: Look for paint that is lightfast, such as Winsor & Newton. Your painting will retain its true color and vibrancy when proudly out on display.

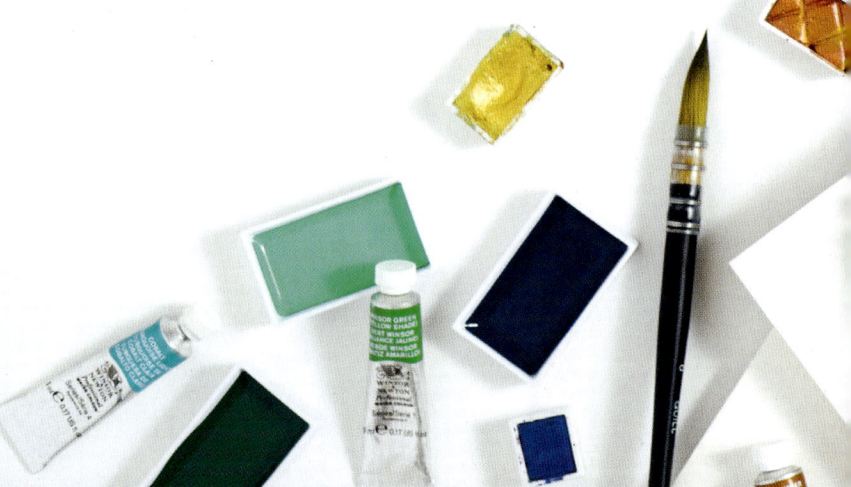

PAPER

Quite literally the foundation of your work, your paper dictates how colors blend, how the water washes across the page, and how the paint pigments settle. The right paper can help to create a variety of patterns through its texture alone.

TEXTURE

Watercolor paper usually comes in three main types.

- **Smooth:** Also known as "hot pressed", the very smooth surface allows you to create small and intricate details.

- **Cold pressed:** Also called NOT, as in *not* hot pressed, this is my preferred paper. Its pleasing texture reveals the natural properties of watercolor, and it is suitable for beginners.

- **Rough:** The most heavily textured paper used in watercolor. It feels similar to the thicker, grainier texture of handmade paper and is ideal for very loose abstract pieces.

WEIGHT

All watercolor paper, whatever the texture, is labelled to show its weight. The measurement used is "gsm" (grams per square meter). I recommend starting out with 300gsm paper – it's sturdy and good to experiment and practice on.

FORMAT

Paper comes in many formats – here are the four main types.

- **Loose sheets:** Inexpensive, so ideal for building muscle memory, practicing techniques, and generally having fun!

- **Sketchbook:** Keeps all your work together, so great for beginners and trying new techniques or ideas. As you grow in skills, you can flick through to chart your progress! Spiral binding keeps the pages flat and stable as you paint.

- **Pad:** Pages of paper glued along one edge. The "pages" can be kept together, or removed to give you loose sheets.

- **Glued block:** Pages glued along all four edges; a small opening lets you lift away each finished page. The top page is kept taut by the pages beneath, so is less likely to buckle or ripple (similar to watercolor board but more budget-friendly). So, you don't have to wet and pre-stretch your paper – this feels like a lot of work, and so I never do!

- **Watercolor board:** A very rigid board with a sheet of watercolor paper already adhered to one side. This allows you to use lots of paint and water, and the paper won't buckle or bend (this can happen with thinner paper). Look for watercolor board covered with cold-pressed paper.

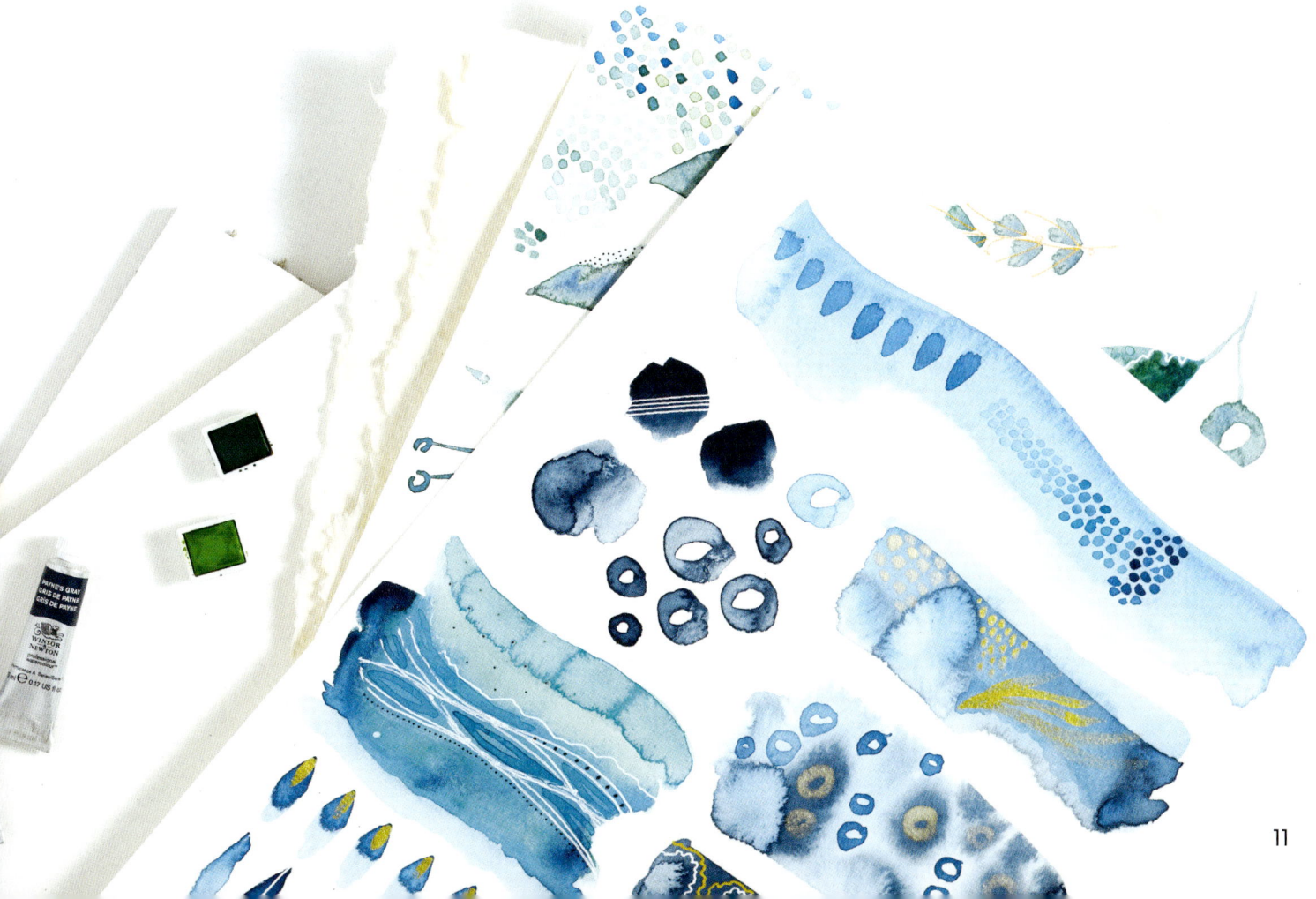

BRUSHES

I feel as if I've tried most of the many, *many* brushes out there! Early on I purchased several, but used only a handful on repeat. A few basics available from art suppliers is all you need to get started. Here is what I use and recommend.

QUILL BRUSH

This is a great all-round brush. Its full "belly" and fine point allow you to make both full, sweeping marks and delicate details. Quill brushes also hold lots of paint or water, meaning you can paint for longer before returning to your palette.

I use... the Jackson's Icon quill brushes. I have a range of sizes, but size 0 is a must, size 000 is useful for finer details, and size 4 is for large washes.

ROUND BRUSH

Another great all-round brush for mark making and details. Sizes 0, 4 and 8 provide a useful range for getting started.

I use... Daler Rowney round brushes – I've built a small collection over the years.

FILBERT BRUSH

The wider flat side and narrower edge of this versatile, sturdy brush create lots of interesting marks. The bristles form a flattened oval head, which I use to create my raindrop spots.

I use... an ancient Daler Rowney filbert brush – a keepsake from my art student days! Size 3 or 4 is the most useful.

MASKING SUPPLIES

Where your paint *doesn't* go is as important as where it does! I use a couple of products to create everything from tiny details to sharp, bold borders.

MASKING TAPE

Good tape is an absolute essential in your beginner's tool kit! Used to mask off simple shapes and create soft torn edges, it's also a must for preserving a crisp white border (*see* Techniques: Masking Borders). I use Frog Tape Yellow Delicate Surface Painter's Tape in 24mm (1in) and 36mm (1½in) widths. The tape can also be used instead of masking fluid to cover simple shapes or areas you want to protect from paint.

MASKING FLUID

What if you want to mask off more complex shapes? This is where masking fluid comes into its own! For example, you might want to retain clean white shapes, free of paint, in your design but still use bold watercolor washes. Masking fluid would be applied to those shapes first. Once dry, you can paint over the paper and the masking fluid, then remove the fluid when the paint is dry (*see* Techniques: Masking Shapes and Highlights).

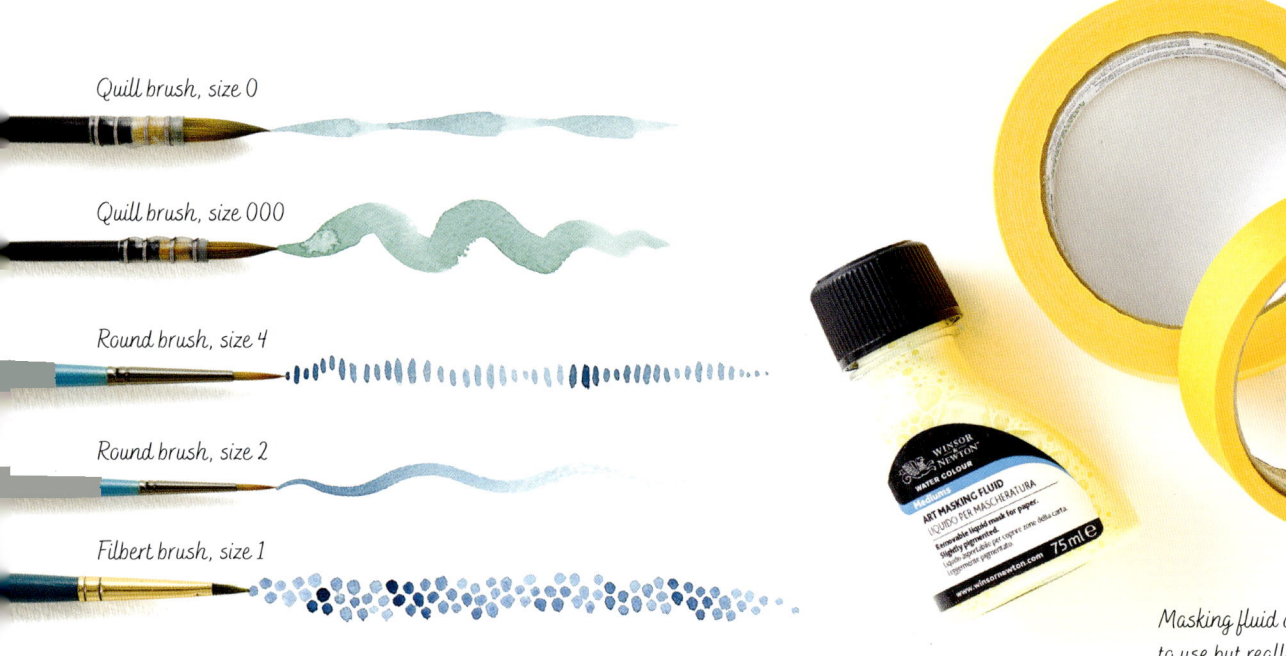

Quill brush, size 0

Quill brush, size 000

Round brush, size 4

Round brush, size 2

Filbert brush, size 1

Masking fluid and tape are simple to use but really elevate your art.

INK AND PENS

In addition to paint, there are other mediums that play nicely with watercolor, allowing you to add refined details and embellishments to your art.

METALLIC INK

As I've already mentioned, I love to embellish my work by painting metallic details and highlights over the watercolor base. There are fantastic metallic watercolors on the market, but I find that metallic inks create the best color and shine! I enjoy the Winsor & Newton metallic inks. The thick metallic pigment and clear liquid solution separate in the bottle, so shake well to combine before use. Use a filbert brush for spots, or a small round brush for other details.

PENS

Much like metallic inks, pens can be used on top of your finished painting to add texture, new color, or details. This is sometime called "mixed media" – using extra materials over your watercolor base. I use a range of pens to add lines, dots, details, and more. These are the best pens I've found:

White and metallic gel pens

Uni-ball Signo gel ink pens flow well and add nice opaque coverage, even when working over darker colors. I use the size "Broad", which is actually only 1mm! This size allows for well-defined line work as well as delicate details.

White paint pens

Posca paint pens are fantastic for dots, dashes, and other embellishments. I wouldn't be without them in a range of sizes to suit the scale and style of piece I'm working on.

Black fineliners

These are a great tool to add to your kit – they make adding details easy and precise. I use a range of sizes, from ultra-fine 0.1mm for very delicate lines up to 0.8mm for larger dot work.

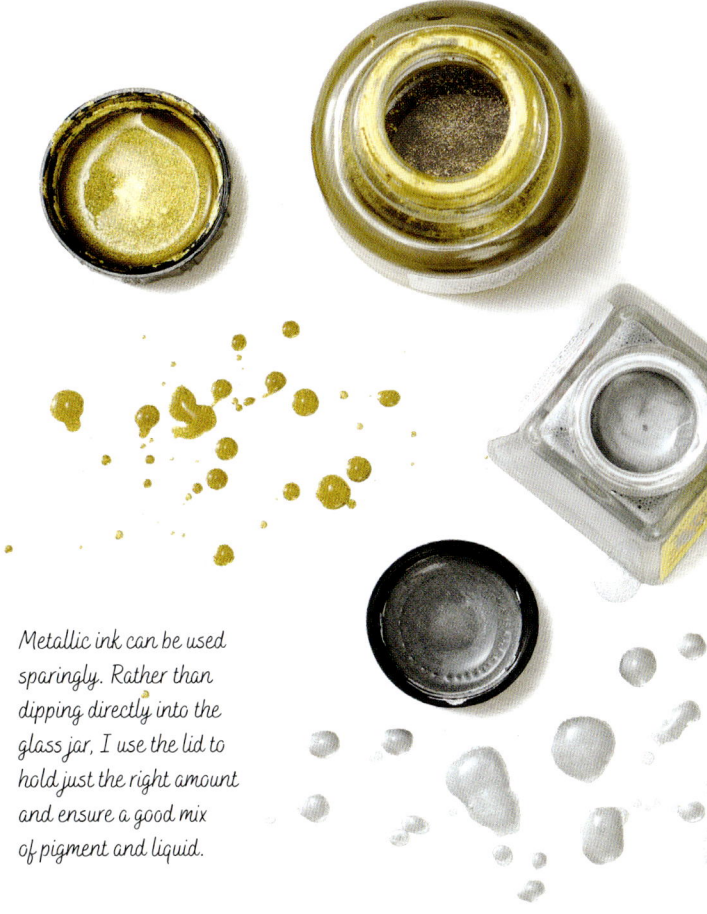

Metallic ink can be used sparingly. Rather than dipping directly into the glass jar, I use the lid to hold just the right amount and ensure a good mix of pigment and liquid.

Top Tip: If adding paint over ink pens, make sure that the pens are waterproof to avoid your marks smudging and running!

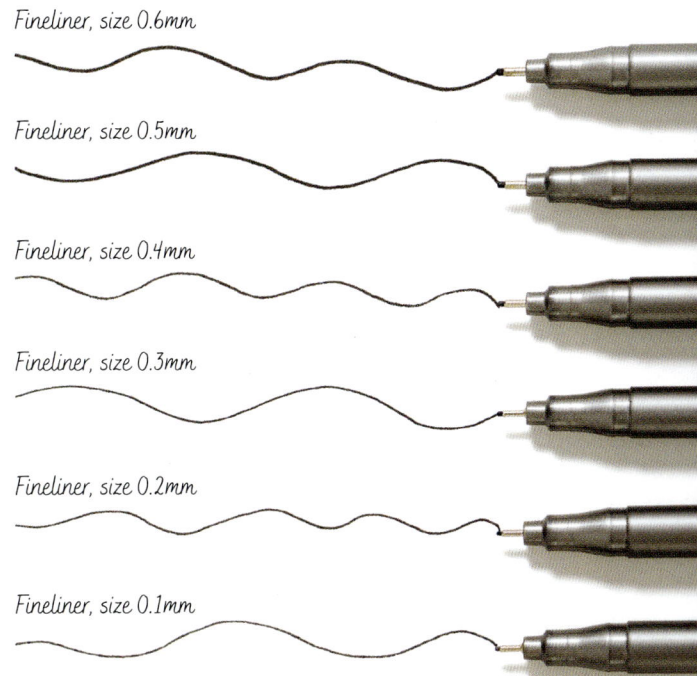

Fineliner, size 0.6mm

Fineliner, size 0.5mm

Fineliner, size 0.4mm

Fineliner, size 0.3mm

Fineliner, size 0.2mm

Fineliner, size 0.1mm

Color Philosophy

When writing this book, I knew I would have to give an overview of color – both how it is used and my own particular preferences. Having studied art at college and university, I must have covered the color wheel and traditional color theory at some point – but that very much feels like the dim and distant past! Picking up my paints over twenty years later, I'm very relaxed with my color choices, preferring to work with hues I'm naturally drawn to rather than the prescribed colors that supposedly "work" together. In this section, I'll guide you through a few of my favorite colors and palettes, and how I use them.

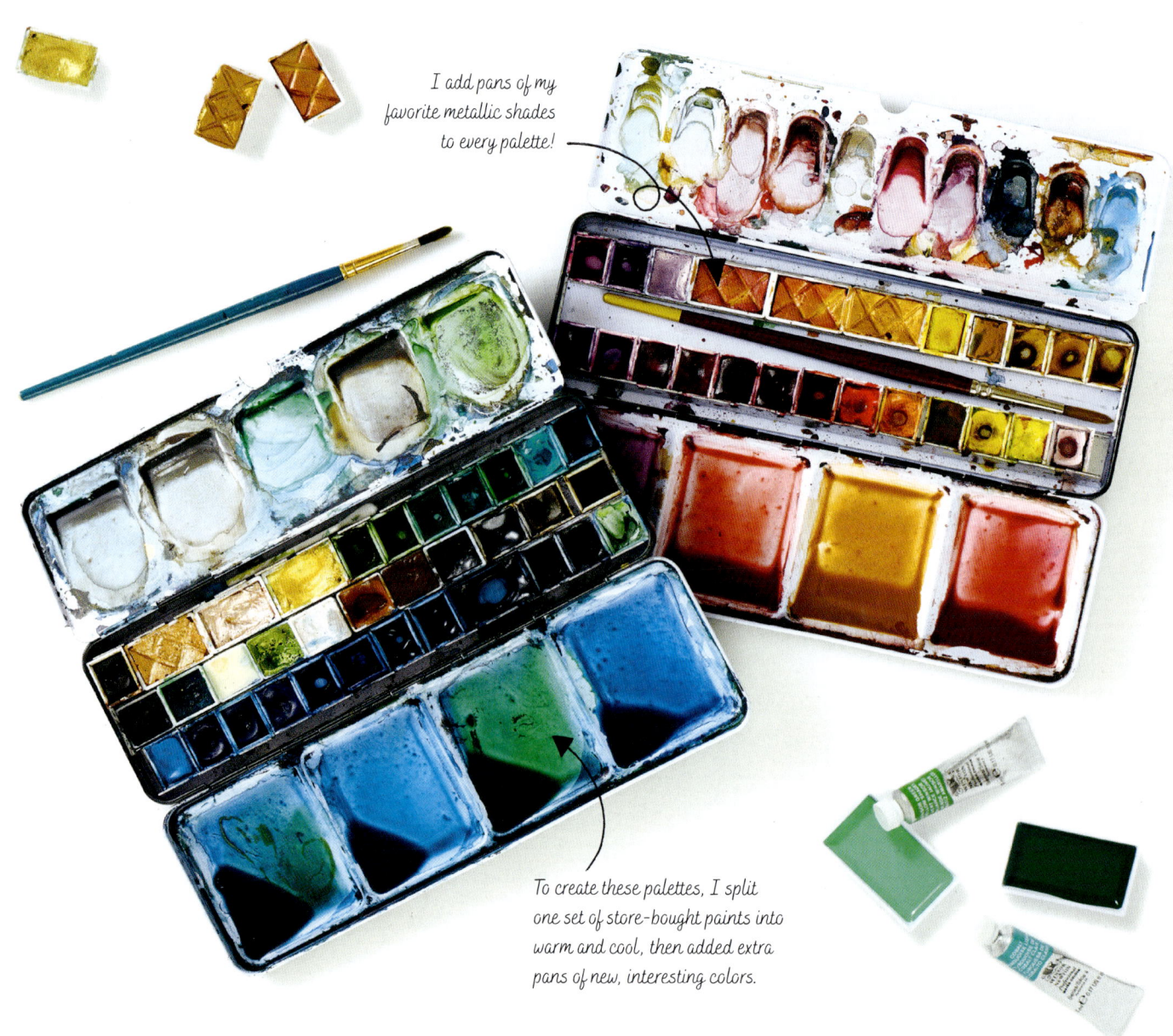

I add pans of my favorite metallic shades to every palette!

To create these palettes, I split one set of store-bought paints into warm and cool, then added extra pans of new, interesting colors.

ANALOGOUS PALETTES

Looking at my work in preparation for this chapter, I saw that I not only like to work with the warm *or* cool side of the color wheel, but I also choose an even narrower "slice". These groups of adjacent colors are often referred to as "analogue" palettes – colors that sit together on the color wheel. Analogue palettes are a safe bet when creating a harmonious look that's pleasing to the eye, with no one color standing out too prominently. I often use a pop of metallic (gold in particular) to help add highlights and contrast.

Top Tip: To add interest, you can use an "accent" color that stands out from the rest. You're most likely to find these colors on the opposite side of the color wheel from your analogous segment.

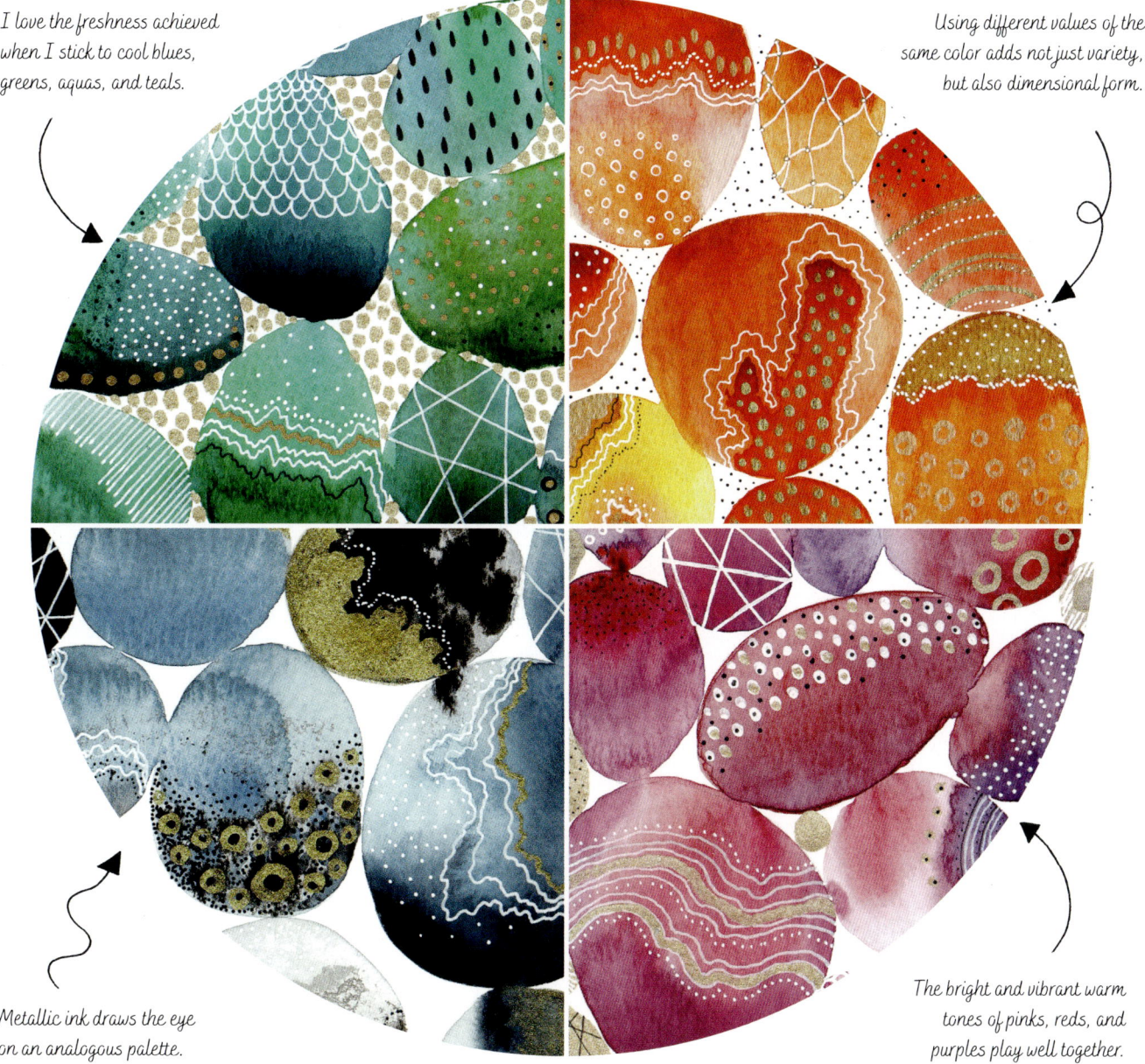

I love the freshness achieved when I stick to cool blues, greens, aquas, and teals.

Using different values of the same color adds not just variety, but also dimensional form.

Metallic ink draws the eye on an analogous palette.

The bright and vibrant warm tones of pinks, reds, and purples play well together.

PAYNE'S GRAY

My favorite and most used color is Payne's Gray. I have pans and tubes of it, and have tried a variety of brands. This color is both beautiful and versatile. Try using it to deepen colors for rich, muted tones; it gives a much softer look than the traditional Ivory Black included in most paint sets.

Monochrome palette

Payne's Gray can also be used in various strengths (mixed with more or less water) to create a soft, inviting palette of beautiful blue-gray. This kind of palette is often called "monochrome" – the use of a single color to create a design.

Top Tip: If your monochrome piece looks a little "flat", wait for it to dry, then add contrast with a second layer of paint (*see* Techniques: Wet On Dry). This will add depth and contrast while retaining the monochrome effect.

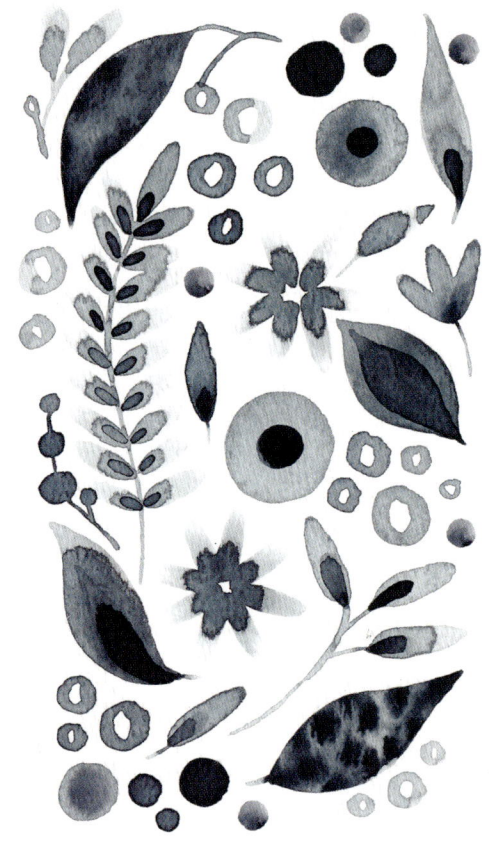

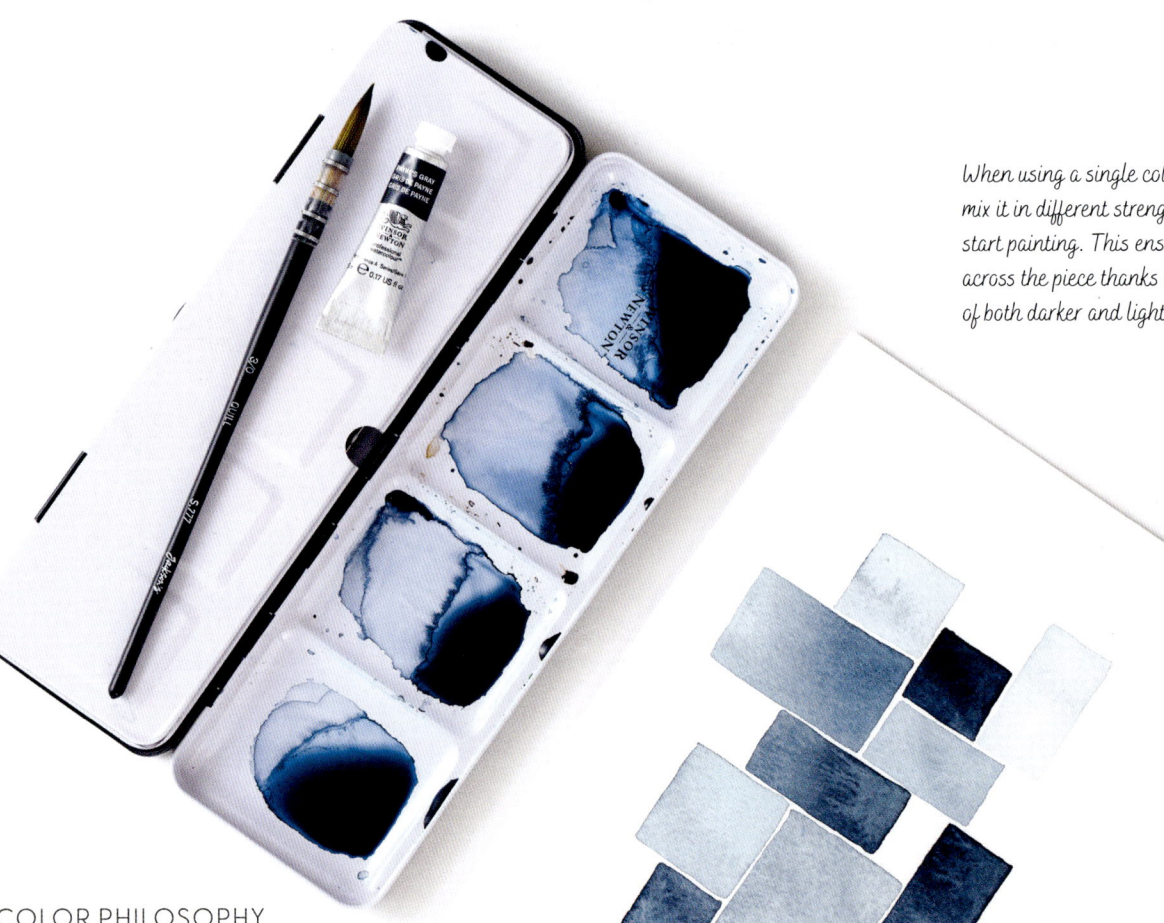

When using a single color, I like to mix it in different strengths before I start painting. This ensures contrast across the piece thanks to the presence of both darker and lighter tones.

COLOR MIXING

Color is a wonderful way to evoke a particular feeling or mood, and with watercolors you will often create a multitude of new colors and tones as the paint moves and merges. I love to mix my own colors in the palette, often creating new and interesting tones. This also doubles the size of your palette using only the existing shades.

The projects

At the start of each project, I'll tell you which paint colors I have used to create the palette shown. However, it's entirely up to you which colors and mixes you use, and I also share ideas for alternative palettes. Keep trying different shade mixes to create a million different and subtle color combinations.

Mix it up

The following exercise is all about experimenting and having fun! Mix up, or squeeze out from the tubes, your three main colors, and have your mixing mediums at hand. Mix the colors in varying ratios to form different colors – use a palette with sections to keep the mixes separate. Add Payne's Gray to darken your mixes, or lighten them by adding more water. White will soften colors and transform your existing mixes in to pastel shades. I also mix everything with everything and see what I come up with – experimentation is key!

3 core colors

Alizarin Crimson

Emerald

Intense Green

3 mixing mediums

White

Payne's Gray

Water

Mix up 30 new hues!

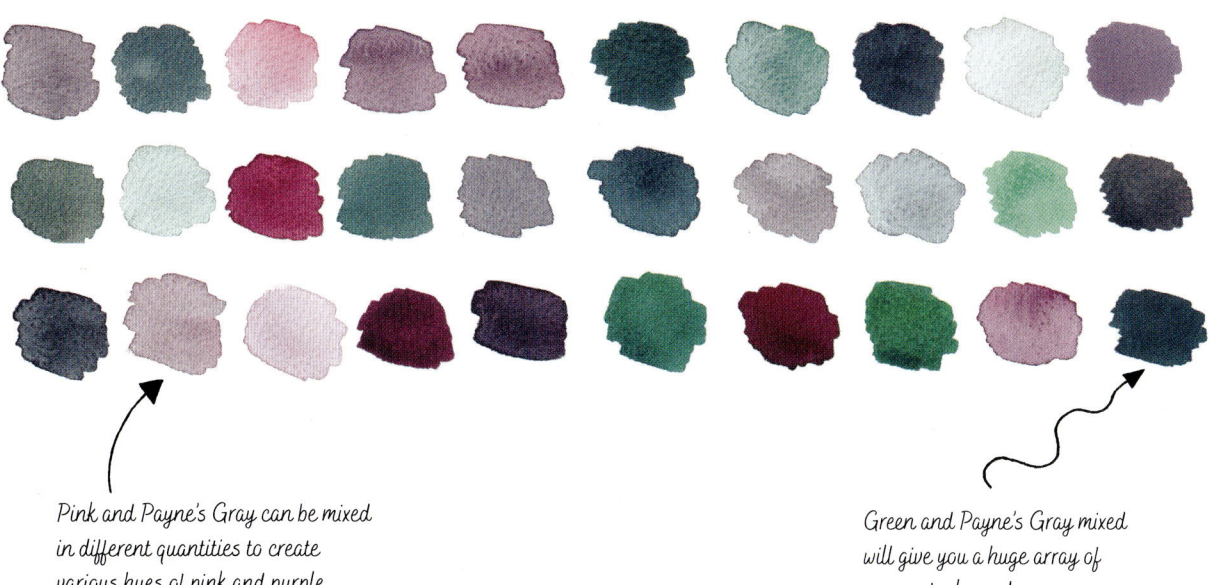

Pink and Payne's Gray can be mixed in different quantities to create various hues of pink and purple.

Green and Payne's Gray mixed will give you a huge array of greens, teals, and sea green.

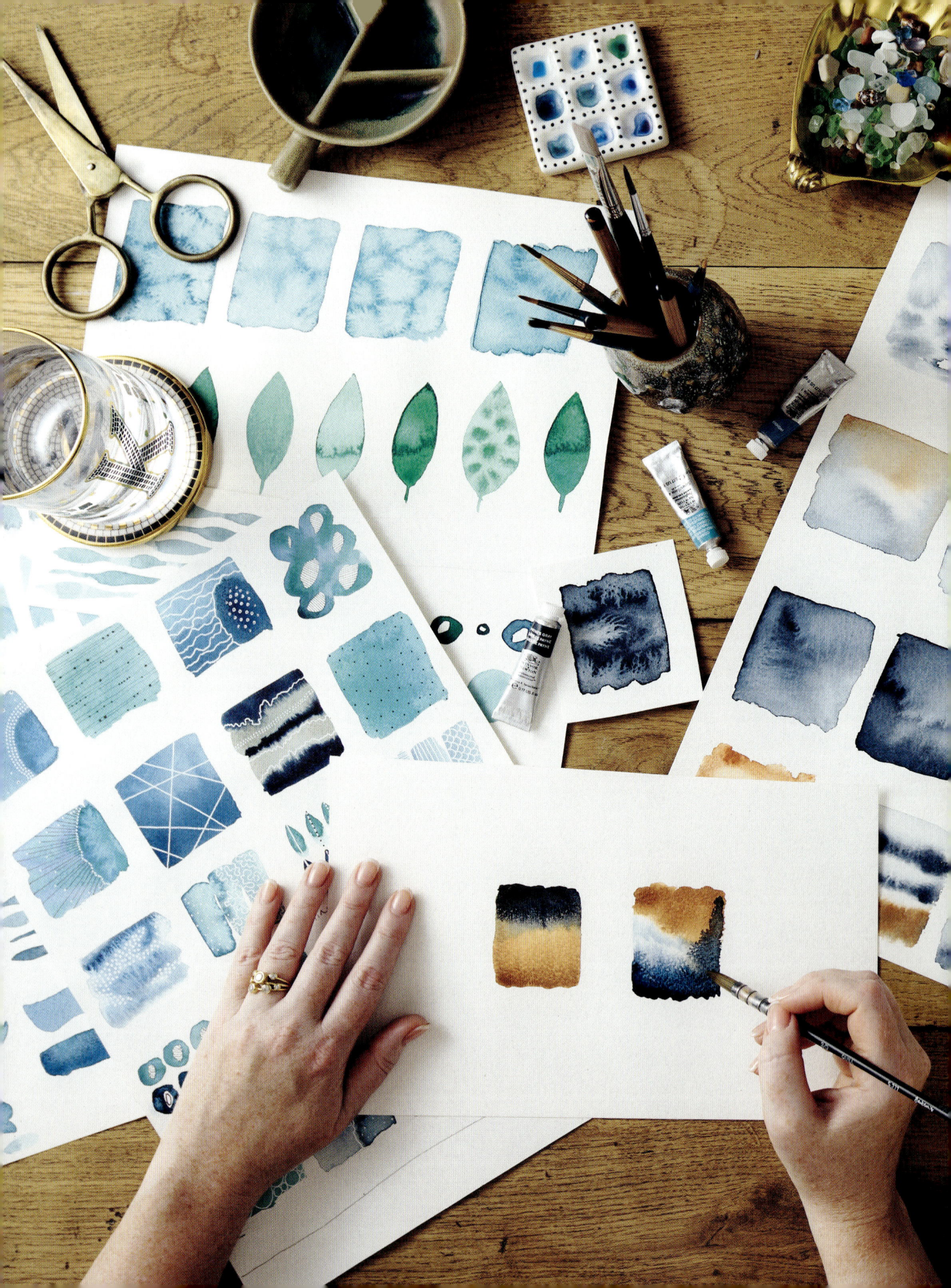

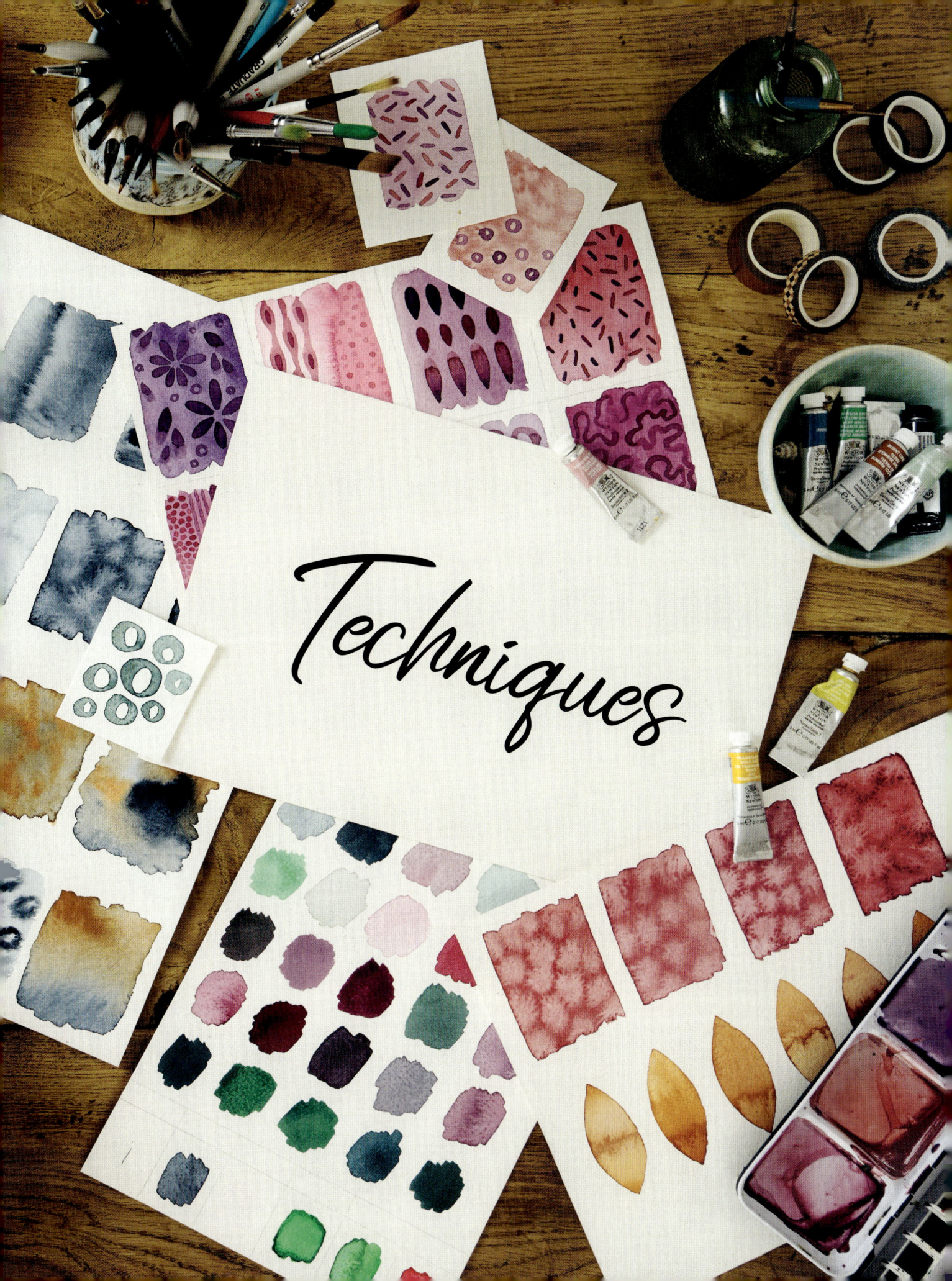

Techniques

GETTING STARTED

It's time to learn basic techniques that you can practice and refine as you progress through the projects. We'll cover basic watercolor processes such as wet on wet, wet on dry and water blooms, plus a selection of my favorite mark-making techniques. Mastering these will introduce a repertoire of new shapes and textures into your watercolor practice.

Top Tip: Practice really does make perfect! At the start, it's natural to struggle with some techniques, but the more you play and experiment, the more relaxed you will feel with your paints and mark making.

Paper choice

When your first try these techniques, start with cheap copier or scrap paper. Practice will help you build "muscle memory" as you learn how to paint key shapes and marks, and you'll feel freer to experiment and build those muscles when using cheaper paper.

Once you're more confident, move on to watercolor test sheets where you can practice on textured paper. Practice should be fun (not a chore!), helping you discover new ways of painting and effects you enjoy. Make notes on how you created different effects and your favorite colors and marks.

Don't forget to have fun!

Practice the techniques somewhere relaxed – a desk in your home office, the dining table, or simply on your kitchen counter (just push the toaster to one side!). I love that watercolors are so low maintenance – your brushes and palette can be quickly cleaned with water rather than specialist solutions. Just pick up a brush and go for it!

"There is no must in art because art is free"

Wassily Kandinsky

Working on loose sheets to play and experiment is a super-fun way to practice because there's nothing at stake!

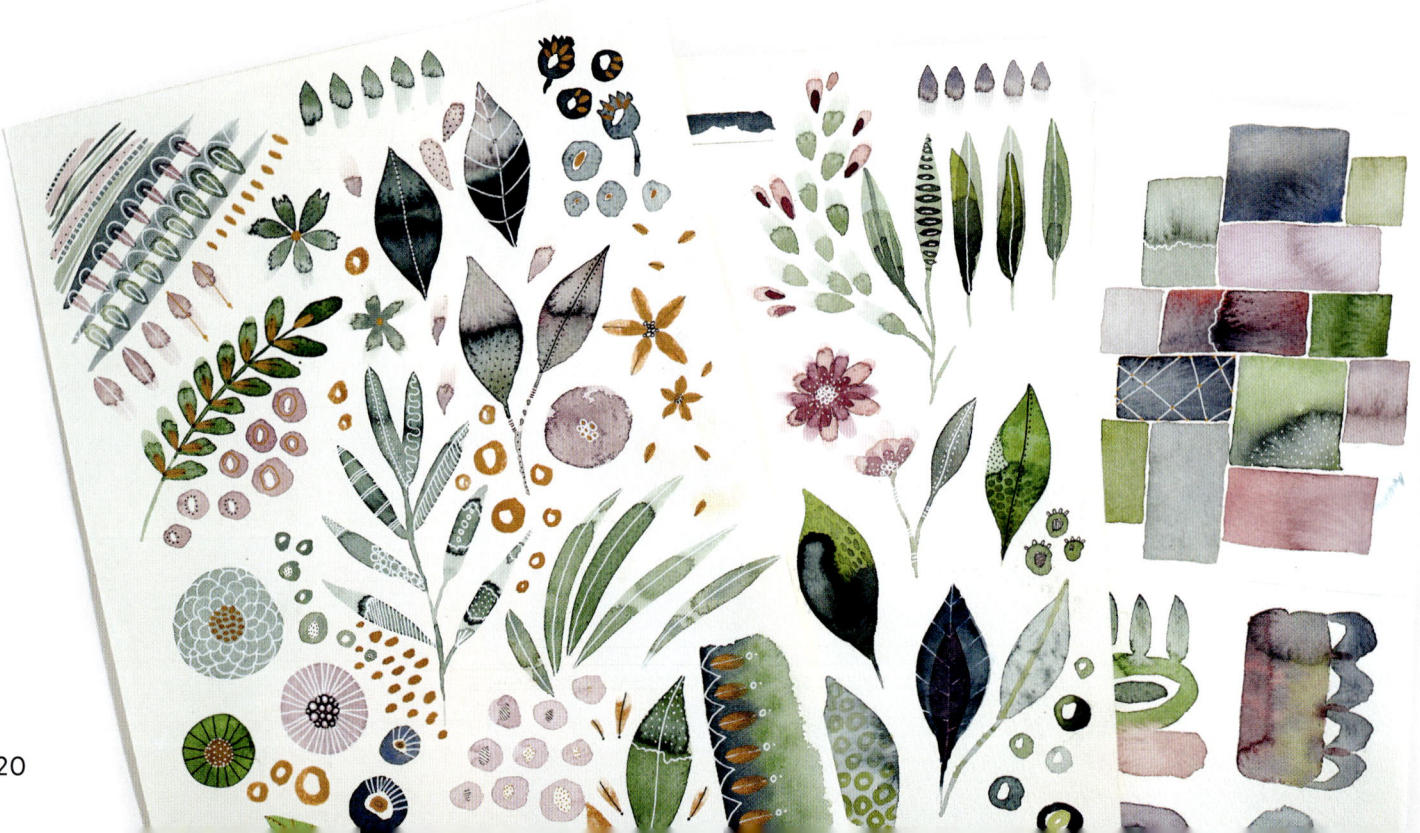

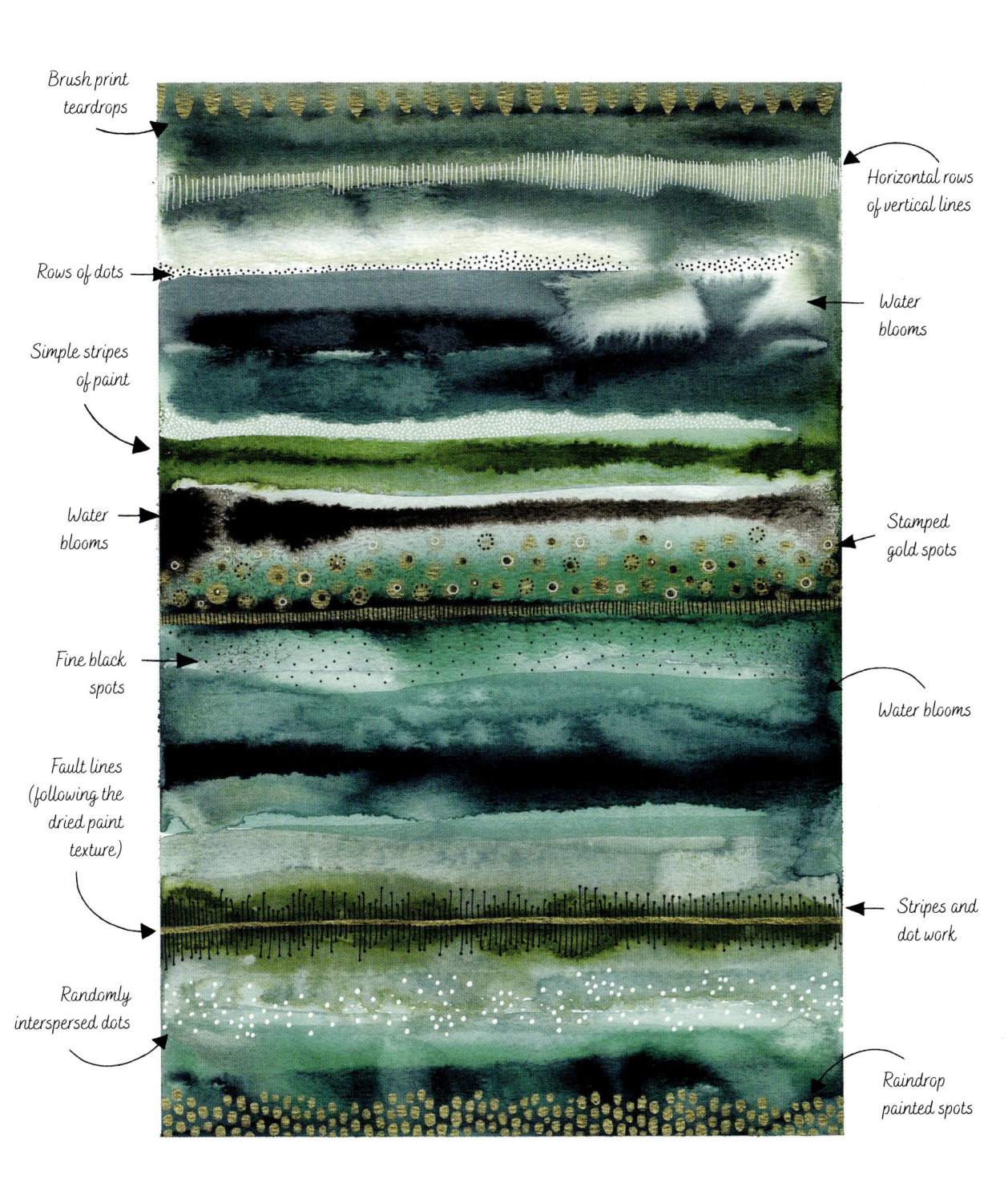

Brush print teardrops

Horizontal rows of vertical lines

Rows of dots

Water blooms

Simple stripes of paint

Water blooms

Stamped gold spots

Fine black spots

Water blooms

Fault lines (following the dried paint texture)

Stripes and dot work

Randomly interspersed dots

Raindrop painted spots

WET ON WET

This is the technique of putting down a layer of water or wet paint and then, rather than waiting for it to dry, working straight into it. This gives interesting effects as the new paint reacts with the wet layer beneath. It can create beautiful merges of color, shapes in the paint as the pigments move, and textures created as the paint dries.

PAINT ON WATER

1. Paint a square using clean water and add a color along one edge.

2. Choose a second color to flood the opposite edge.

3. As the paint settles, the water will allow the two colors to merge together.

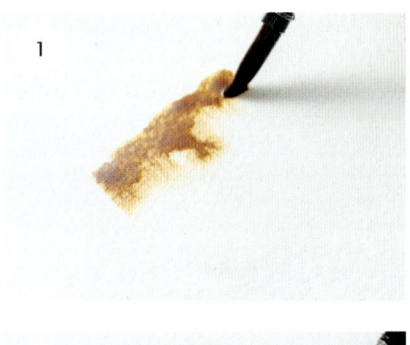

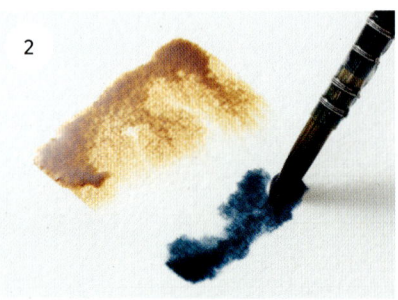

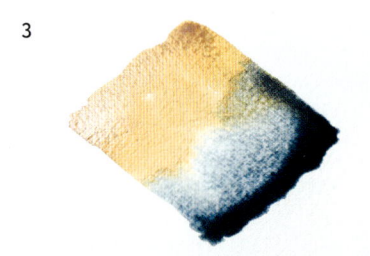

WATER ON PAINT

1. Paint a square of color, using plenty of paint for a bold effect.

2. Once the square has settled for a few minutes – but is still wet – drop in dots of clean water from the end of your brush to creates water blooms.

3. The paint will dry to a textured effect.

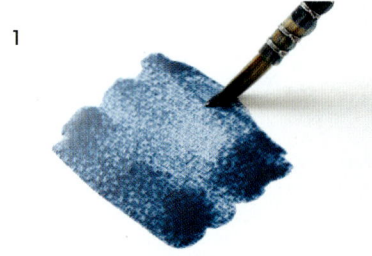

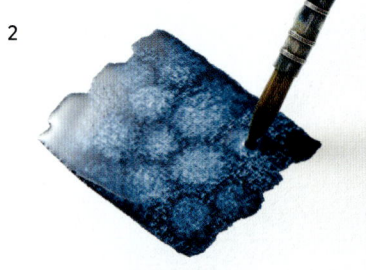

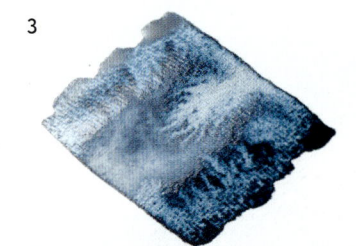

PAINT ON PAINT

1. Paint a square, making it nice and wet. Here, I've add more paint on one side for interest.

2. From the end of your brush, drop in dots of a second color.

3. New shapes will appear as the new color moves across your base color.

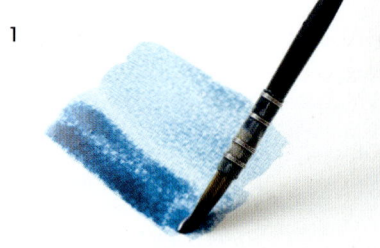

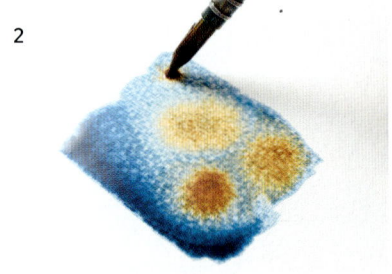

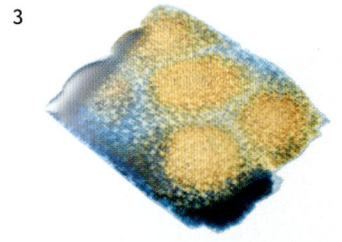

PAINT ON WATER

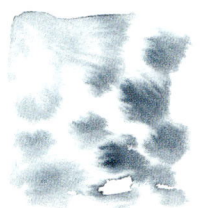

*Watercolor spots
into clean water*

*Watercolor spots
into clean water*

*Wash of water with dark pigment
bleeding from edge to edge*

*Wet square of paper with
thin lines of deep pigment*

*Wet square with a lighter
toned border of color*

*Blocks top and bottom with
center mixed to form a gradient*

*Clean water with a colored
stripe added top and bottom*

*Wet square with pigment border
around spots of clean water*

WATER ON PAINT

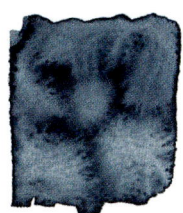

*Droplets of water added
onto a dark wash*

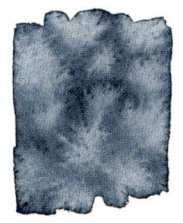

*Droplets of water added
into a mid-color wash*

*Droplets of clean water
added into a light wash*

*Colored background with
contrasting color droplets added*

PAINT ON PAINT

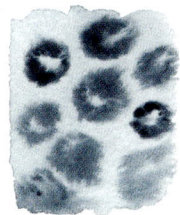

*Light wash of color with dark
circles painted in while wet*

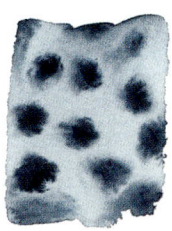

*Wash of watercolor with spots
and drops of darker paint added*

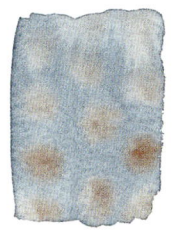

*Wash of watercolor with a
contrasting color spot added*

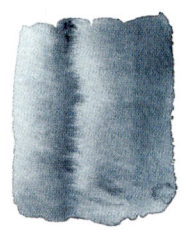

*Thin wash of diluted color with
vertical stripes of darker paint*

WATER BLOOMS

Often called water blooms (aka "cauliflowers", which I love!), this effect is caused by one area of paint drying faster than the others. When paint is applied in a thin layer and a pool of pigment collects, an interesting effect is created. The thin layer dries while the other areas are still very wet, forming fantastic natural textures. Here are some of my experiments.

Top Tip: Water blooms are hard to control, so you'll have to (literally) go with the flow and expect the unexpected! Lean into it – the more water, the more exciting the results!

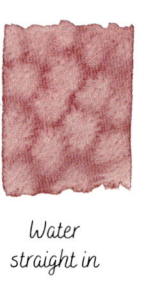
Water straight in

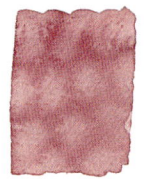
Water after 1 minute

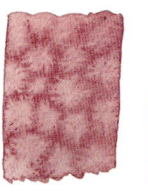
Water after 2 minutes

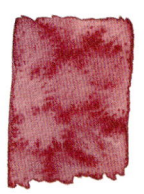
Water after 3 minutes

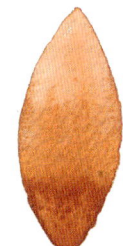
Pooling paint at each end

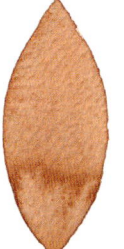
Soft wash with pigment at one end

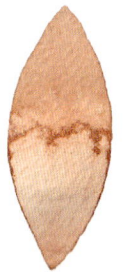
All over coverage

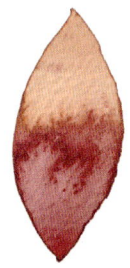
Lots of water at one end

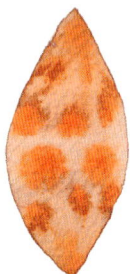
New color added

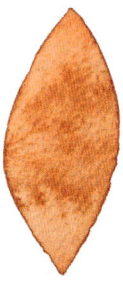
Spots of paint

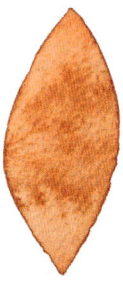
Spots of water

CREATING WATER BLOOMS

1. Mix a light wash of your chosen color and paint a shape (a square in this case). For the best results, apply the color in a thin, even layer.

2. Using a clean brush loaded with fresh water, add drops of water to the wet paint.

3. As they sit on the wet paint, the dots will spread outward to create your water blooms!

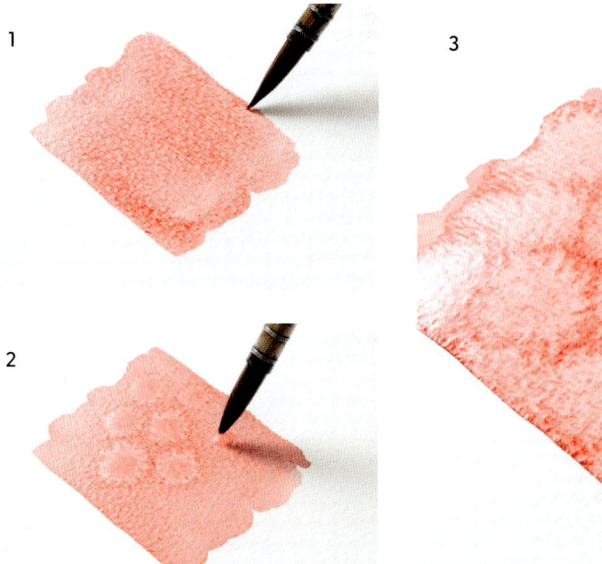

SPOTS AND CIRCLES

Lovely soft, organic circles and spots work beautifully in all sorts of compositions, from decorative borders and sea pebbles to the center stamens of abstract flowers. Here are a few of the basic spots and circles I like to use in my work – try them out and experiment to discover more of your own!

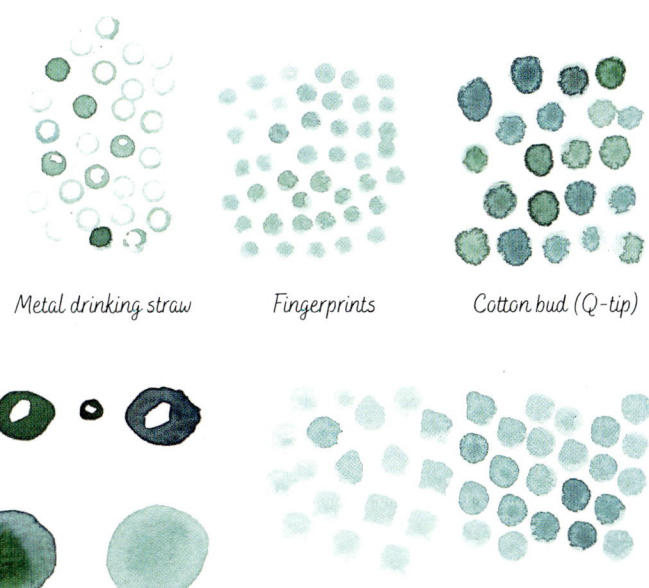

Metal drinking straw   *Fingerprints*   *Cotton bud (Q-tip)*

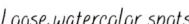
  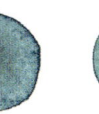 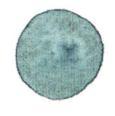 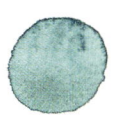 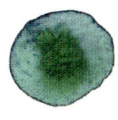 

Loose watercolor spots

Plain   *Central dot*   *Edge of paint*   *Half and half*   *Spot*   *Drier brush*

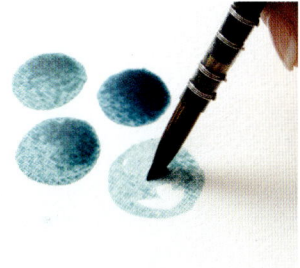

light paint   heavy paint
Foam stamp

PAINTING CIRCLES AND SPOTS

1. Mix up some loose, wet watercolor in your palette and load your brush. Make circular outlines – these should be nice and juicy, using lots of the paint and water mixture.

2. Make the same circle shapes, but fill them in to create spots.

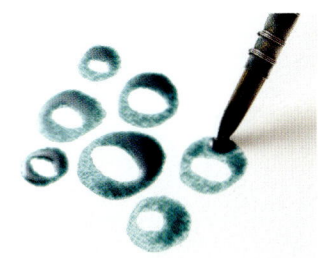

1   2

USING OTHER TOOLS

I've used a variety of implements to create spots and marks in my paintings. These include a foam stamp, cotton bud (Q-tip), a metal drinking straw and even my finger!

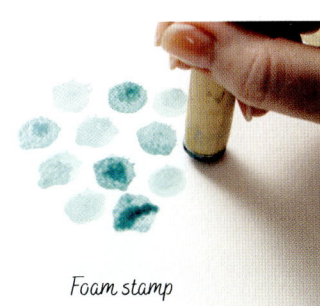

Foam stamp   *Cotton bud (Q-tip)*

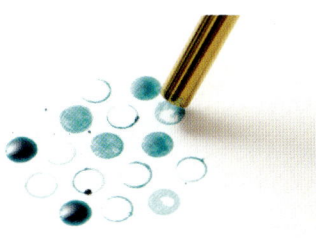

Metal drinking straw   *Finger print*

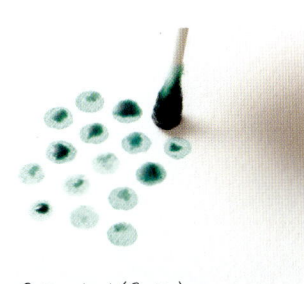

WET ON DRY

Wet on dry is as simple as it sounds, adding wet paint to a layer of dry paint. This lets you create defined shapes and stops colors from mixing. It's a great way to add details and texture to a dry wash that looks a bit flat – you can see here how simple shapes can add lots of visual interest.

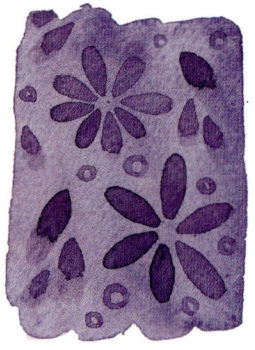

Flower brush prints and circles

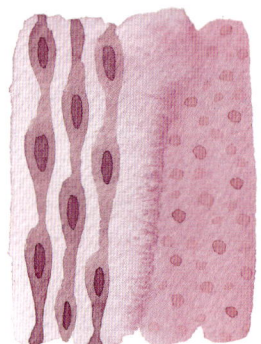

Wavy lines and raindrop spots

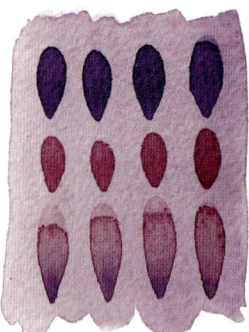

Brush prints in different colors

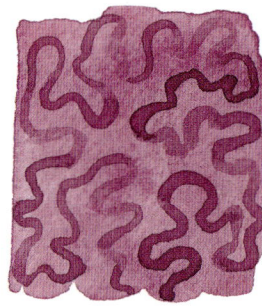

Freehand squiggle line

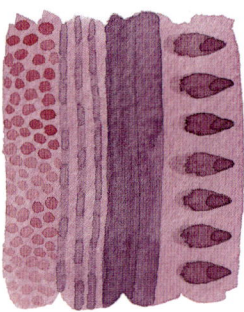

Dots, lines and brush prints

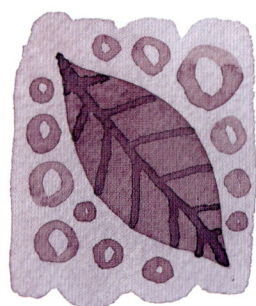

Freehand leaf painting with loose circles

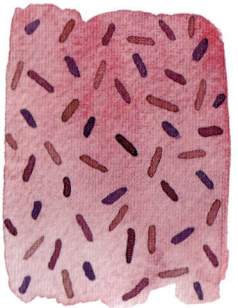

Small lines to create a sprinkles effect

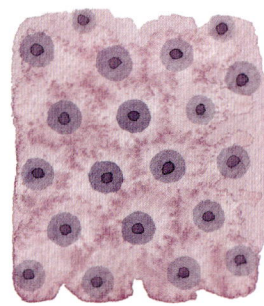

Layered circles and spots

ADDING WET-ON-DRY DETAILS

Start with a square of fully dry watercolor, then paint wet details. The dry base allows for defined marks.

Here, I've used the brush to stamp sprinkles across a solid background. I also painted soft watercolor circles to accentuate water blooms. Once dry, I'll add a center to each one.

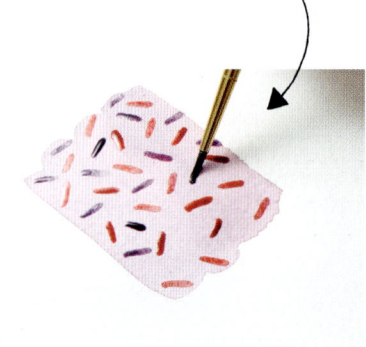

Stamping across a plain, dry wash

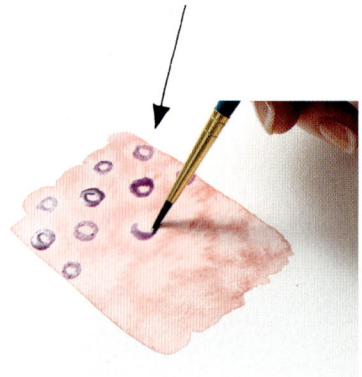

Accentuating dry texture

MASKING SHAPES AND HIGHLIGHTS

Masking fluid is a great tool to have in your kit. Applying it to the paper creates a barrier from any paint applied over it, allowing you to retain the fresh white paper (or other color or texture you've already painted) beneath.

The method is simple – paint masking fluid (*see Materials: Masking Supplies*) on the area you want to protect and let it dry completely (it will feel tacky, but shouldn't feel wet, sticky, or come off when touched lightly with a finger). Once it's dry, add your layer(s) of paint and leave them to dry completely. Use a soft eraser (or a clean finger!) to lightly rub away the masking fluid to reveal the shapes now highlighted below.

Top Tip: Masking fluid is quite gluey and can ruin your brush, so use a special masking fluid brush (or an old brush dedicated to the job). Wash it in soapy water straight after use to stop the fluid drying in the bristles.

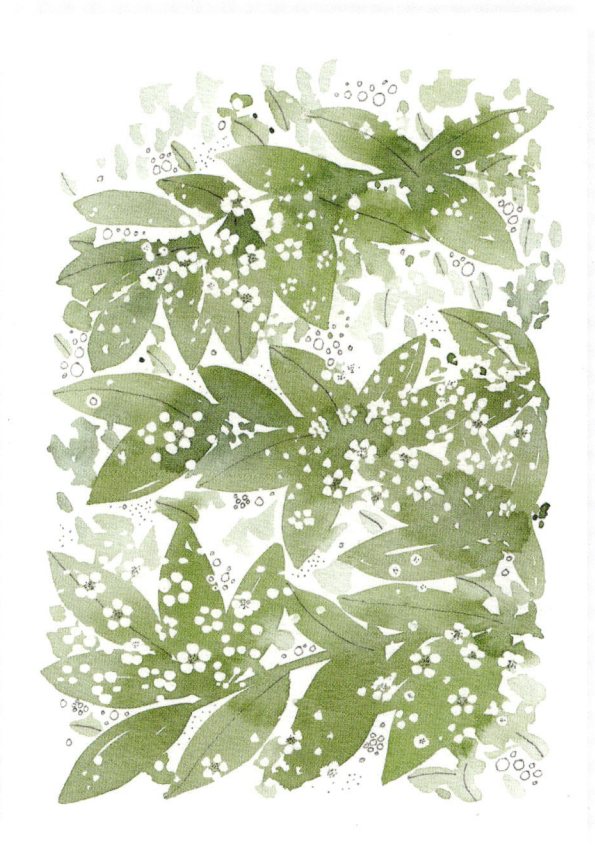

Spots of masking fluid placed randomly across the page create delicate flowers within the leaves.

USING MASKING FLUID

1. Pour a little masking fluid into the lid of the bottle. Dip your brush into the lid to load it, then dot small circles on to the paper to create flower shapes.

2. When the fluid has dried completely (it will darken in color), paint a wash of color directly over it.

3. When the paint is dry, use an eraser or a finger to rub away the fluid, revealing clean white flowers below.

4. Leave the flowers with the paper showing through, or paint them – the white paper will make the petals pop!

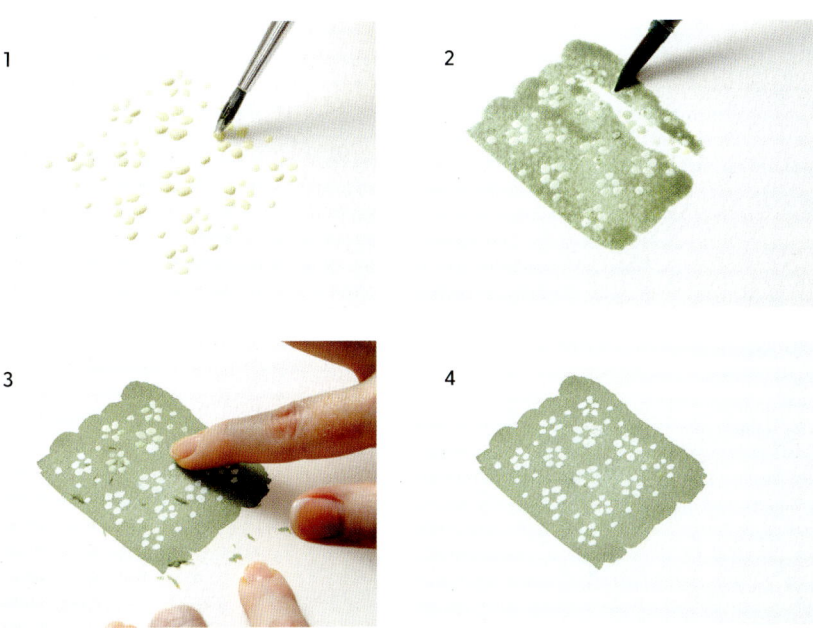

EASY ORGANIC BRUSHWORK SHAPES

My favorite brush is a quill (*see* Materials: Brushes). It has a lovely point for fine details, a wider base for thicker marks, and holds loads of water and paint, making it a dream for easy brushwork. Most of the shapes, patterns, and textures in the projects are created using basic equipment – see below for examples.

SOFT SPOTS

To create soft spots, use a filbert brush (or small round brush) loaded with very wet paint. The more watery the paint, the darker the spot will be when dry.

STAMPED SHAPES

Load your quill brush with watery paint. Gently press the length of the bristles onto the paper, using the brush as a "stamp" to create the shape.

Use the same stamping technique to form different shapes, such as this flower. Work the petals around a clock face until the circle is complete.

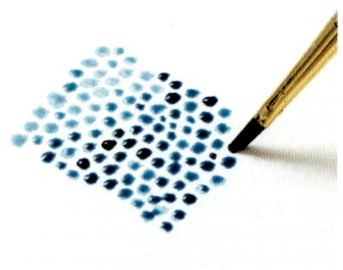

Mixing light and dark spots adds texture

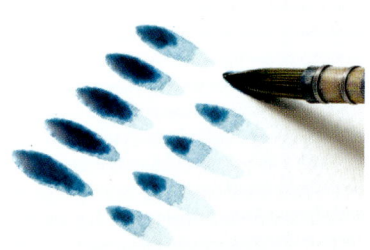

The brush holds enough paint for multiple shapes

Turn the paper rather than your brush or arm

WAVY LINES

1. Load your quill brush with lots of very watery paint. Begin painting the line using only the tip of the brush, then add pressure to push its full belly onto the page to create a thicker line.

2. While still pulling the brush toward you, gently release the pressure and watch as the line become thinner until only the tip of the brush is touching the paper again.

3. Continue painting the line in this way to produce a series of waves. The more you practice, the more intuitive this flowing (and meditative!) movement will become.

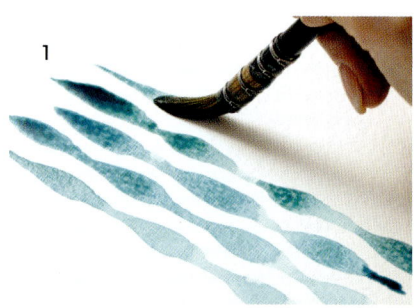

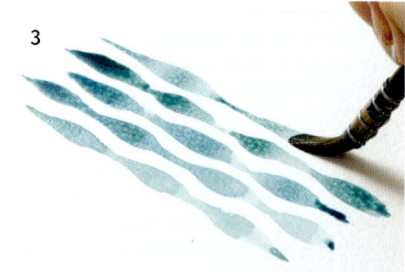

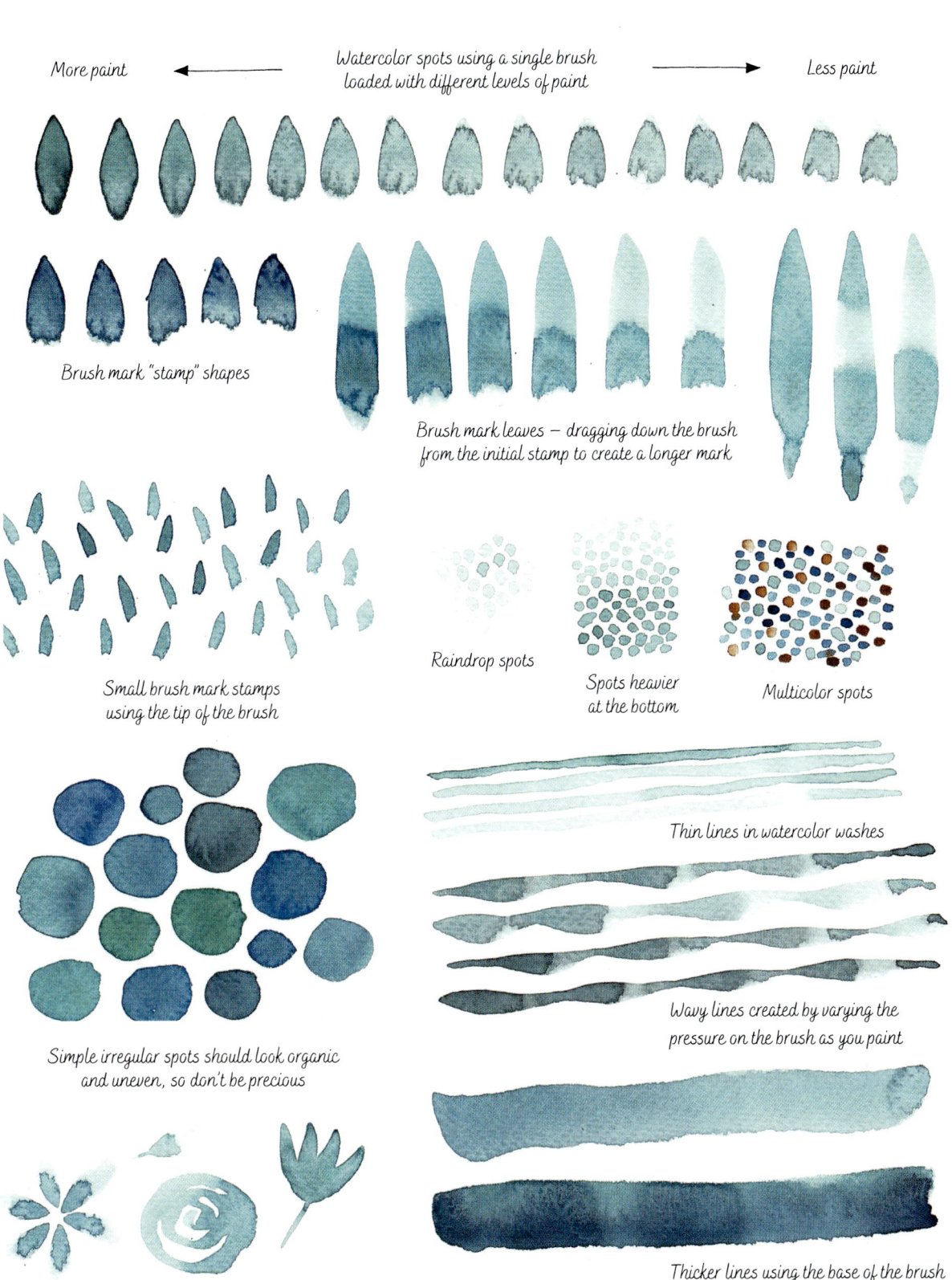

More paint ← Watercolor spots using a single brush loaded with different levels of paint → Less paint

Brush mark "stamp" shapes

Brush mark leaves — dragging down the brush from the initial stamp to create a longer mark

Small brush mark stamps using the tip of the brush

Raindrop spots

Spots heavier at the bottom

Multicolor spots

Simple irregular spots should look organic and uneven, so don't be precious

Thin lines in watercolor washes

Wavy lines created by varying the pressure on the brush as you paint

Thicker lines using the base of the brush

Flowers created using simple stamps of the brush or quick painted shapes

MARK MAKING

People often comment on the decorations and embellishments in my work. These marks transform watercolor paintings into mixed media – the pens and inks add texture, detail, highlights, and contrast. While I admit to being a maximalist ("more is more" in my eyes!), these details not only accentuate the areas of your work you love, but can also "save" any areas that need a helping hand. Here are some of the marks I use.

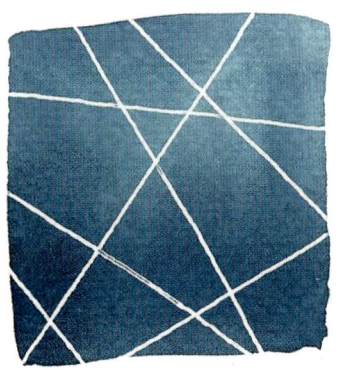

Intersecting lines:
white gel pen

BASIC MARKS

These simple marks can be made on most surfaces and backgrounds. They use one tool, one color, and simple lines, yet create a dynamic effect (*see* Materials: Ink and Pens for my favorite black and white pens).

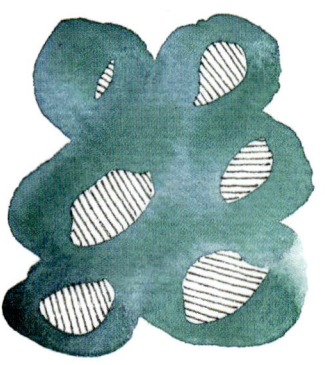

Black line work:
black fineliner pen

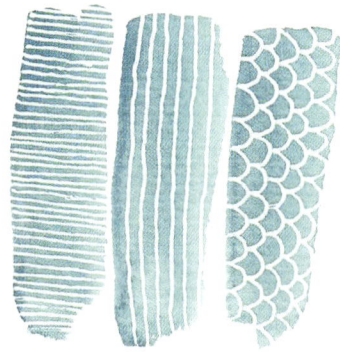

White line work:
white gel pen

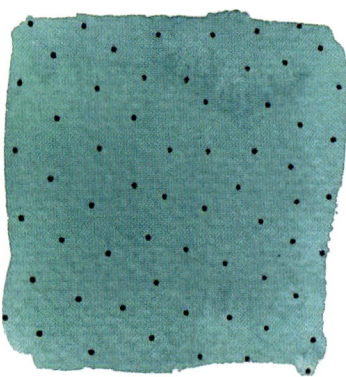

Black spots:
black fineliner pen

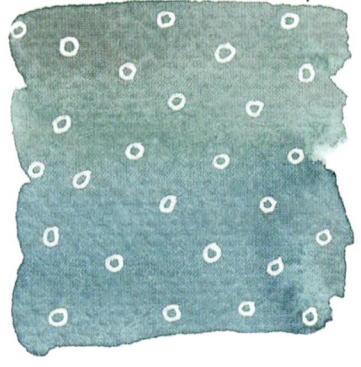

Small circles:
white gel pen

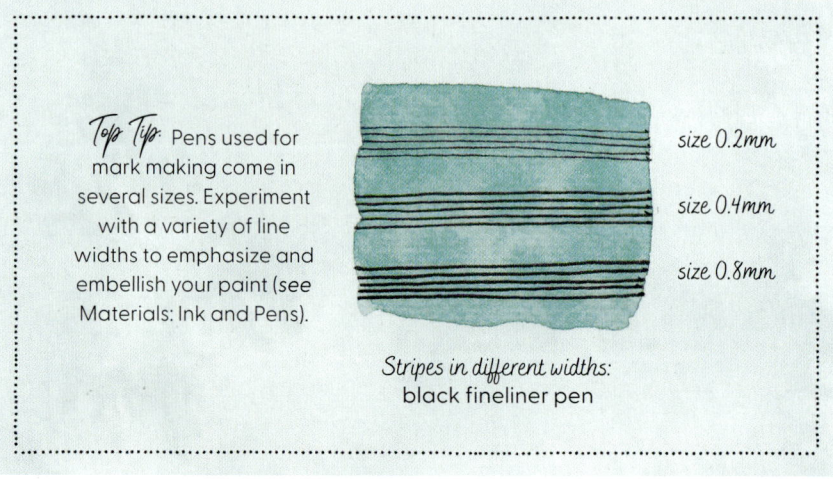

Top Tip: Pens used for mark making come in several sizes. Experiment with a variety of line widths to emphasize and embellish your paint (*see* Materials: Ink and Pens).

size 0.2mm

size 0.4mm

size 0.8mm

Stripes in different widths:
black fineliner pen

MARKS GUIDED BY BLOOMS AND BRUSHWORK

Whether created deliberately or by a happy accident, brushwork and blooms provide infinite opportunities for abstract mark making (*see* Techniques: Wet On Wet, Water Blooms, and Spots and Circles). They may inspire recognisable shapes, such as circles, or more freestyle marks that play on fault lines and edges created by the paint.

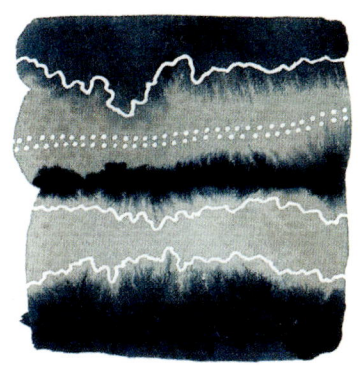

Fault lines and dots:
white gel pen

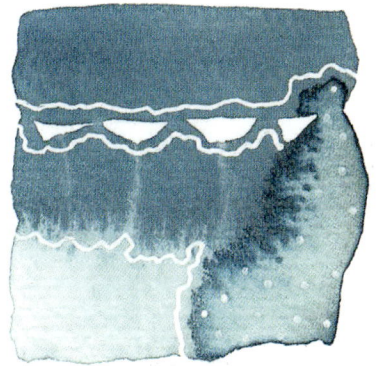

Fault lines:
white paint pen

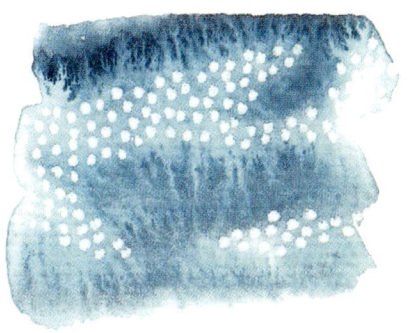

Large cluster spots:
white paint pen

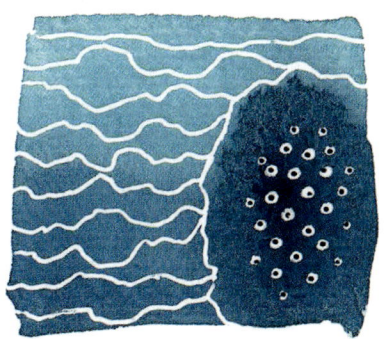

Lines and spots:
white paint pen
black fineliner pen

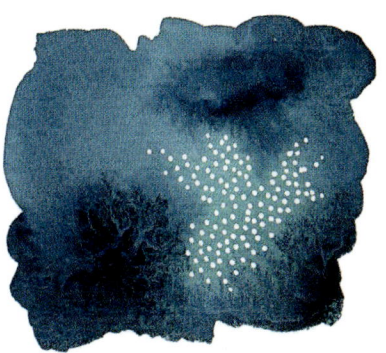

Spot clusters:
white gel pen

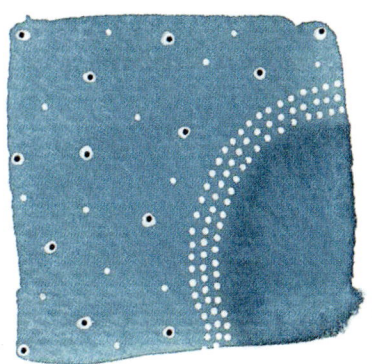

White dots, rows, and spots:
white gel pen
black fineliner pen

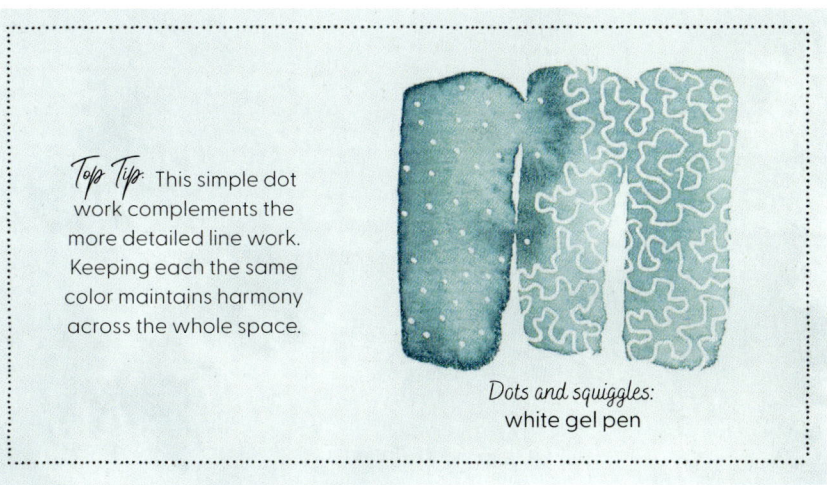

Top Tip: This simple dot work complements the more detailed line work. Keeping each the same color maintains harmony across the whole space.

Dots and squiggles:
white gel pen

CREATING YOUR OWN SWATCH LIBRARY

I like to create swatches of colors to use as testers when trying out different embellishment ideas. Why not do the same and try out different marks, pens and inks to find your favorites? The examples on this page are some of my favorite styles.

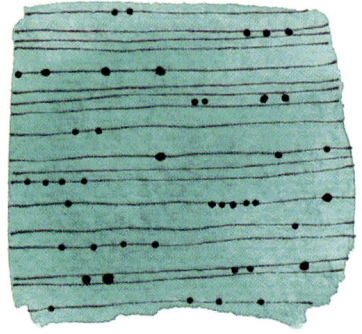

Stripes and dot work:
black fineliner pen

Simple florals:
white gel pen
black fineliner pen

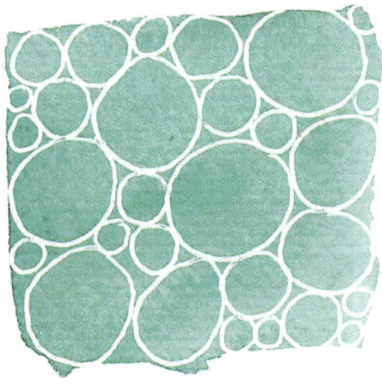

Circles in various sizes:
white paint pen

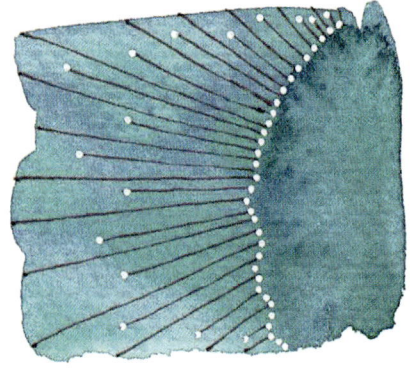

Sunburst lines with spots:
white gel pen
black fineliner pen

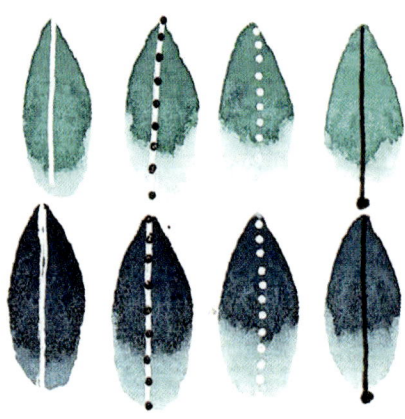

Lines and dot work:
white gel pen
black fineliner pen

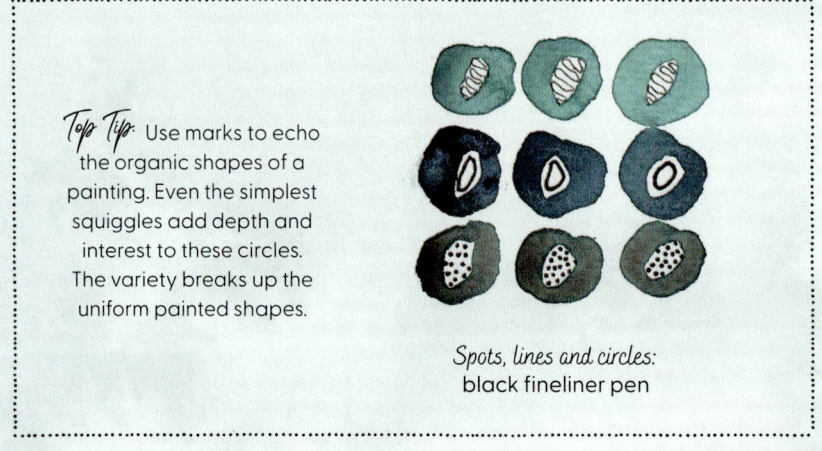

Top Tip: Use marks to echo the organic shapes of a painting. Even the simplest squiggles add depth and interest to these circles. The variety breaks up the uniform painted shapes.

Spots, lines and circles:
black fineliner pen

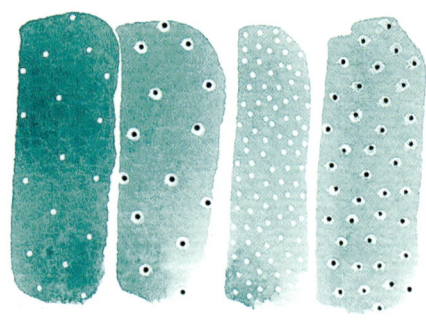

Spots in different sizes:
white gel pen
black fineliner pen

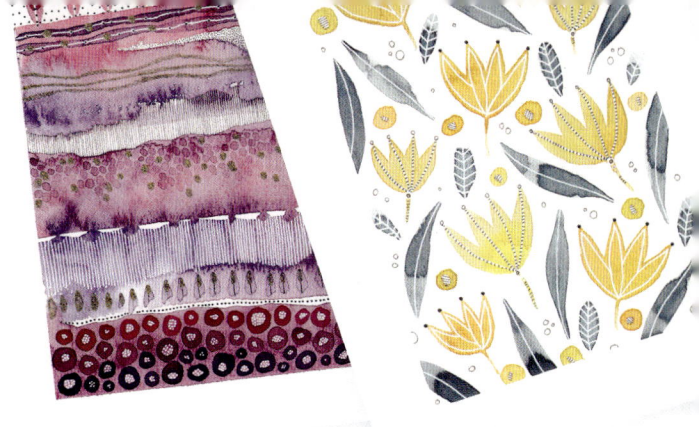

MASKING BORDERS

I use masking tape mainly for creating a crisp border around my painting. The border gives your artwork room to breathe and contrasts well with the clean white paper. I use lots of strong colors and textures, so the contrast is all the more vibrant. But even the softest colors and textures benefit from the straight line created by the masked border.

TIPS FOR MASKING YOUR BORDER

- **Selecting a size:** Choose the best width of border – and therefore masking tape – for your painting.

- **Testing your tape:** After much trial and error, I found a tape that doesn't lift or tear the paper when removed (*see* Materials: Masking Supplies). However, always test the tape on a scrap (or the back) of the paper before using it on your artwork.

- **Creating a strong bond:** Ensure that each strip is well adhered to the paper by firmly rubbing the inner edges and corners of the tape.

- **Checking the corners:** Take special notice of the corners where the tape overlaps. This is the area where paint is most likely to bleed under the tape.

- **Removing the tape:** To remove the tape safely, without ripping the paper, peel it away slowly, pulling it toward you at an acute angle. If you pull the tape "up" rather than across the page, it can lift and ruin the paper below.

- **Using heat:** If your tape proves difficult to remove, run a warm hair dryer over it to slightly melt the glue – this should make it much easier for you to peel away.

CREATING CRISP BORDERS

1. Starting with the long sides, align the outside edge of the tape with the edge of the paper for neat, vertical borders. Repeat for the short sides, overlapping the tape at each corner to ensure no paint seeps underneath. Use your fingertips to smooth down the inner edges and corners.

2. Paint your piece – don't flood the tape with water or paint, but don't be afraid to work right up to and onto it.

3. When the paint has completely dried, remove the tape from the short sides first, gently pulling it back on itself to avoid damaging the paper.

4. Now remove the tape from the long sides to reveal a lovely sharp border!

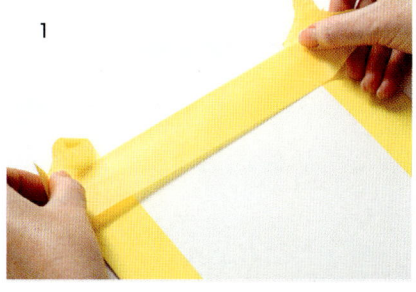
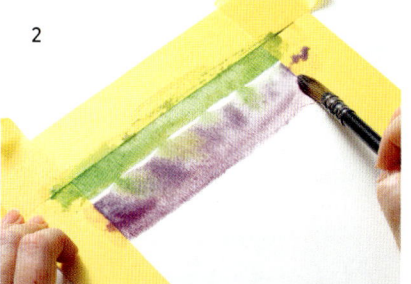
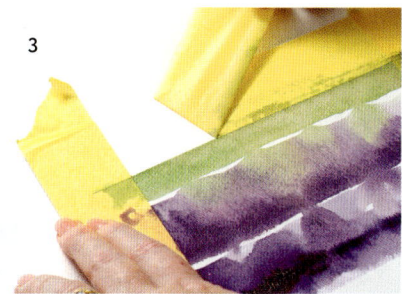
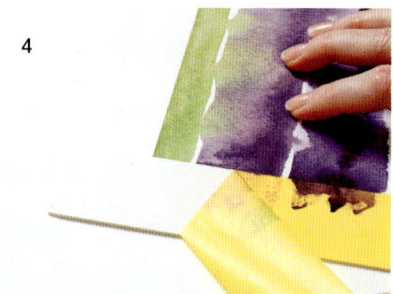

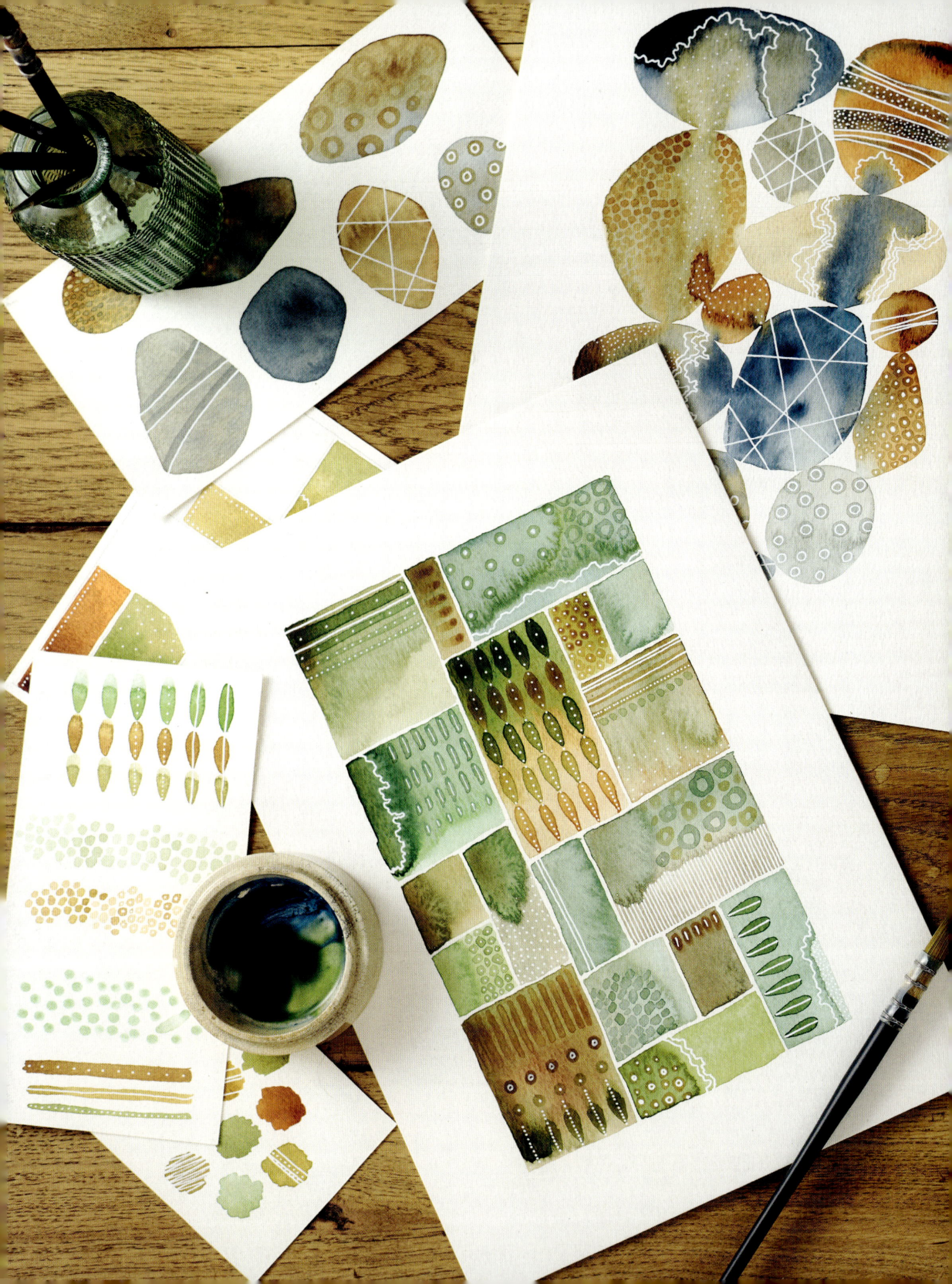

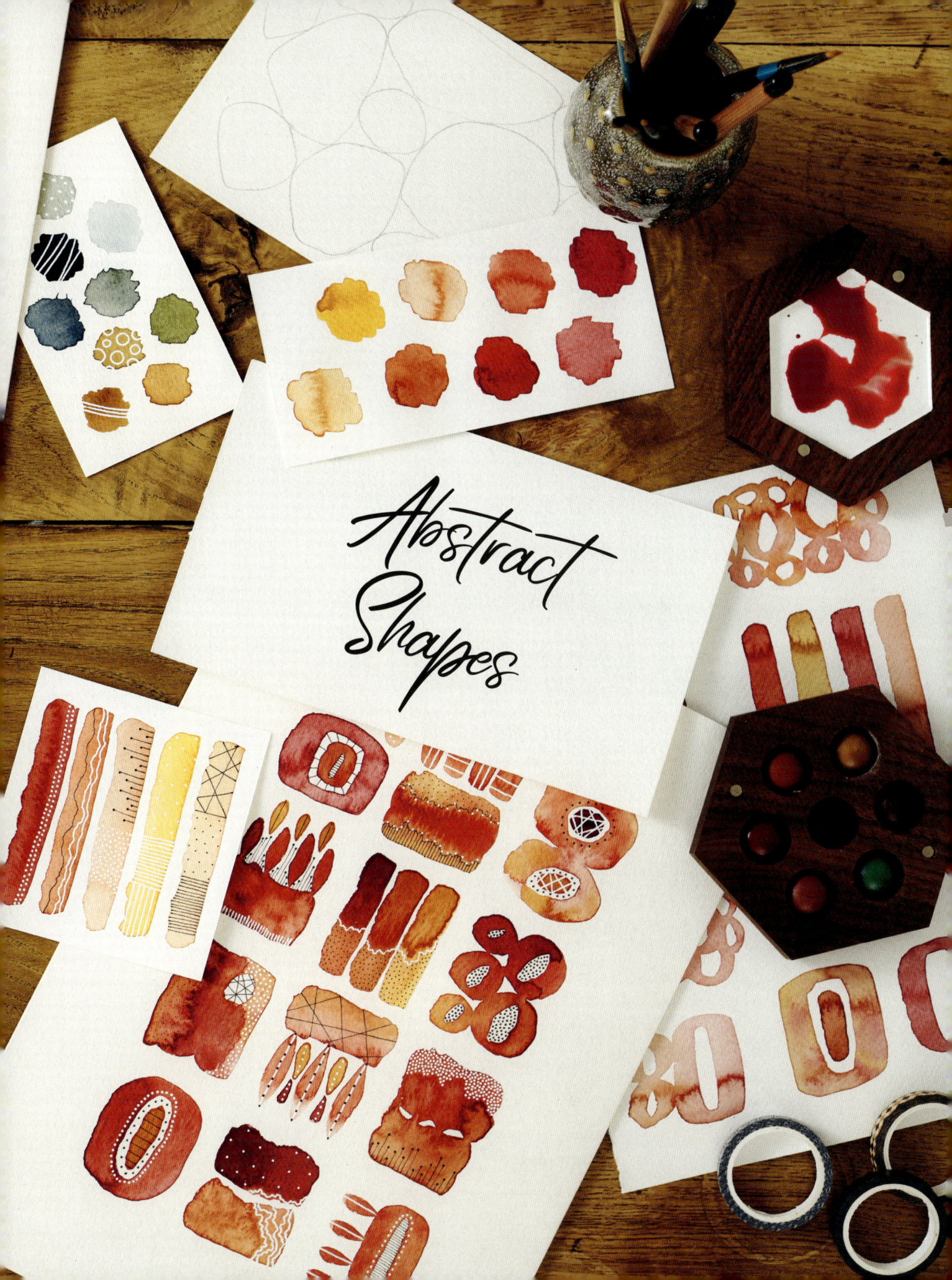

Abstract
Shapes

Experimental Sampler

This sampler is an excellent way to experiment with color, shapes, and textures, and build your watercolor confidence. I've suggested simple shapes, but you can go wild – there's no right or wrong with abstract watercolors! Circles, stripes, squiggles and color blocks all sit harmoniously when you use a pared-back color palette to tie the whole piece together.

MATERIALS

- Winsor & Newton professional watercolors
- Daler Rowney Aquafine Artboard
- Jackson's quill brush – sizes 0 and 10/0
- Filbert and round brushes
- Uni-ball Signo pen – white, 1mm (Broad)
- Posca paint pen – white, 0.7mm (Ultra Fine)
- Staedtler pigment liner – black (in a variety of sizes/thicknesses)
- Winsor & Newton Drawing Ink – gold
- Ruler and pencil

COLOR CHOICES

As in all my projects, I've suggested a palette, but do go with your gut and select colors that speak to you, are your favorites, or simply feel right for the project! Here I've selected a fiery palette of yellows, oranges, and red, which give a lovely warm glow to the finished piece.

WINSOR & NEWTON COLOR REFERENCES

- Burnt Umber
- Cadmium-Free Red
- Cadmium-Free Yellow
- Winsor Orange

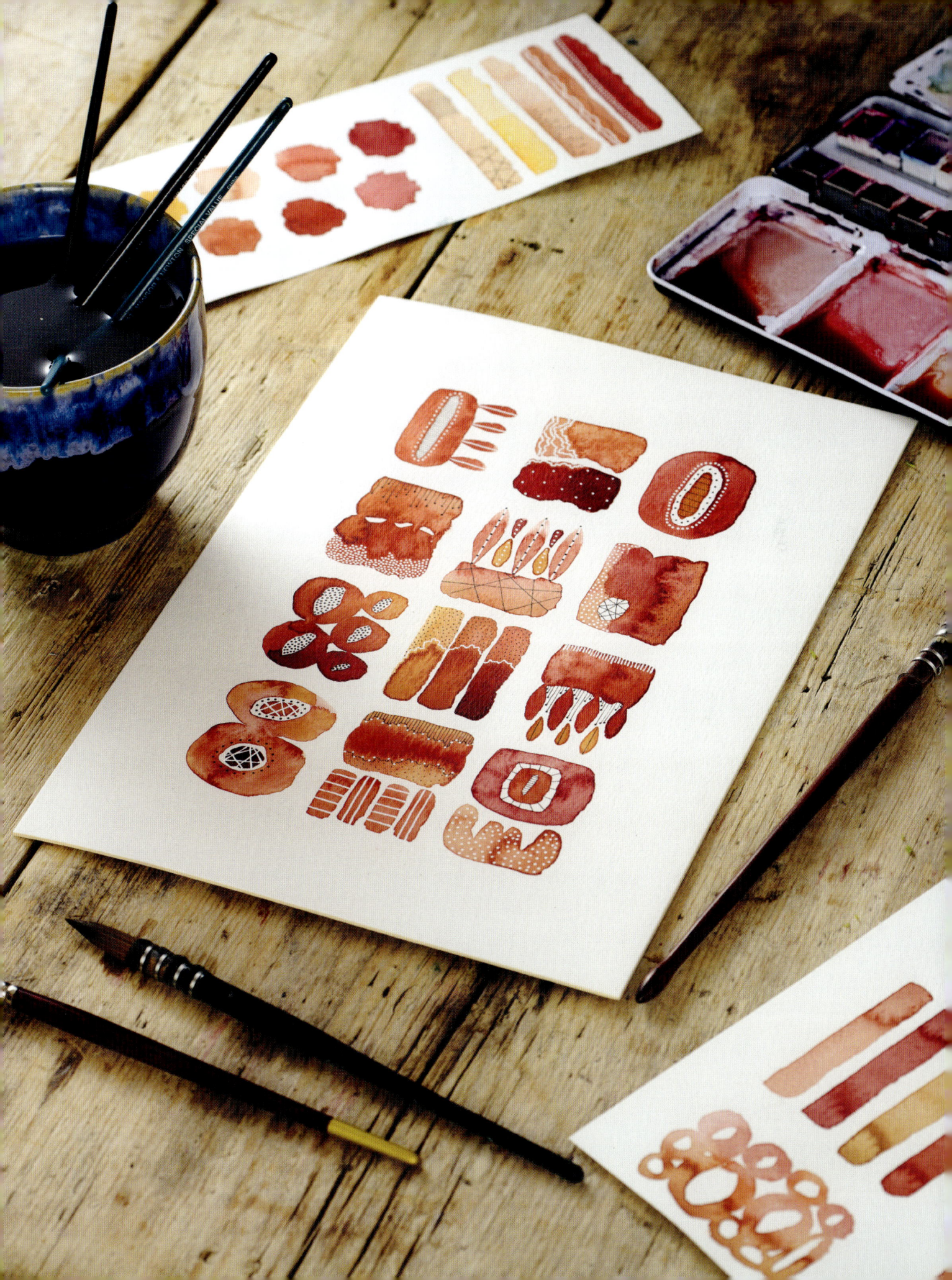

Step 1: **WET PAINT**

Start by masking your page (*see* Techniques: Masking Borders).

Use a pencil and ruler to divide your page into a grid of rectangles (or squares if you prefer). This doesn't have to be perfect – it's simply giving you a rough guide.

Mix up paint in your palette – you'll want it nice and wet (make sure the paint is diluted with plenty of water). I mix up four or five colors – the base colors listed with a few variations where I mixed two colors together to give a new shade.

Paint a design in each pencil box. These can be made up of shapes and colors – I like to use a variety of color on each one (although you could use a single color in each box if you like). Once you've filled all your squares, let the piece dry completely before moving on to our next step.

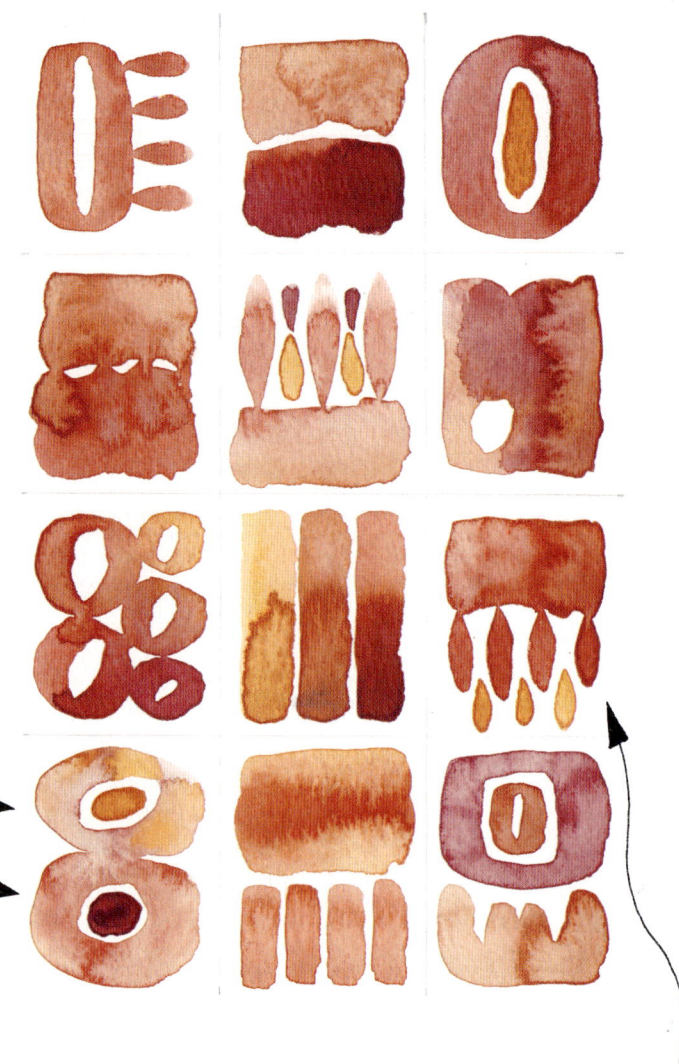

Try painting a shape with one color, then drop a different shade into the wet paint to create a color merge.

Load your brush with plenty of water to create loose rings of paint.

Simply rest a loaded quill flat on the paper to create a teardrop shaped brush mark. The more heavily you press, the larger the mark.

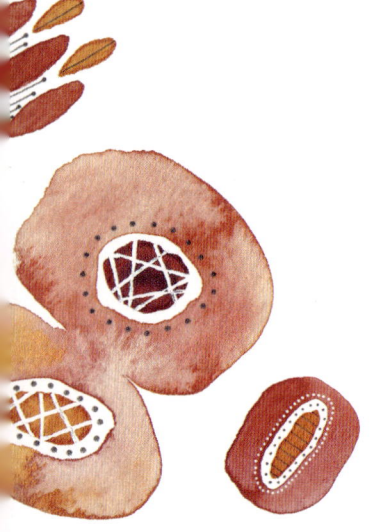

Top Tip: When painting this style of sampler, vary the types of shapes and marks to create balance. For example, use a mix of straight and curved lines on each row, rather than all curved, or all straight.

Step 2: **EMBELLISHMENTS**

Now for my favorite step – the embellishments! I've used a range of white and black pens as well as gold ink to add interest and detail. When everything is dry, erase the pencil lines to complete the sampler.

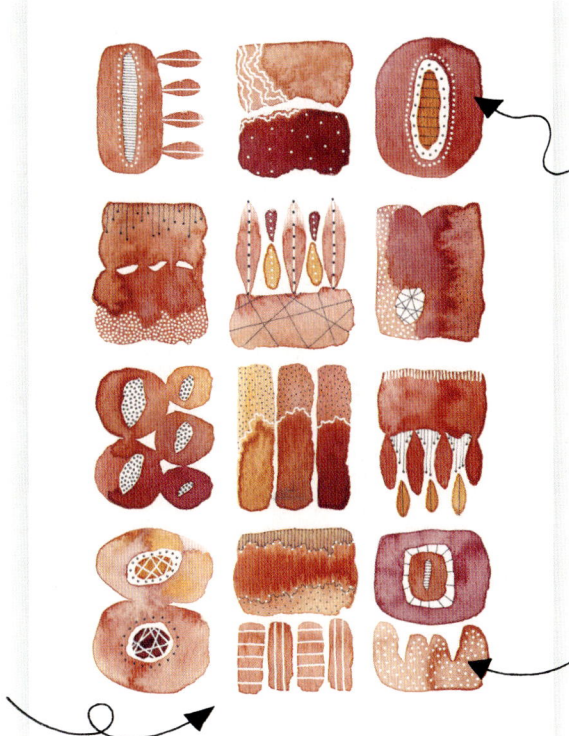

Vary the pen's thickness to create smaller or larger dots in rows or an allover pattern.

When drawing rows or single lines, think about your color choice and size of pen.

White dots look striking against a dark color; black works best on pale colors.

More inspiration

Try different color palettes and techniques to create different samplers as your confidence grows.

Here, I created a sampler with another set of mark making, bold shapes, and decorative embellishments. The cool blues and minty greens give this piece a totally different vibe to the warm reds and vibrant oranges.

Although originally created to practice my brushwork, these pieces look lovely framed with a wide mat (mount) to showcase the intricate details.

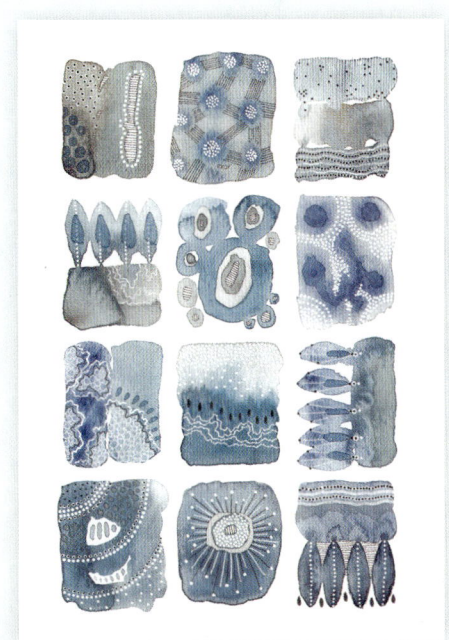

Loose Stripes

Stripes are one of my favorite patterns to paint. I love letting the paint lead the way and often get the best results from "happy accidents", where colors merge and bleed to create exciting shapes and new tones. After masking off the outer border in the first step, you can't go wrong – just wash the colors across the page and let the paint work its magic!

MATERIALS

- Winsor & Newton professional watercolors
- Daler Rowney Aquafine Artboard
- Jackson's quill brush – sizes 0 and 10/0
- Filbert and round brushes
- Uni-ball Signo pen – gold, 1mm (Broad)
- Posca paint pen – white, 0.7mm (Ultra Fine)
- Staedtler pigment liner – black (in a variety of sizes/thicknesses)
- Winsor & Newton Drawing Ink – gold

COLOR CHOICES

You can create this loose watercolor stripe in whatever colors you like. Feel free to experiment and go wild – the results may surprise you! I've worked with a limited palette of purples and pinks. Whichever colors you pick, include at least four or five. I've used a deep purple, mauve, and magenta, as well as mixing two of those colors to create a complimentary shade.

WINSOR & NEWTON COLOR REFERENCES

- Permanent Magenta
- Permanent Rose
- Winsor Violet (Dioxazine)

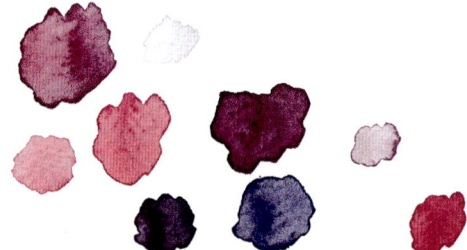

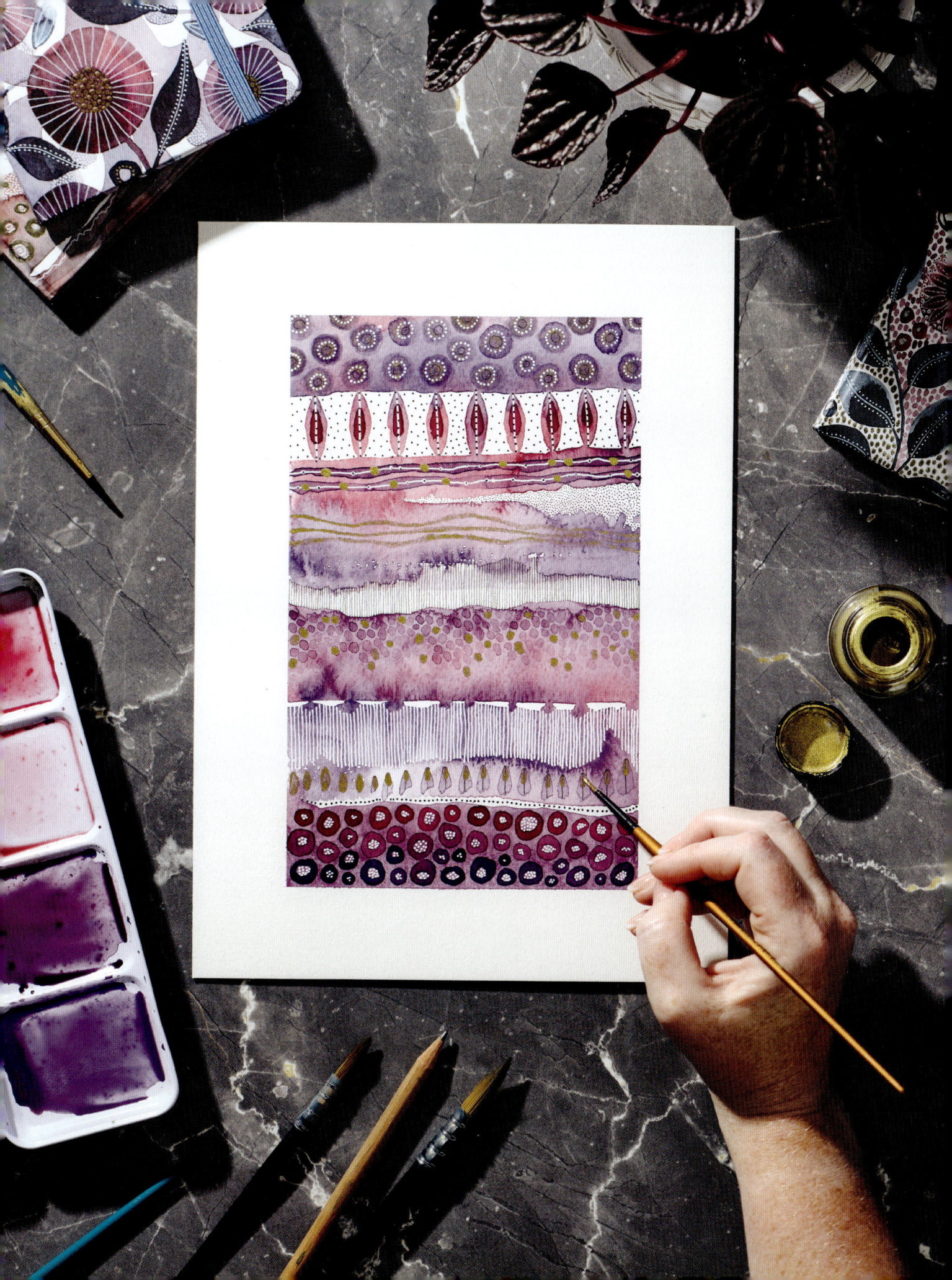

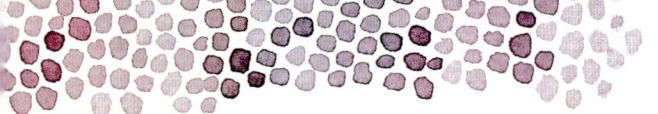

Step 1: WET PAINT

Start by masking your page (*see Techniques: Masking Borders*).

Next, wash a layer of paint in a band across the sheet to create your first stripe. Then continue with these stripes, working down the page. When you're happy with the colors and patterns, let this first layer dry completely.

Top Tip: Keep your stripes uneven and organic – the variation adds visual interest.

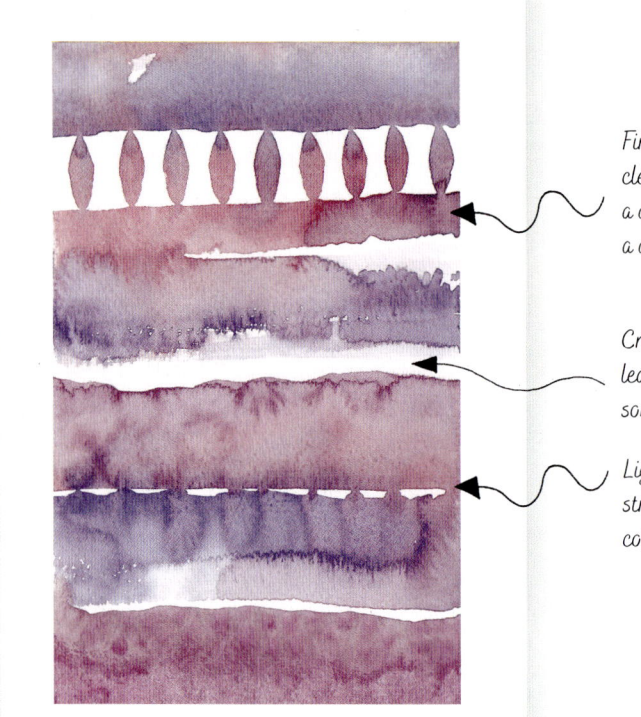

First, paint stripes on clean, dry paper. Use a drier brush to give a different effect.

Create white space by leaving gaps between some stripes.

Lightly connect other stripes to allow the colors to run together.

Step 2: WET ON DRY

Move on to brush your second layer of paint on top of the dried first layer (*see Techniques: Wet On Dry*). This is your chance to add extra color to build contrast. When happy with the overall look, let this second layer dry.

Dip your quill brush in the paint and gently press the side of the brush down to create teardrop-shaped marks.

Vary or graduate the colors to create further interest and depth.

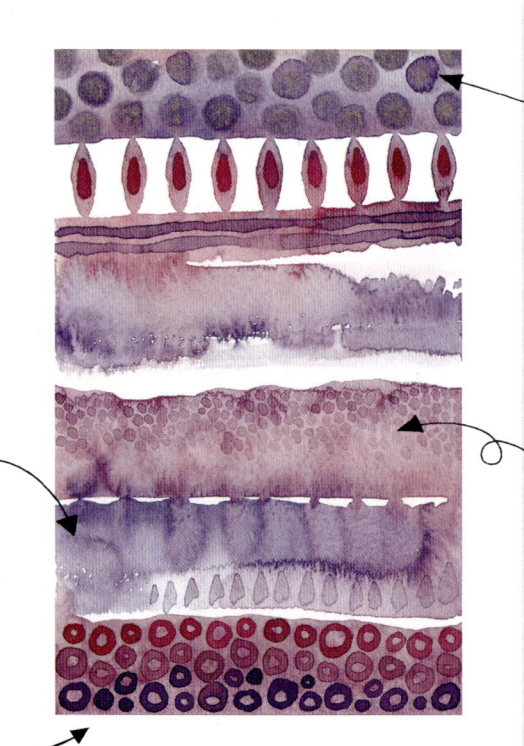

Mix the scale of your painted details. Large circles next to tiny raindrop marks add dimension.

I like to add soft raindrop dots (small dabs of very watery paint) to create texture and pattern.

Step 3: **EMBELLISHMENTS**

Use a range of different embellishments and details, again varying the size and scale to create interest.

Top Tip: When adding embellishments, I'm guided by how the paint has dried. Embrace "wobbly" lines, following them with your pen in rows of dots or simple line work to accentuate interesting shapes and textures in the paint.

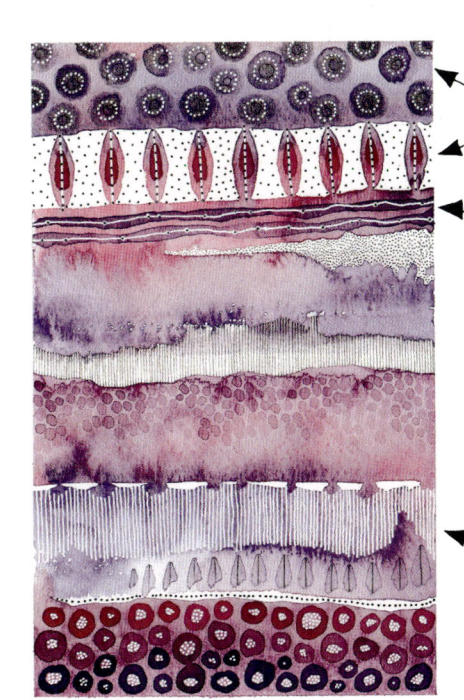

I added dot work in black and white ink. Space out some of these dots and cluster others together to create different effects.

I've used line work both vertically and horizontally to create contrast.

Try adding thicker lines with paint, as well as thinner lines using a fineliner pen.

Step 4: **GOLD HIGHLIGHTS**

The final step of the piece – gold! I always leave this stage until the end so I can judge the full piece. Look at balance and textures, then add gold only where needed. Experiment with metallics such as gold, silver, and bronze, but stop and stand back occasionally to ensure you don't overdo it. A wise person once said, "You can always add more but you can't take it away!" – so true!

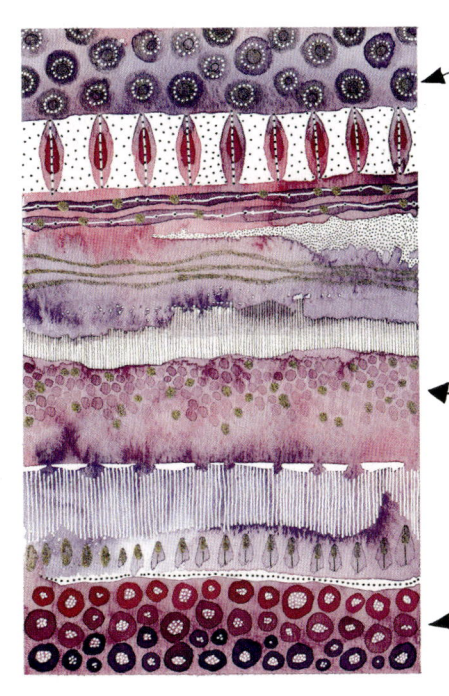

I've used gold ink here, creating diffused spots with the brush, rather than opaque marks.

Gold is a simple but effective way to highlight key areas of the design.

I've left parts of the picture free of gold highlights. With metallics, I take the "less is more" approach.

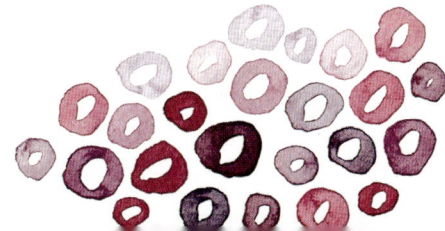

Concentric Circles

These simple concentric circles are easy to paint and fun to embellish. I always fall into a calm state when working on this style of painting – the repeat circles are so relaxing to create, it almost feels like mindfulness. The final piece looks striking and has real impact without the need to worry about composition.

MATERIALS

- Winsor & Newton professional watercolors
- Daler Rowney Aquafine Artboard
- Jackson's quill brush – sizes 0 and 10/0
- Filbert and round brushes
- Uni-ball Signo pen – white, 1mm (Broad)
- Posca paint pen – white, 0.7mm (Ultra Fine)
- Staedtler pigment liner – black (in a variety of sizes/thicknesses)

COLOR CHOICES

I've opted for cool blues and aquas – it feels quite cold and icy, almost like the center of a snowflake. You could try this piece in a variety of colors or even in rainbow hues, with each circle painted a different color.

WINSOR & NEWTON COLOR REFERENCES

- Aqua Green
- Cerulean Blue
- Cobalt Turquoise Light

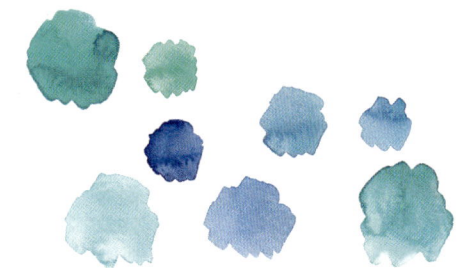

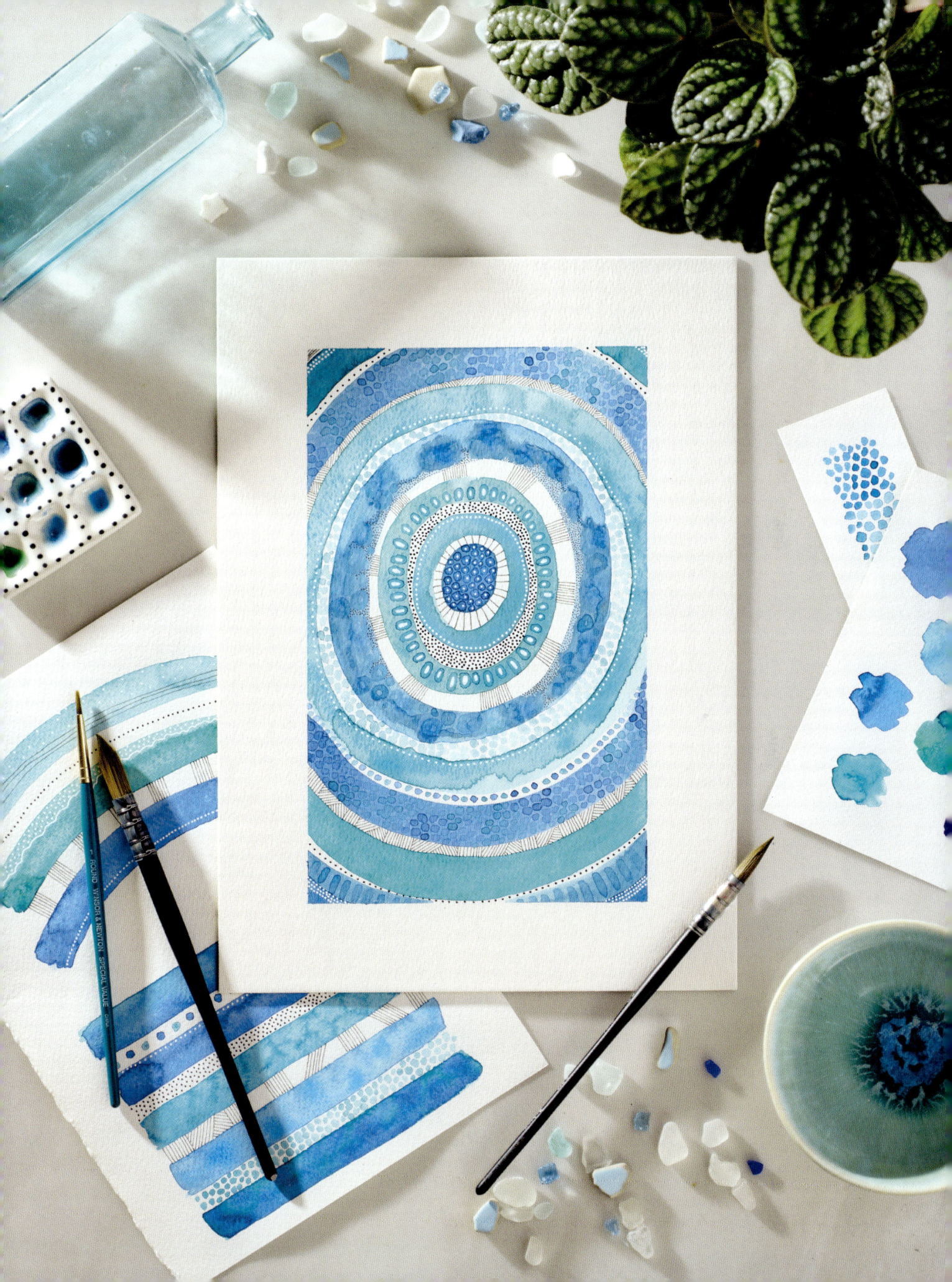

Step 1: WET PAINT

Start by masking your page (*see Techniques: Masking Borders*).

Mix three colors of paint in your palette, diluting with plenty of water, and use these as transparent washes to build color. You can also create darker areas by dipping directly into the pans for strong, undiluted color. Let the piece dry completely before moving on to the next step.

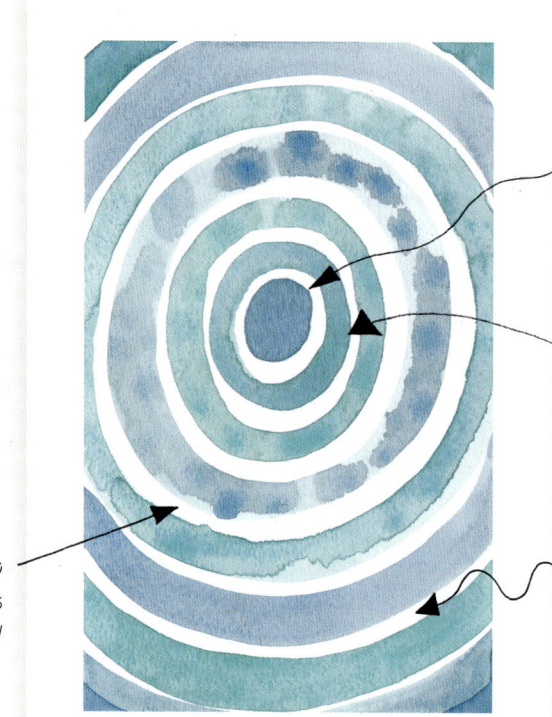

Begin roughly in the center of the page with a circle about 2.5cm (1in) in diameter.

Leaving an even gap of white around the circle, add the first ring of paint. Repeat until you have filled the page.

The painting doesn't have to be perfect – happy accidents can yield the best results!

For a organic feel, vary the widths of both the rings and the white spaces between them.

Step 2: WET ON DRY

Once the first layer is dry, you can add a second layer of wet paint onto your initial design. This can be used to add more color and contrast, or details and texture (*see Techniques: Wet On Dry*). Leave to dry.

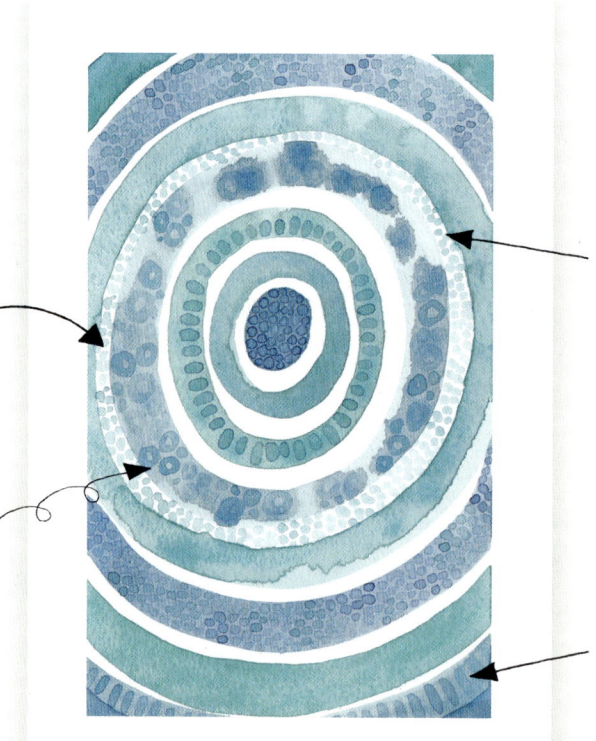

Try adding raindrop spots to the white area to create a more subtle blend between the rings.

The painted circles and spots echo the shape of the larger rings.

Loose circles made with a filbert brush contrast with the smaller raindrop spots.

Create rectangular dashes by pressing down on the side of a wet, round brush loaded with paint.

Step 3: EMBELLISHMENTS

You can see I've used a variety of embellishments and types of mark making (*see* Techniques: Mark Making). With this circular piece, I recommend leaving some circles lighter and some darker; some heavily embellished and some plain. This adds contrast, letting each circle stand out against its neighbour. If all of the circles were too similar with lots of decoration, the whole painting would lose definition and become a single mass of color.

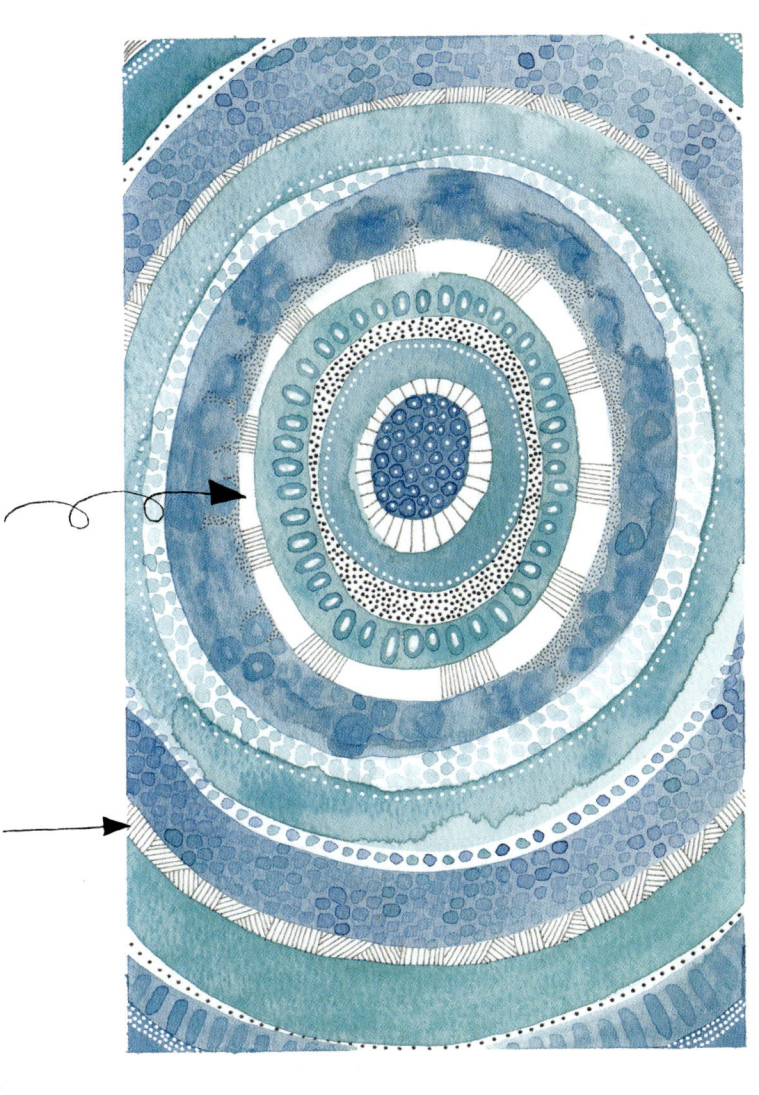

Hold back from adding embellishments to some rings to create a sense of calm.

Take advantage of areas of white space to create detailed line work.

Top Tip: Sometimes even I refrain from adding metallic embellishments! To me, this piece evokes a rippling ocean and soothing shapes, so I've left it free of metallics. But this is personal choice – who knows what shimmering effects could be achieved!

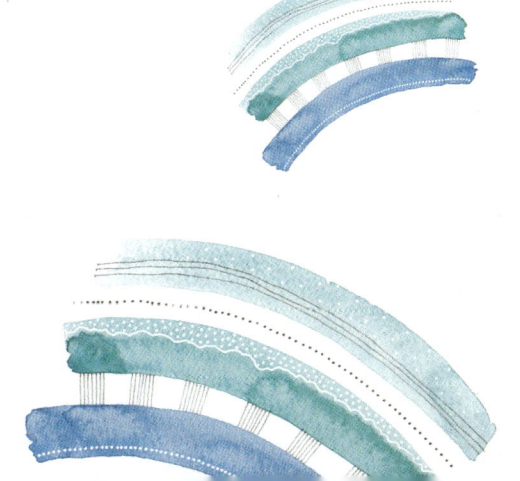

Bold Blocks

Squares and rectangles are a joy to paint – they allow you to experiment with colors, patterns, and textures. They're also great fun to embellish, and usually end up looking pretty good! You will also learn how to control the paint and keep a steady hand. I work freehand, but you can draw a simple pencil grid or outline to guide you when you're starting out.

MATERIALS

- Winsor & Newton professional watercolors
- Daler Rowney Aquafine Artboard
- Jackson's quill brush – sizes 0 and 10/0
- Filbert and round brushes
- Uni-ball Signo pen – white, 1mm (Broad)
- Posca paint pen – white, 0.7mm (Ultra Fine)
- Staedtler pigment liner – black (in a variety of sizes/thicknesses)
- Ruler and pencil

COLOR CHOICES

In abstract art, your color choices are guided by personal preference and inspiration. When I was painting this, the surrounding countryside was flourishing in seasonally warm weather. I admired the rich, brown trunks and budding leaves of trees, and green shoots emerging from fresh soil. But in the past, I've painted squares in every color of the rainbow – go crazy and enjoy the techniques.

WINSOR & NEWTON COLOR REFERENCES

- Burnt Sienna
- Burnt Umber
- Hooker's Green
- Permanent Sap Green
- Yellow Ochre

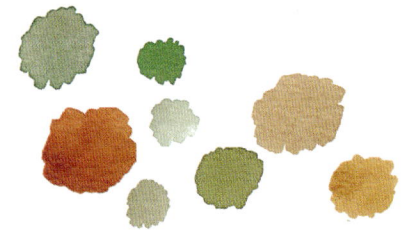

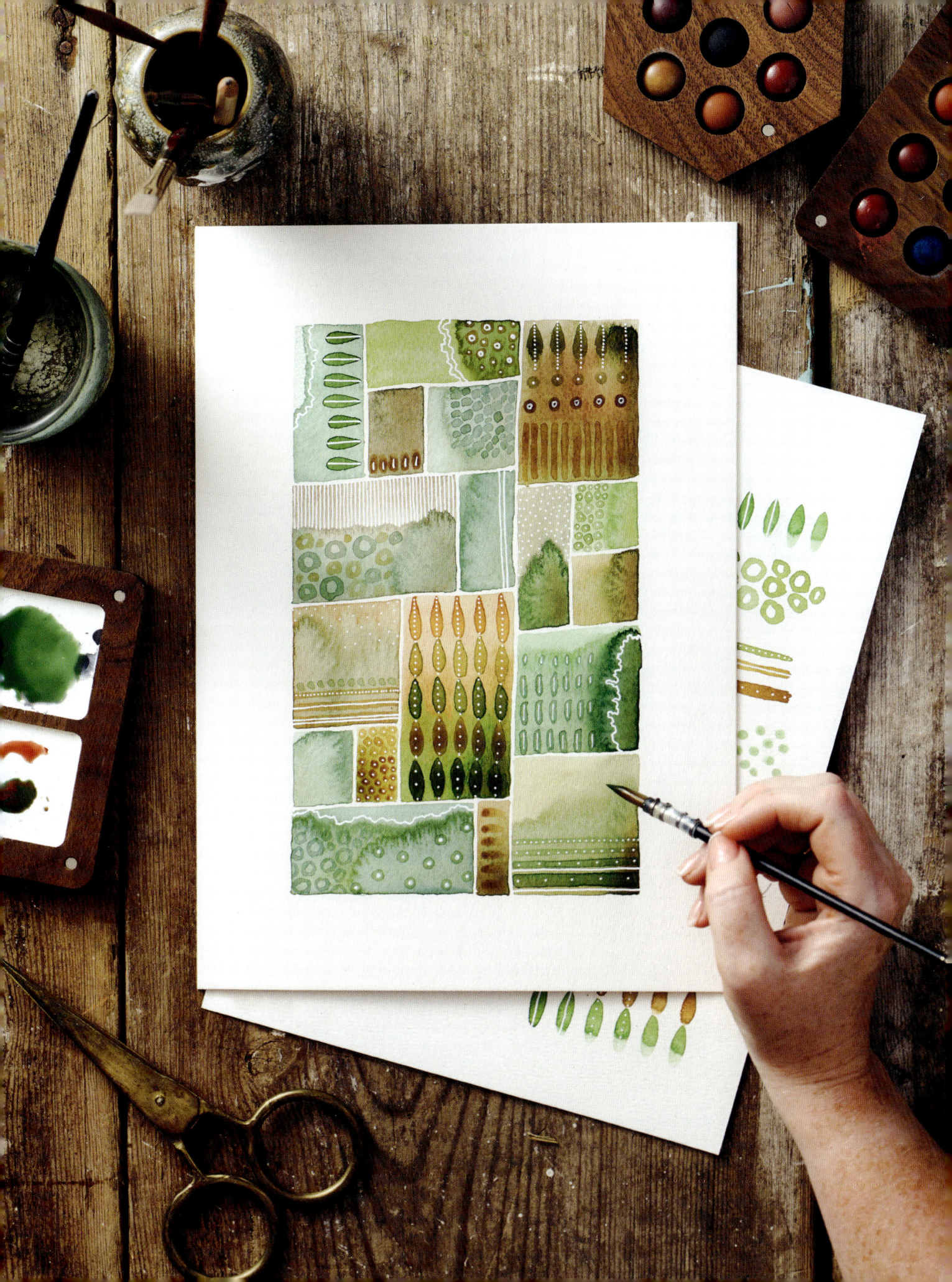

Step 1: WET PAINT

Start by masking your page (*see* Techniques: Masking Borders).

Use a pencil and ruler to mark a grid of different-sized squares and rectangles across the page, keeping them random and organic. Don't worry about being neat – lines can be erased or hidden with embellishments later.

Mix your colors in a palette. Start at the top of the grid to avoid smudging wet paint as you work. I use my brush to paint the outline of the square, then begin to fill it in. I've painted graduated squares by using a thin layer of paint at the top, then flooding the bottom with more paint. This helps to create lovely blooms and textures when dry. Fill the grid and allow to dry.

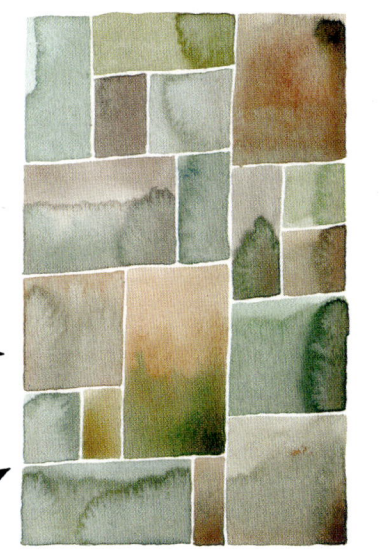

Mix the block colors across the page to create an organic effect.

Leave a thin border of paper between each block.

Step 2: WET ON DRY

With your piece totally dry, you can begin your wet-on-dry layer (*see* Techniques: Wet On Dry). I tend to like a mix of patterned and plain squares in my work to stop things from looking too busy or overdone.

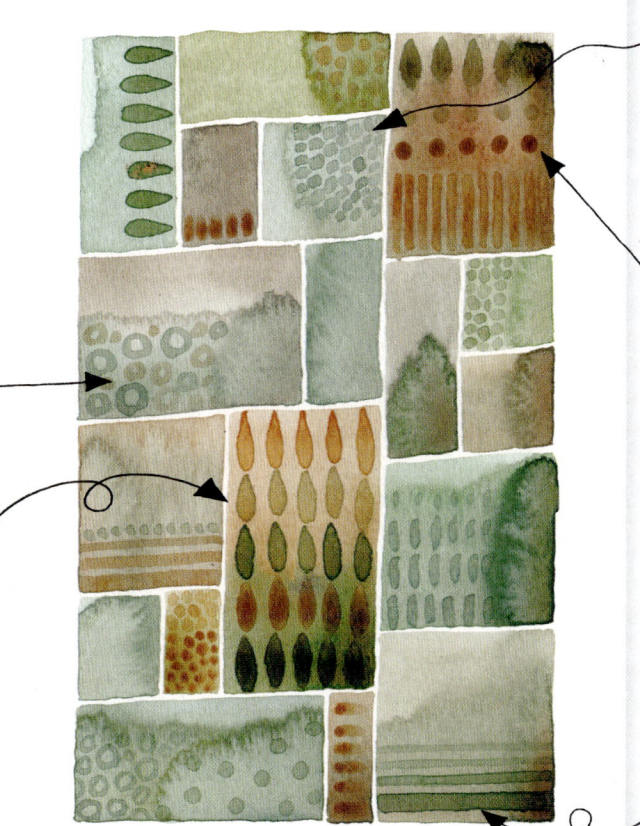

Paint loose watercolor circles in a variety of sizes.

Load a quill brush with paint and press down on the page for a teardrop-shaped mark.

Using a small round brush, create raindrop spots that match or contrast with the base color.

A cotton bud (Q-Tip) can be dipped into paint and used to stamp dots.

The quill brush creates lines in different thicknesses. Paint thin lines with the tip and add pressure for thicker lines.

Step 3: EMBELLISHMENTS

Now's the time to go wild with more decoration! I've embellished random squares using various techniques (*see* Techniques: Mark Making).

The combination of simple marks gives a highly decorative result.

White lines along the center of leaf shapes feel very organic.

Structure is added with vertical lines.

I added white fault lines where paint has bled and dried into interesting shapes.

Cleverly spaced white dots add a sense of depth to this block.

More inspiration

It's fun to experiment with color palettes and techniques with this design. You'll create different squares while building your watercolor repertoire.

Here, I've masked the edges of the paper to retain a white border, but instead of painting right up to the edge of the tape, I've left some blocks slightly short. This creates a lovely broken edge that adds variety to your block paintings. You may prefer the neat, straight edge to this more dynamic approach, but it's nice to have both styles to choose from!

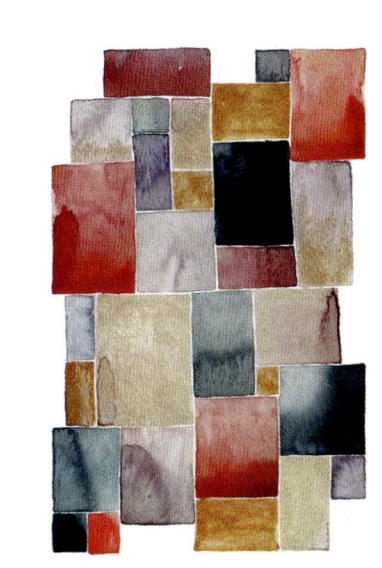

Irregular Pebbles

Pebbles are a favorite subject and one of the first things I created when I started painting. I enjoyed the process massively! There's no right or wrong, so don't try to be too precise. Let them be round, rectangular, flat, and varied in size. Think about the pebbles found on a beach or riverbed – Mother Nature doesn't care for symmetry!

MATERIALS

- Winsor & Newton professional watercolors
- Daler Rowney Aquafine Artboard
- Jackson's quill brush – sizes 0 and 10/0
- Filbert and round brushes
- Uni-ball Signo pen – white, 1mm (Broad)
- Posca paint pen – white, 0.7mm (Ultra Fine)
- Staedtler pigment liner – black (in a variety of sizes/thicknesses)
- Foam stamp

COLOR CHOICES

A recent trip to the beach inspired this soft, natural palette. Earthy browns and rich Burnt Sienna contrast so well with the cool, blue tones of Payne's Gray. Try mixing a little of the blue into the brown to create a variety of mid-tones and subtle washes (such as those seen at the top of this piece).

WINSOR & NEWTON COLOR REFERENCES

- Burnt Sienna
- Burnt Umber
- Payne's Gray
- Raw Umber

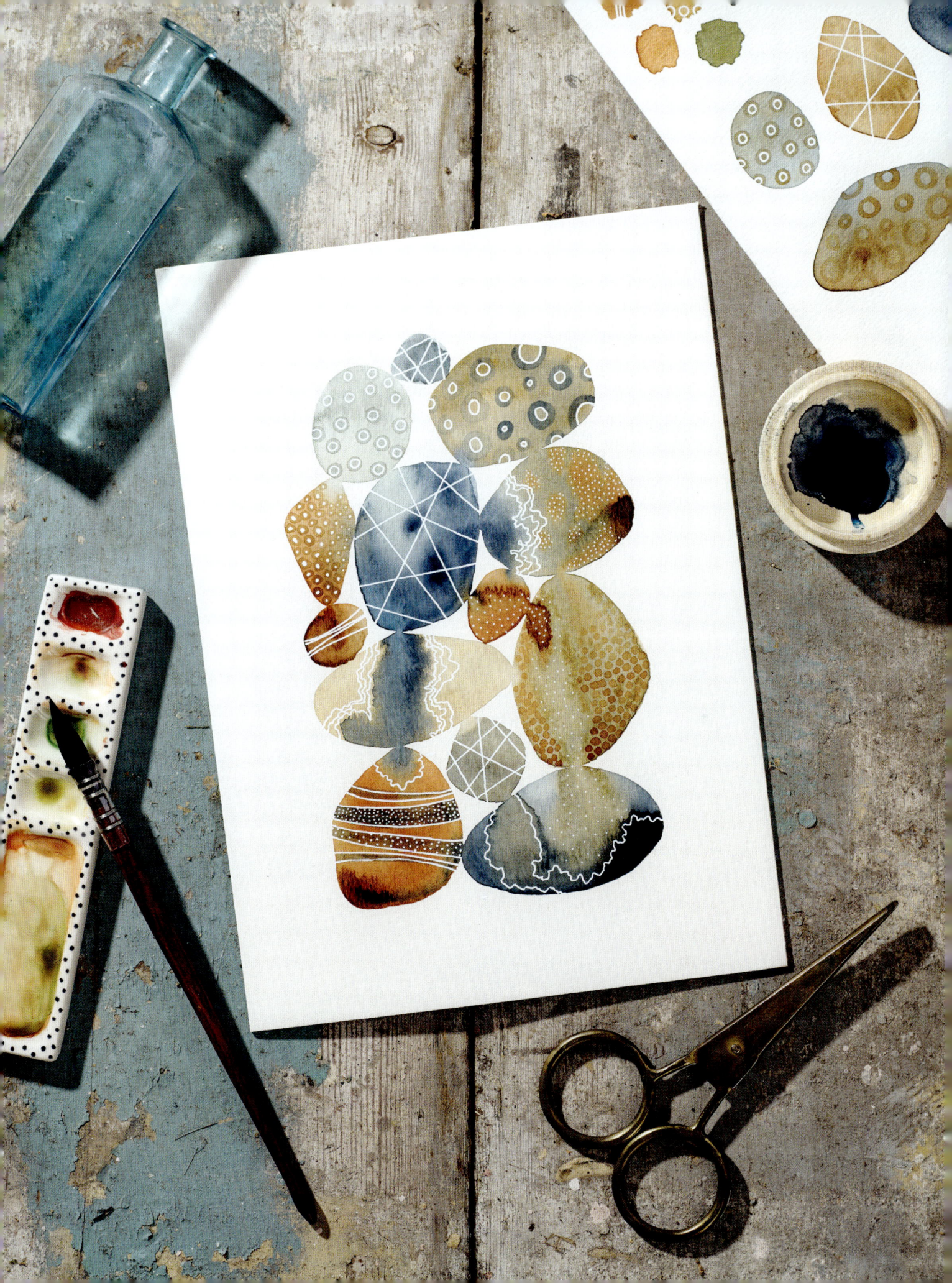

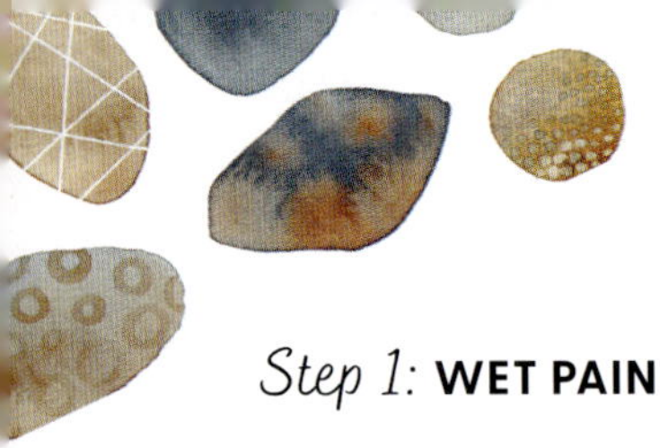

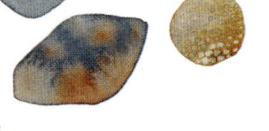

Step 1: WET PAINT

Start by masking your page (*see* Techniques: Masking Borders).

Before painting, put a small object such as an eraser under the top edge of the paper. This will make a slope that allows the wet paint to run and "pool" at the base of each pebble.

Mix your colors in a palette. Starting at the top of the page, paint a pebble, then paint another touching the first. Let the paint flow from one pebble to the next, "connecting" them. Add connecting pebbles until you have filled your page, or are happy with the composition.

Top Tip: Ensure colors flow and pool by loading your brush with plenty of paint. Leave this layer to dry completely before moving on to Step 2. If you use a lot of paint, you might have to be patient!

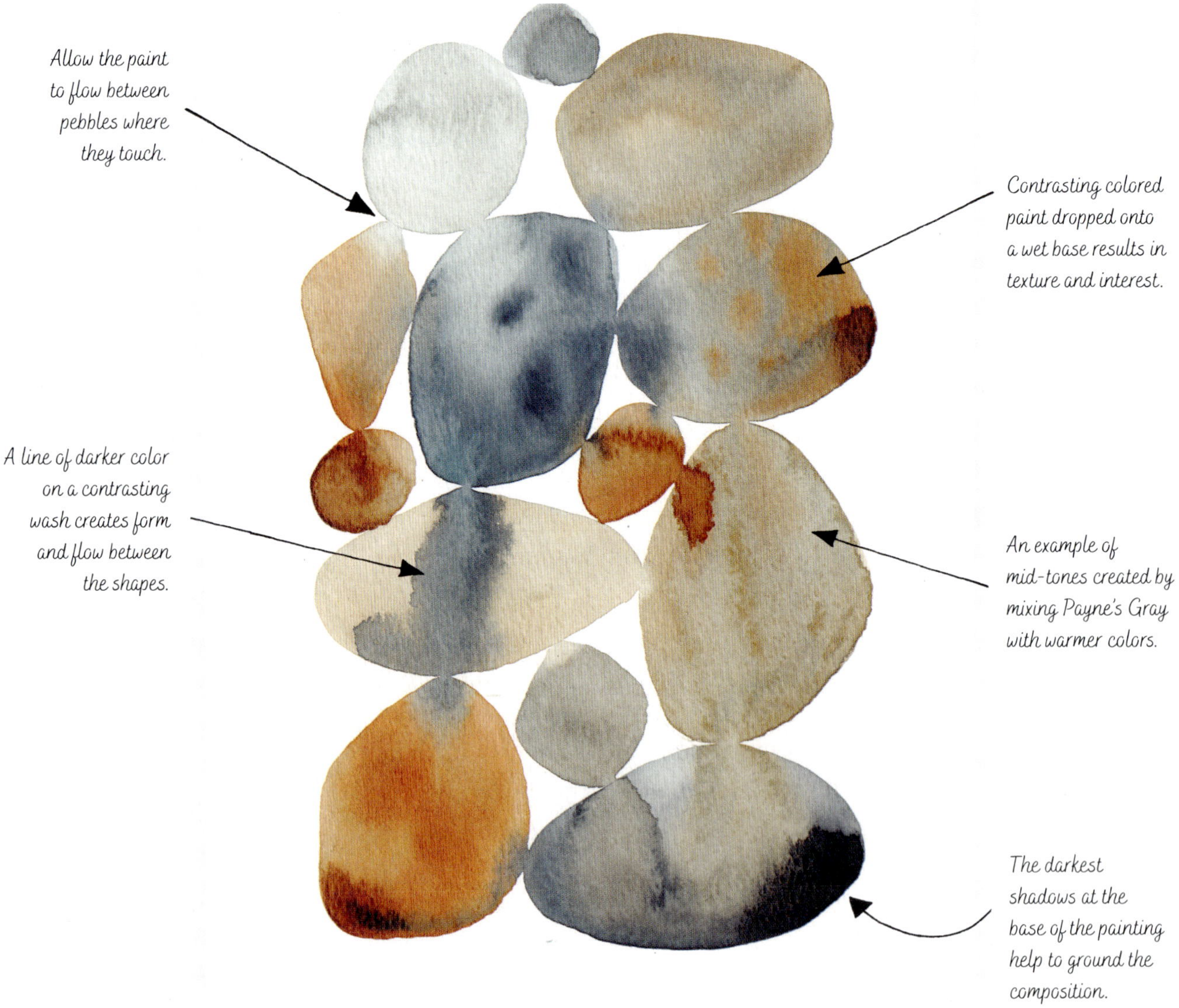

Allow the paint to flow between pebbles where they touch.

Contrasting colored paint dropped onto a wet base results in texture and interest.

A line of darker color on a contrasting wash creates form and flow between the shapes.

An example of mid-tones created by mixing Payne's Gray with warmer colors.

The darkest shadows at the base of the painting help to ground the composition.

Step 2: WET ON DRY

Once the first layer of paint is completely dry, you can begin adding the wet-on-dry layer of paint to create decorative marks and designs (*see Techniques: Wet On Dry*). I've referenced natural pebbles for this painting, with their random marks, circular patterns, and lines that cut across the surface.

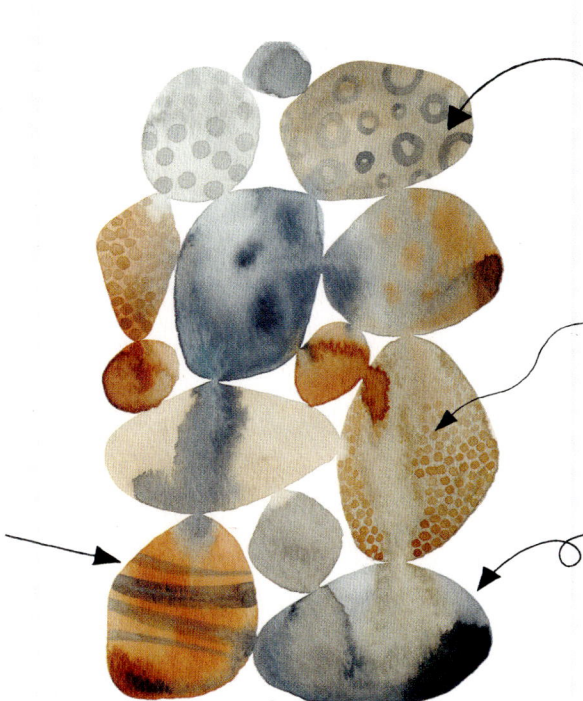

Spots of varying sizes fade and seem to disappear around the side of the pebble.

A foam stamp creates circles, leaving gaps where paint flows into the other pebbles.

I left a couple of pebbles free of extra paint as their blooms already form interesting shapes.

Stripes retain their form using the wet-on-dry technique.

Step 3: EMBELLISHMENTS

Once the paint is dry, add white details to create interest and texture (*see Techniques: Mark Making*). Draw single lines or multiple marks, depending on what you prefer. I've also used my usual array of circles, spots, and dots to decorate each stone. Leave to dry, and you're done!

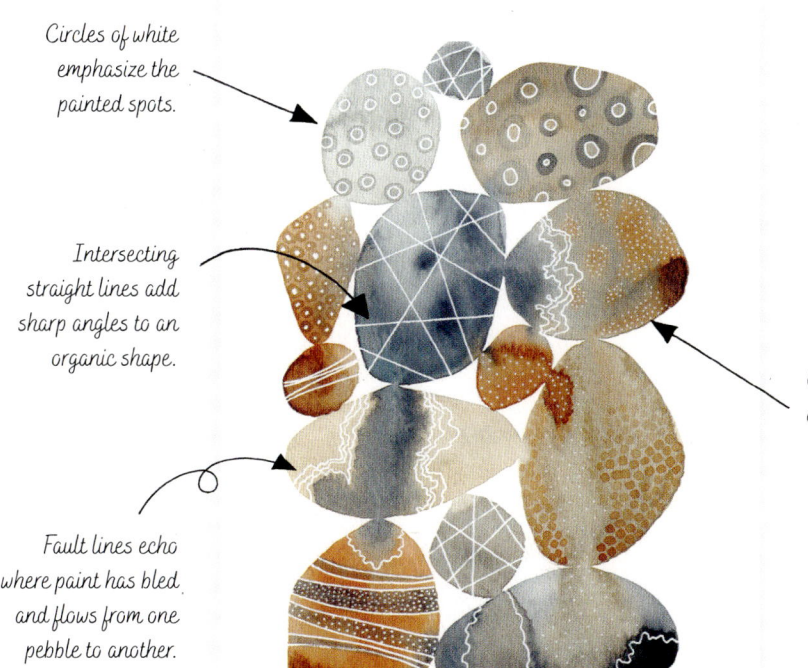

Circles of white emphasize the painted spots.

Intersecting straight lines add sharp angles to an organic shape.

Fault lines echo where paint has bled and flows from one pebble to another.

Clusters of tiny dots add texture.

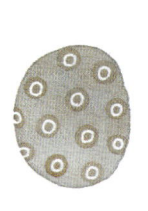

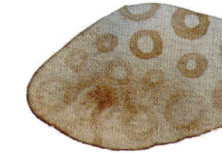

Soothing Scallops

This fun project allows you to focus entirely on colors, textures, and embellishments without the need to consider composition or form. The scallop shape is simple, yet these overlapping curves are the perfect basis for a dynamic effect. It's also a great way to experiment – try a new technique in each shape as well as creating an impressive final piece!

MATERIALS

- Winsor & Newton professional watercolors
- Daler Rowney Aquafine Artboard
- Jackson's quill brush – sizes 0 and 10/0
- Filbert and round brushes
- Uni-ball Signo pen – white and gold, 1mm (Broad)
- Posca paint pen – white, 0.7mm (Ultra Fine)
- Staedtler pigment liner – black (in a variety of sizes/thicknesses)
- Ruler (optional) and pencil
- Foam stamp

COLOR CHOICES

Scallop shapes always make me think of mermaids' tails, so I've stuck with that under-the-sea color palette. You could add purples to the mix to create a luxurious peacock palette, or try deep reds, golds, and browns reminiscent of Moroccan architecture and ornate tiles. Be inspired by the colors around you, play, and – above all – have fun!

WINSOR & NEWTON COLOR REFERENCES

- Aqua Green
- French Ultramarine
- Indigo
- Payne's Gray
- Viridian

...and mixes of the above to create lots of new shades.

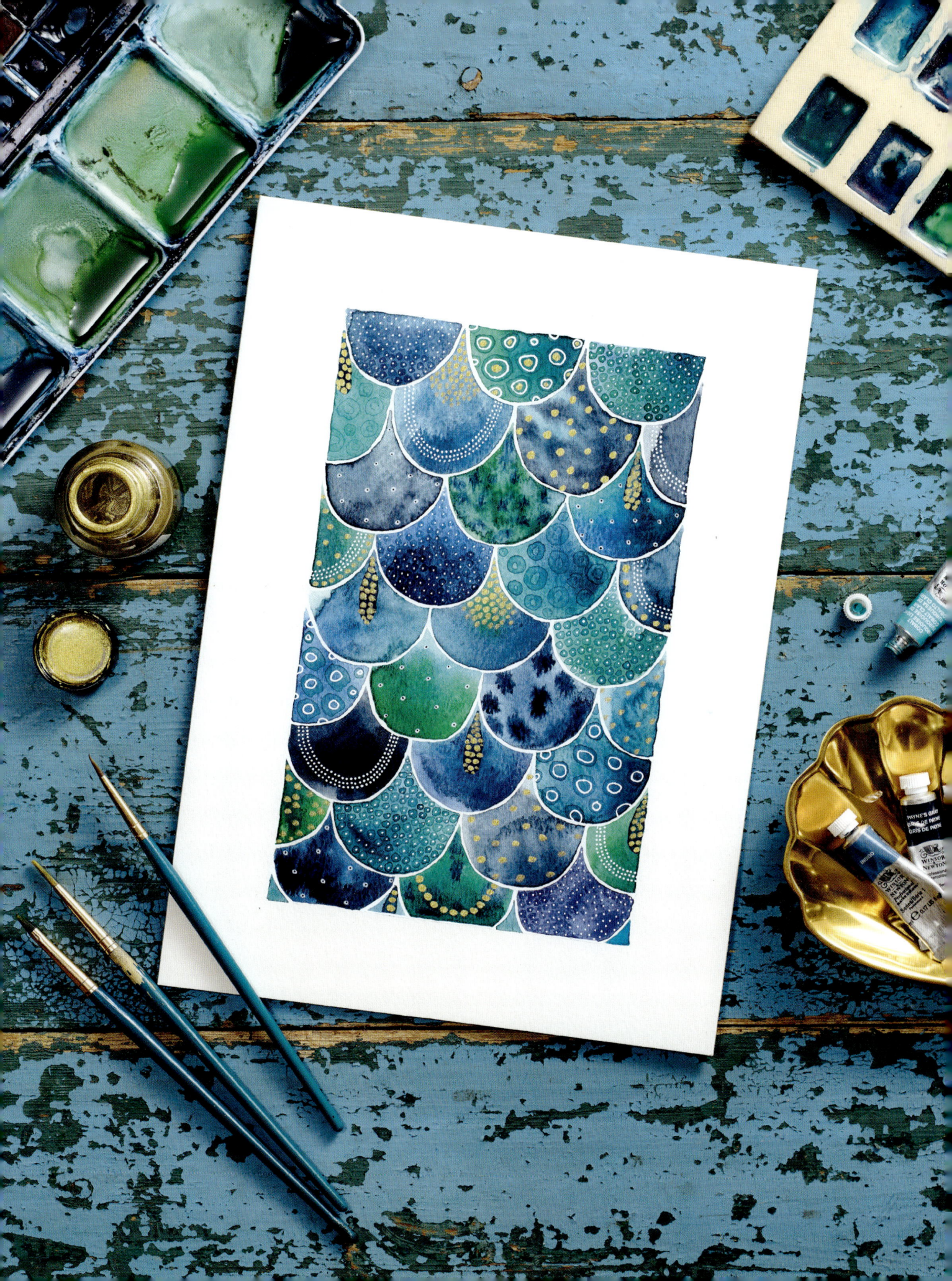

Step 1: PENCIL SKETCH

Start by masking your page (*see Techniques: Masking Borders*).

Using a pencil, sketch out your scallop shapes. Do this freehand if you're confident, or add guidelines to keep the shapes uniform. First, draw two vertical lines evenly spaced down the page. Then, working from top to bottom, add rows of scallops, starting from the center of the scallop above as shown.

Divide the width of your paper into thirds.

Continue the pencil lines onto the masked edges to keep the curved lines smooth.

My shapes aren't perfect, and yours don't have to be either!

The formation resembles a brickwork pattern – each scallop starts from the center of the one above.

Step 2: WET PAINT

With the pencil lines complete, mix your chosen colors in a palette and fill in each scallop. Leave a thin white line around each one to ensure the wet paint of each shape doesn't bleed and merge. I like to use a variety of colors, alternating darker and lighter colors to create contrast.

A happy accident – see the Top Tip!

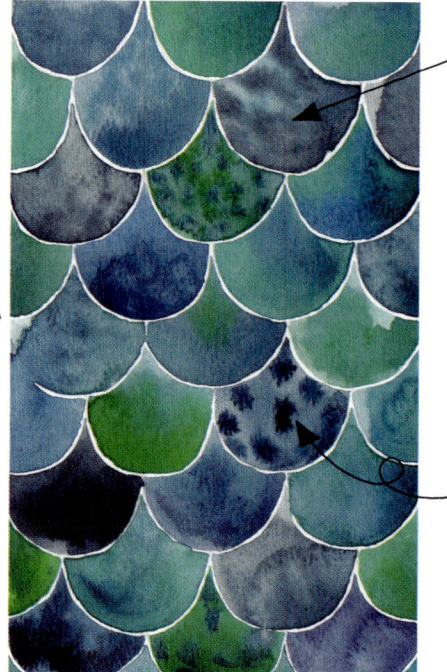

Use several colors together to add varied textures and tones across the shapes.

A watercolor wash with drops of darker paint create bold blooms.

Top Tip: If your scallops touch and bleed (a happy accident!), use a white paint pen to separate the merged shapes and tidy up wobbly edges or mistakes.

Step 3: WET ON DRY

When completely dry, you can add an additional layer of paint to create further texture and tone (*see* Techniques: Wet On Dry). If one area of your design is too light or too plain, add darker tones, spots, dots, and circles to add interest.

Once your second layer of paint is dry, correct any mistakes using your white paint pen, smoothing out lumps and bumps in the white lines.

Top Tip: The white gaps are smoothed and defined with the white paint pen, including the "happy accident" from Step 2.

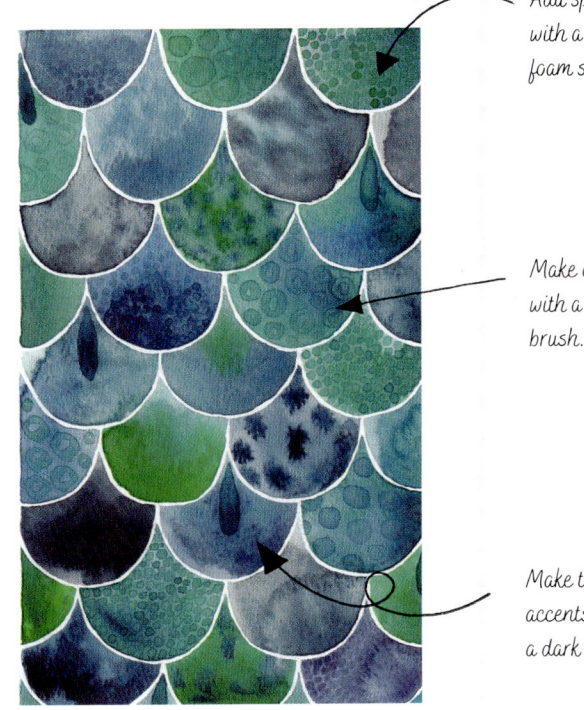

Add spots with a small foam stamp.

Make circles with a round brush.

Make teardrop accents using a dark color.

Step 4: EMBELLISHMENTS

I've used a mix of white and gold highlights to make each scallop shape unique (*see* Techniques: Mark Making). This abstract piece looks quite natural and organic, so don't worry about the embellishments looking perfect. Feel free to play and experiment – the end result will be all the better for it!

A few scallops look great with nothing added, helping to balance the overall embellishments.

Simple white circles let this shy little scallop pop!

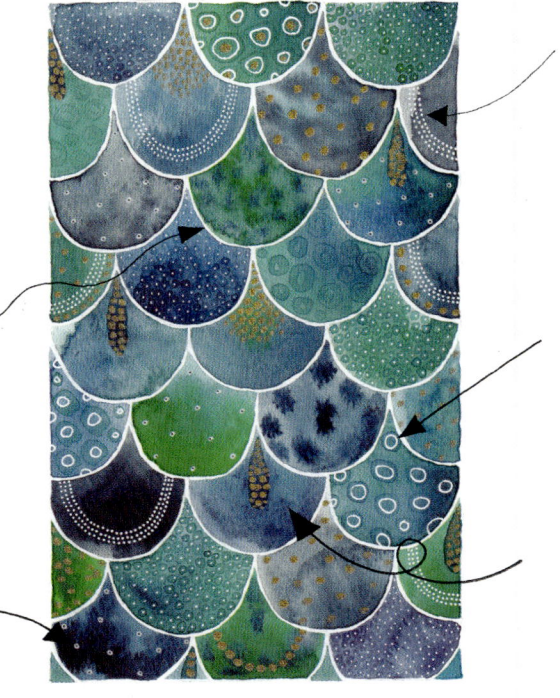

Echo the curves with dot work.

Paint spots are highlighted with white circles.

Embellished with gold, the simple teardrops look ornate.

Freestyle Abstract

We're going to use random shapes to guide our composition here, adding depth and texture with a harmonious color palette. It's when the embellishments are added that this piece really comes alive – white and black details add interest to the watercolor shapes, but the gold highlights really make the composition sing!

MATERIALS

- Winsor & Newton professional watercolors
- Daler Rowney Aquafine Artboard
- Jackson's quill brush – sizes 0 and 10/0
- Filbert and round brushes
- Uni-ball Signo pen – white and gold, 1mm (Broad)
- Posca paint pen – white, 0.7mm (Ultra Fine)
- Staedtler pigment liner – black (in a variety of sizes/thicknesses)
- Winsor & Newton Drawing Ink – gold
- Ruler (optional) and pencil

COLOR CHOICES

I've used bright blues and greens for this piece to create jewel-like tones inspired by emeralds and sapphires. I've painted a similar work (*see More Inspiration*) in rich ambers and browns, which results in a completely different mood. As with all color selection, it's a personal choice, so go for it and freestyle in whichever colors you are drawn to!

WINSOR & NEWTON COLOR REFERENCES

- Aqua Green
- Cerulean Blue
- Winsor Blue (Green Shade)
- Winsor Green (Blue Shade)

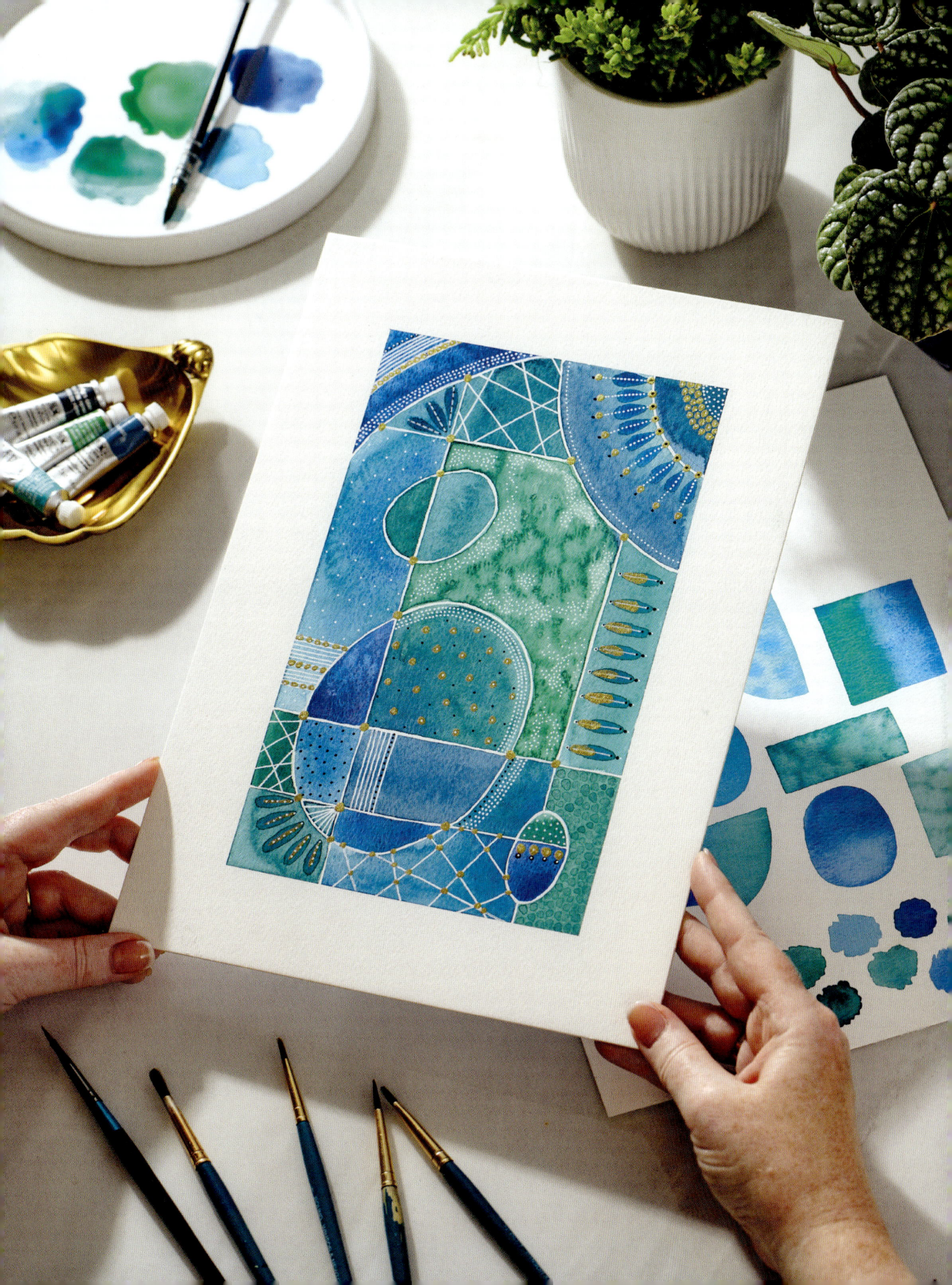

Step 1: **WET PAINT**

Start by masking your page (*see* Techniques: Masking Borders).

Sketch your composition in pencil. I used a ruler to mark "grid lines", then drew curved and circular shapes freehand. With your page masked and design sketched out, you can start to paint. Begin by filling in each shape, being careful to leave a thin strip of white between each area. Leave to dry completely.

Top Tip: To create a balanced composition, place larger shapes at the bottom of the page to avoid the painting feeling top heavy. Also, make sure some shapes intersect others to create interesting color variations.

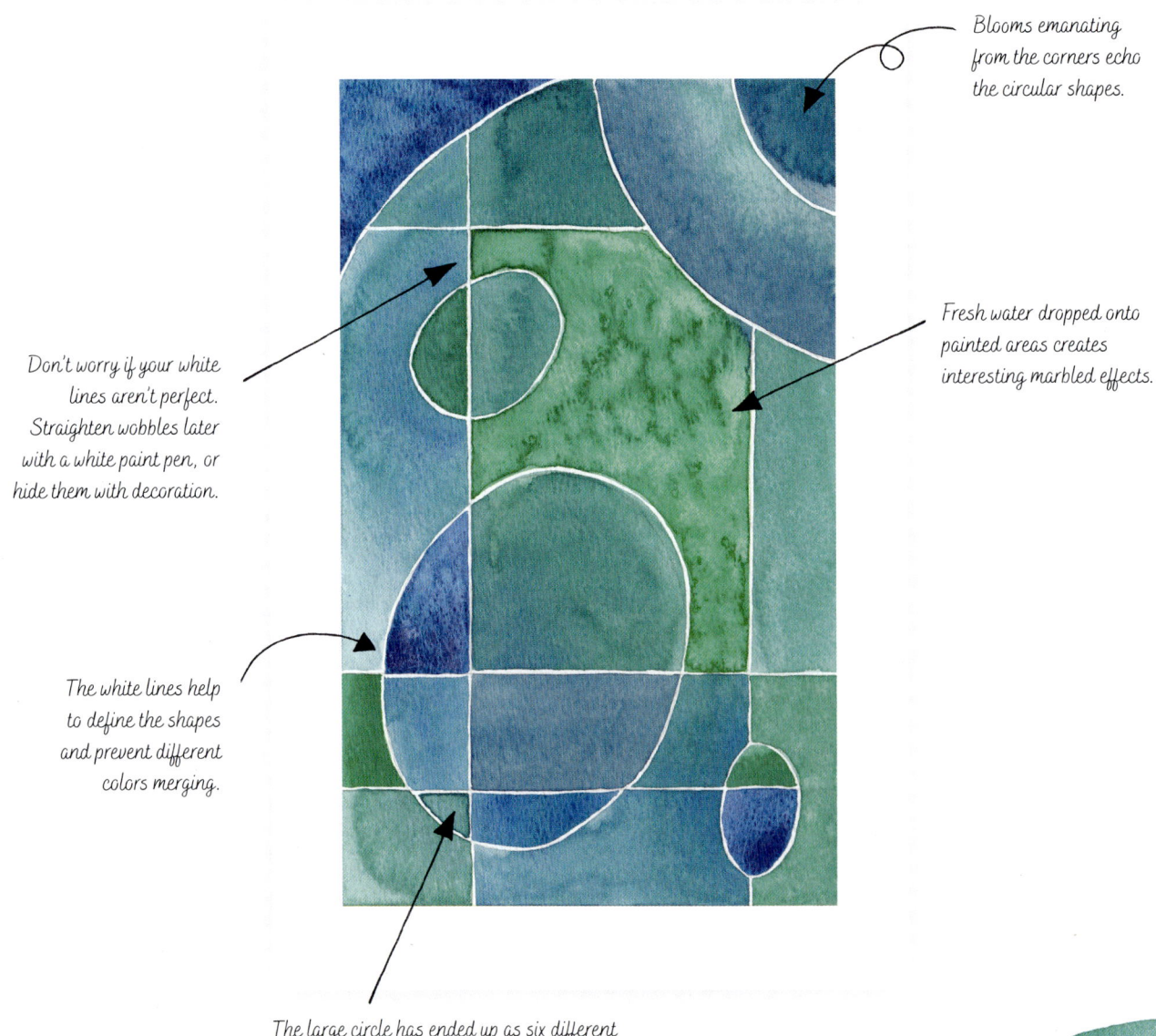

Blooms emanating from the corners echo the circular shapes.

Fresh water dropped onto painted areas creates interesting marbled effects.

Don't worry if your white lines aren't perfect. Straighten wobbles later with a white paint pen, or hide them with decoration.

The white lines help to define the shapes and prevent different colors merging.

The large circle has ended up as six different sections, offering lots of color and texture options.

Step 2: WET ON DRY

I like the simple textures and colors, so haven't done too much at this stage. I just added a few details using my quill brush (*see* Techniques: Easy Organic Brushwork Shapes).

The teardrops look impressive when fanned out in a corner.

A deeper mix of the base color creates elegant tonal details.

I "stamp" my quill brush to create a teardrop shape.

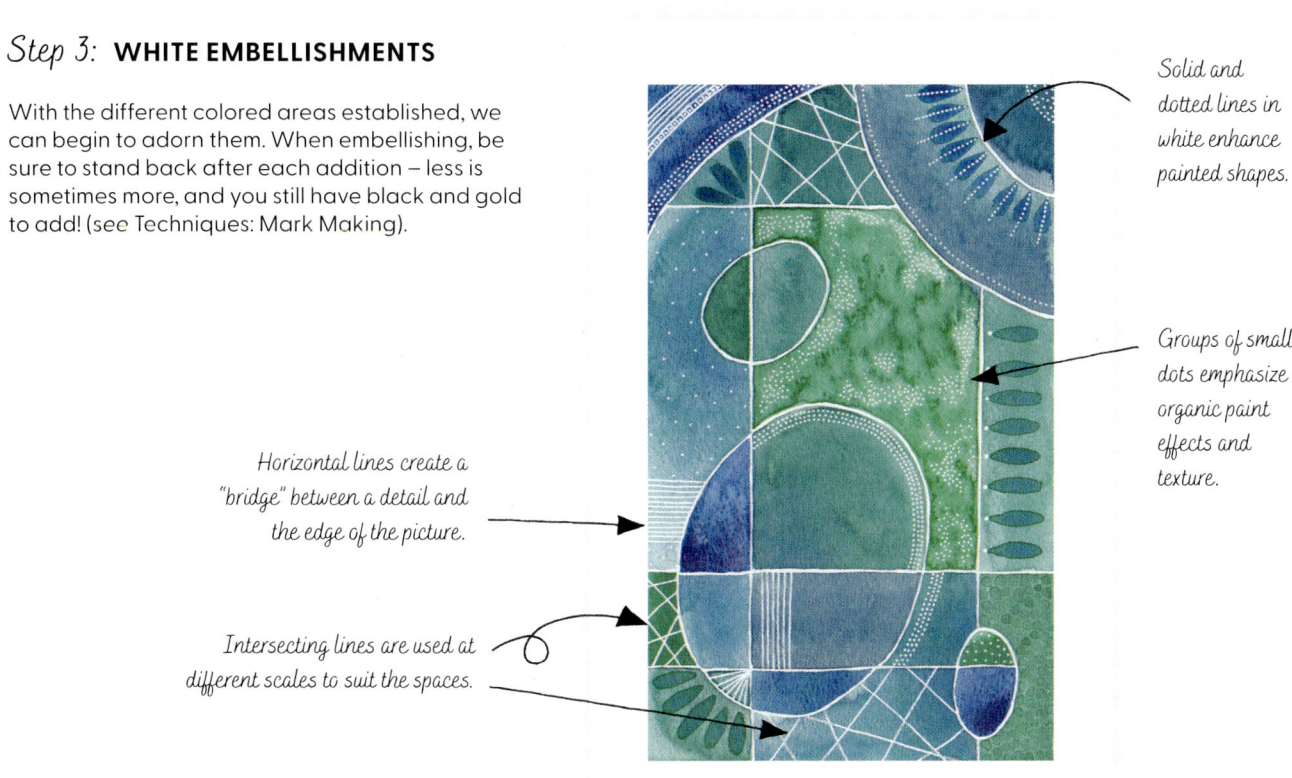

Step 3: WHITE EMBELLISHMENTS

With the different colored areas established, we can begin to adorn them. When embellishing, be sure to stand back after each addition – less is sometimes more, and you still have black and gold to add! (*see* Techniques: Mark Making).

Solid and dotted lines in white enhance painted shapes.

Groups of small dots emphasize organic paint effects and texture.

Horizontal lines create a "bridge" between a detail and the edge of the picture.

Intersecting lines are used at different scales to suit the spaces.

Step 4: GOLD EMBELLISHMENTS

When you're happy with the white details, you can use gold ink to add carefully considered metallic sparkle across the painting.

Give the painted leaves a luxurious feel with gold ink, creating opulent, feather-like shapes.

Highlight where grid lines cross with gold spots.

Add more form and dimension to the smaller intersecting lines with gold spots that guide the eye.

Step 5: BLACK EMBELLISHMENTS

I had originally planned to use only white and gold for this piece. However, when standing back I felt something was missing, so opted to add black details to create more contrast and definition.

Allow your details to dry before carefully removing the masking tape border (see Techniques: Masking Borders). Then stand back and admire your finished piece!

This small row of black dots helps to ground the composition without overwhelming it.

A mix of tiny black and white dots enhance the gold ink, adding depth.

Bolder black dots are used sparingly and kept in a small space.

I used mainly dots for this black layer — sometimes solid black lines can look too heavy.

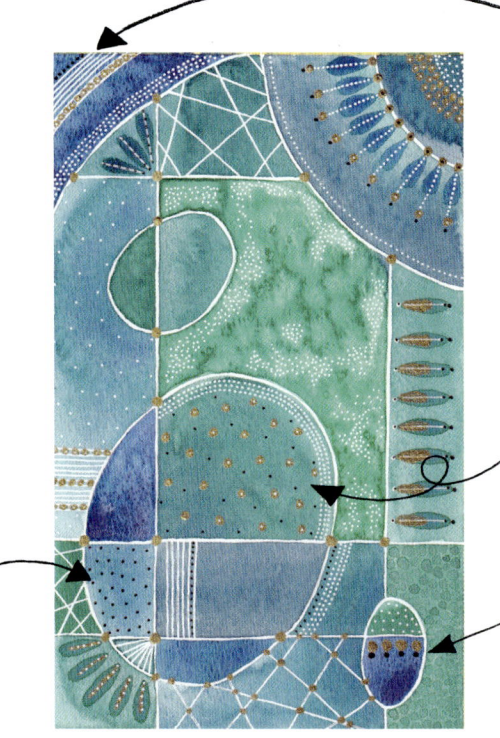

More inspiration

I created this piece in a warm palette of amber, gold, burnt sienna, and a mix of warm browns and oranges I made myself. It was painted during a heatwave, and I think you can tell from my color choices! This gives a rich, jewel-like look – quite different from the cool ocean blues of the main project, but equally as striking.

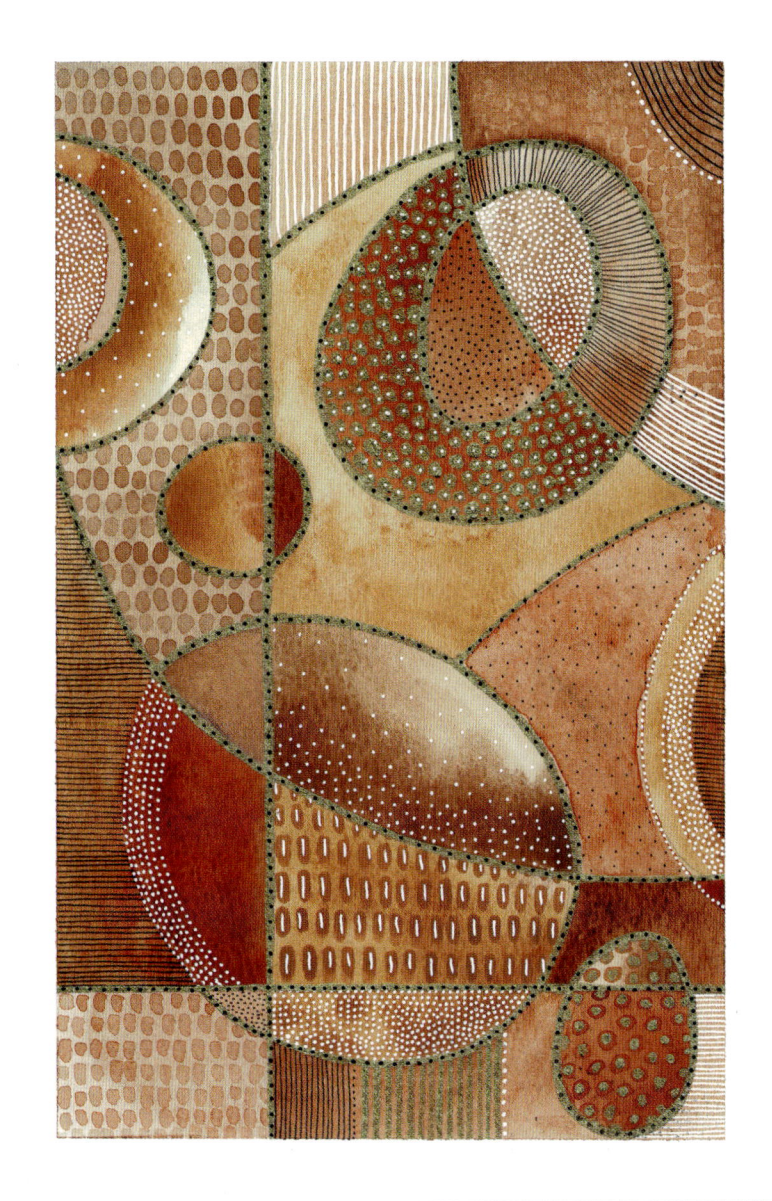

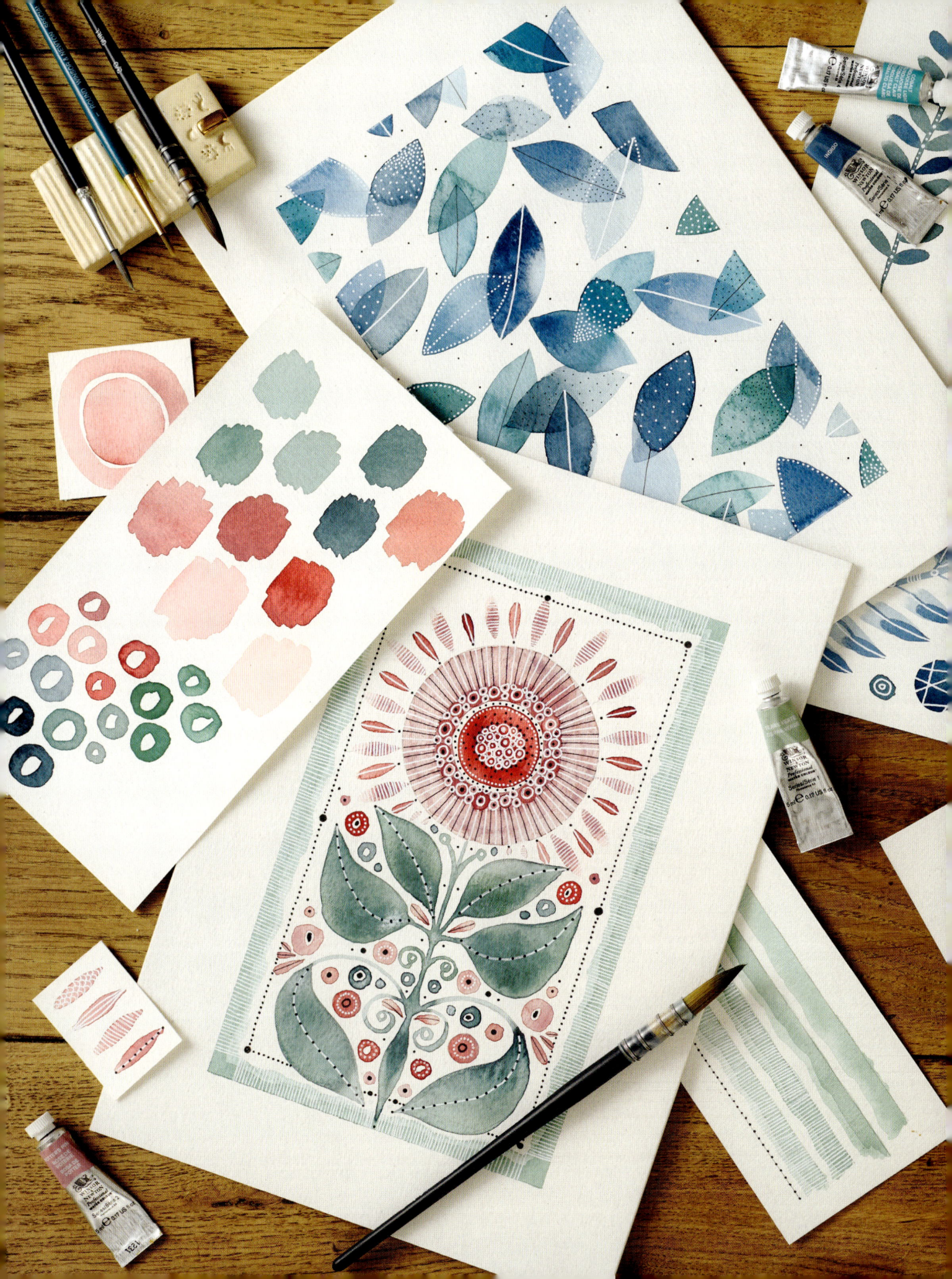

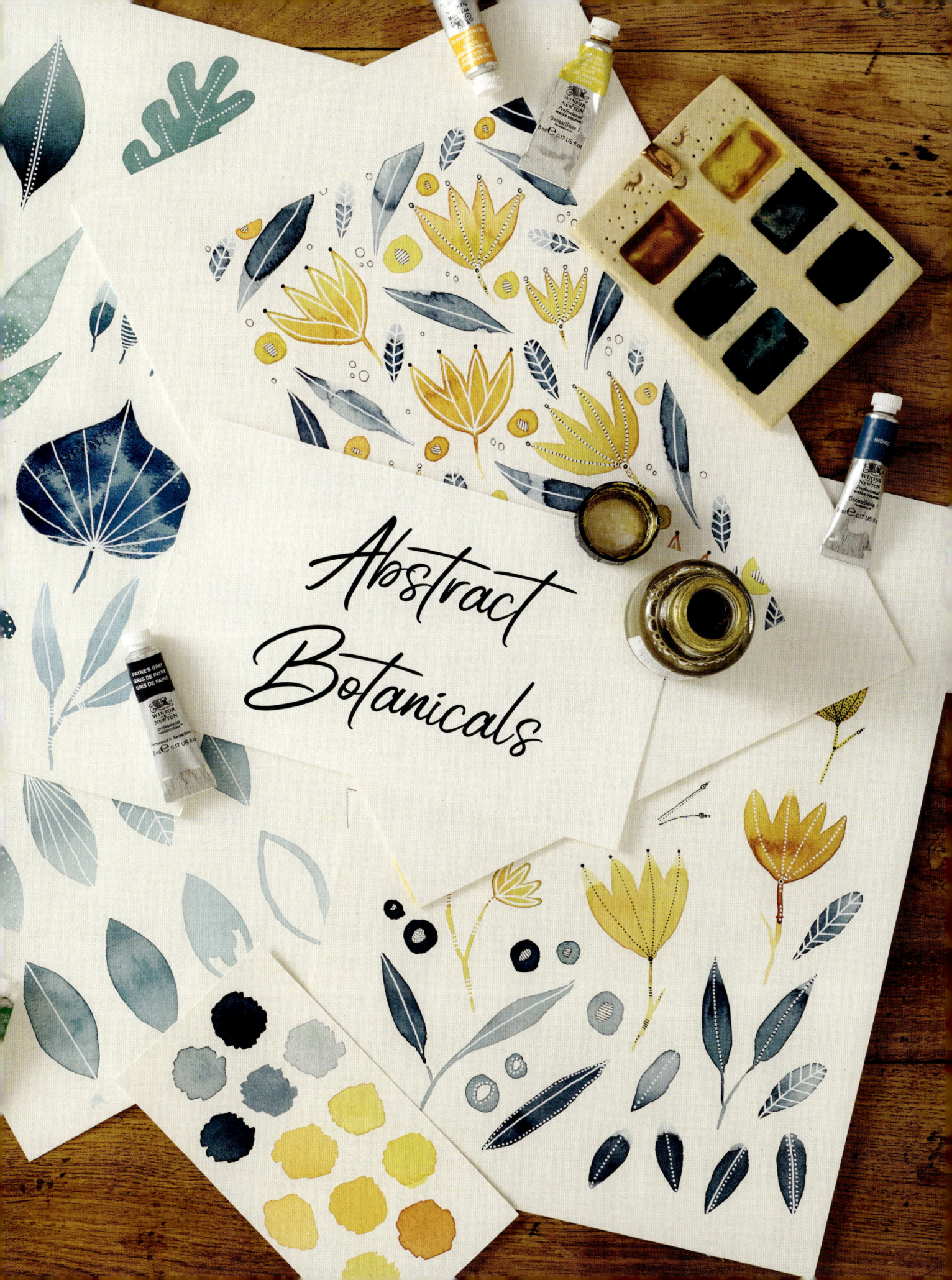

Abstract
Botanicals

Stylized Flowers

Flowers can be tricky to paint if you're trying to recreate a particular variety. So instead, I turn my basic watercolor circles into abstract blooms! Not only is this approach simple and effective, but by varying the size and colors of the circles you can create anything from large, lush bouquets to delicate vines, sprigs, and other floral beauties.

MATERIALS

- Winsor & Newton professional watercolors
- Daler Rowney Aquafine Artboard
- Jackson's quill brush – sizes 0 and 10/0
- Filbert and round brushes
- Uni-ball Signo pen – white, 1mm (Broad)
- Posca paint pen – white, 0.7mm (Ultra Fine)
- Staedtler pigment liner – black (in a variety of sizes/thicknesses)
- Pencil (optional)

COLOR CHOICES

I've gone with a warm, summery palette of pinks, purples, and orange for this piece, but you can create cool winter blooms by using pale greens and icy blues. Or why not go even more abstract with black and navy, which look stunning embellished with white, gold, and silver!

WINSOR & NEWTON COLOR REFERENCES

- Alizarin Crimson
- Cadmium-Free Yellow
- Payne's Gray (optional)
- Winsor Orange
- Winsor Violet (Dioxazine)

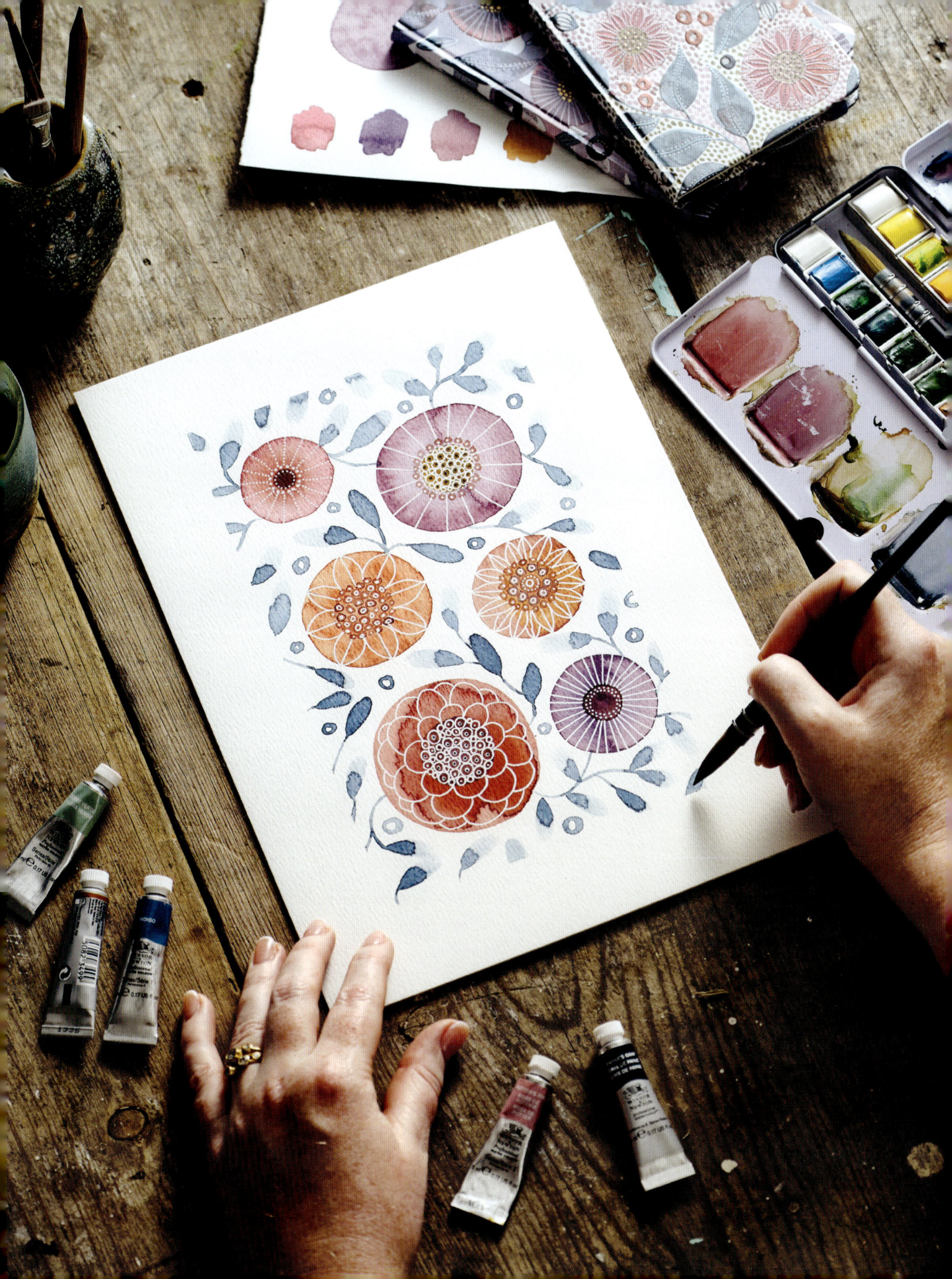

Step 1: **WET PAINT**

Start by masking your page (*see* Techniques: Masking Borders).

Depending on the look you want, begin with any number of circles. I've gone for six circular shapes in various sizes. To start painting, load your brush with plenty of watery paint (if it's too thick, you won't get the lovely effects of the water blooms). Take your brush and gently start to paint the edge of the circles first, then fill the circle from the edge into the center.

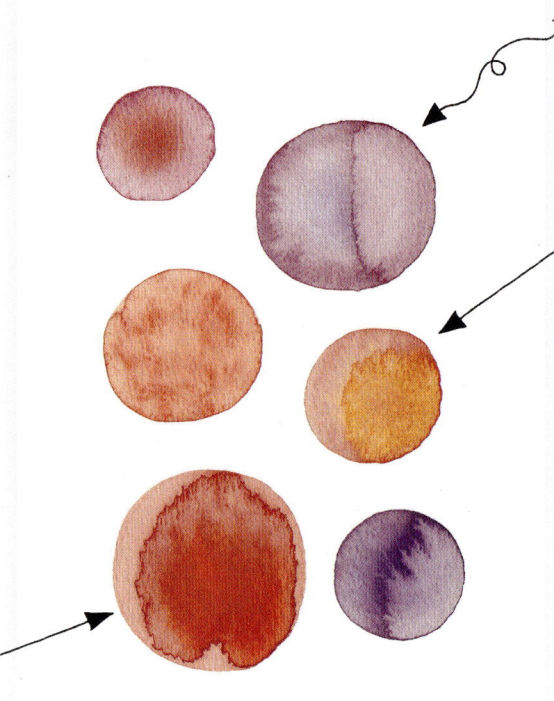

Drop more paint around the edge to get a deeper ring of color.

Until you feel ready to paint freehand, you can sketch circles in pencil first.

Drop another color into the center of a circle to recreate the inner stamens (we'll add details later).

· ·

Step 2: **WET ON DRY**

Paint a second layer of wet paint on top of your dry circles to create extra details and texture. If you prefer a simple, clean look, skip this step and move straight on to embellishment.

Top Tip: Create contrast between the center and outer "petals" of each flower. I've added dark centers to lighter flowers, and vibrant centers to muted ones. These organic shapes have no rules – play and have fun!

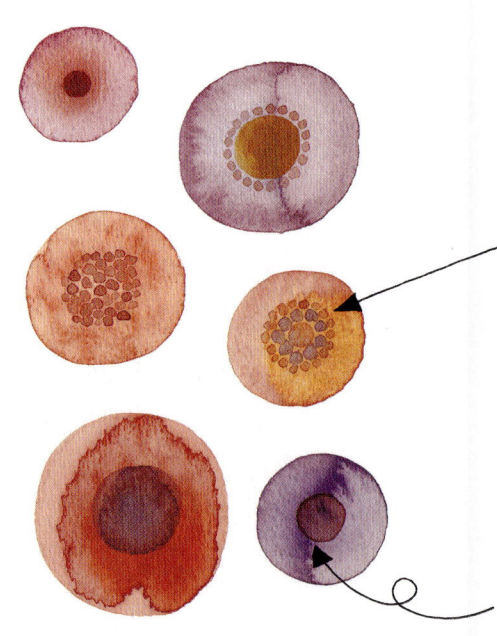

Raindrop spot techniques add definition to the flower centers.

Try adding a more defined and contrasting center circle.

Step 3: EMBELLISHMENTS

To evoke a range of different flower varieties, there are several effects you can use to add interest. I've used a few simple marks to bring the circles to life!

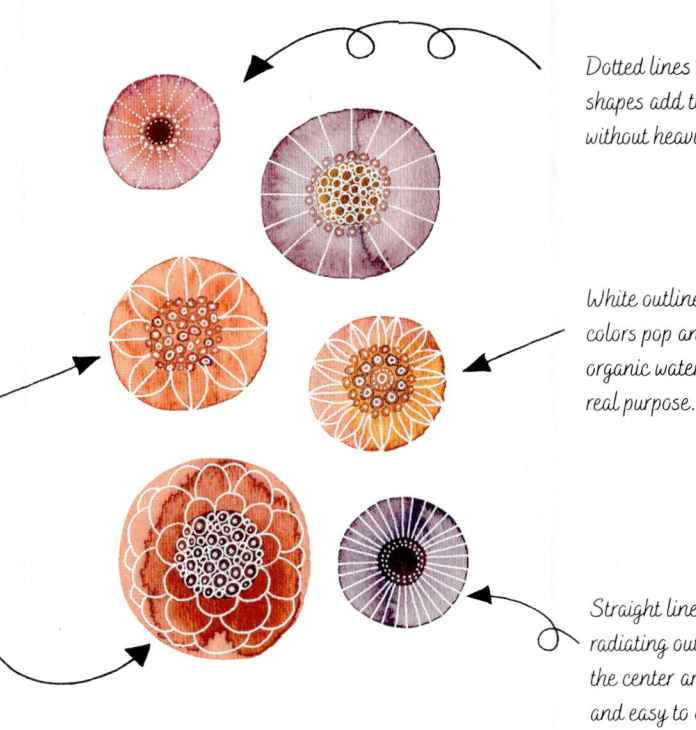

The combination of large petals and tiny circles adds form.

Build concentric circles of scalloped petals around a decorative center.

Dotted lines and shapes add texture without heaviness.

White outlines make colors pop and give organic water blooms real purpose.

Straight lines radiating out from the center are quick and easy to draw.

Step 4: BACKGROUND LEAVES

With your flowers complete, you can stop here as a fun exercise, or carry on and turn them into a final piece. I opted for the latter, mixing a loose wash of Payne's Gray and adding leaves. Start a stem or vine from the edge of each flower. To add a leaf, lay down a quill brush loaded with paint flat on its side. This will leave a leaf-shaped, stamped imprint. I then filled the gaps with loose circles (*see* Techniques: Spots and Circles). When everything has dried, you can remove the masking tape.

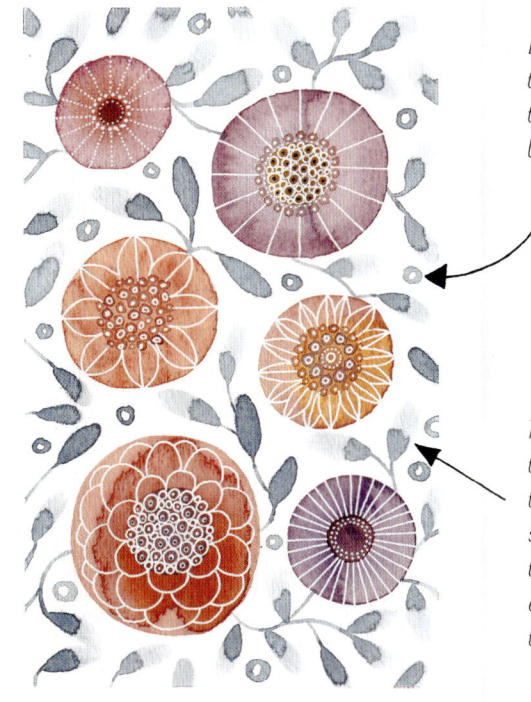

Loose circles in this piece give the impression of little seed pods.

Paint tends to be thicker and darker at the base of the brush, so when you stamp the brush down, you end up with a lovely two-tone effect.

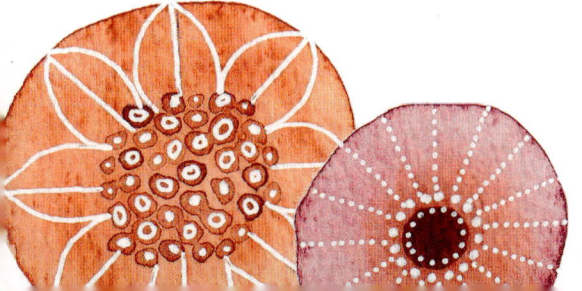

Simple Leaves

Leaves are a lovely way to practice watercolor and play with new paint colors, water blooms, and embellishments. They look simple, but varying the size and color creates beautiful abstract compositions. As you grow in confidence, you can paint repeating patterns that allow you to experiment with fabric, giftwrap, or even wallpaper designs.

MATERIALS

- Winsor & Newton professional watercolors
- Daler Rowney Aquafine Artboard
- Jackson's quill brush – sizes 0 and 10/0
- Filbert and round brushes
- Uni-ball Signo pen – white, 1mm (Broad)
- Posca paint pen – white, 0.7mm (Ultra Fine)
- Staedtler pigment liner – black (in a variety of sizes/thicknesses)

COLOR CHOICES

I've gone with a soft palette of blues, aquas, and greens. While it may be tempting to go for the very literal leafy-green shades, a shift into a more muted, softer palette can help add an air of sophistication to your work. With that said, these shapes work in any color combination, so why not go for deep autumnal reds and oranges, or the unexpected hues of blacks and grays for a steely, monochrome look?

WINSOR & NEWTON COLOR REFERENCES

- Aqua Green
- Indigo
- Payne's Gray
- Winsor Green (Blue Shade)

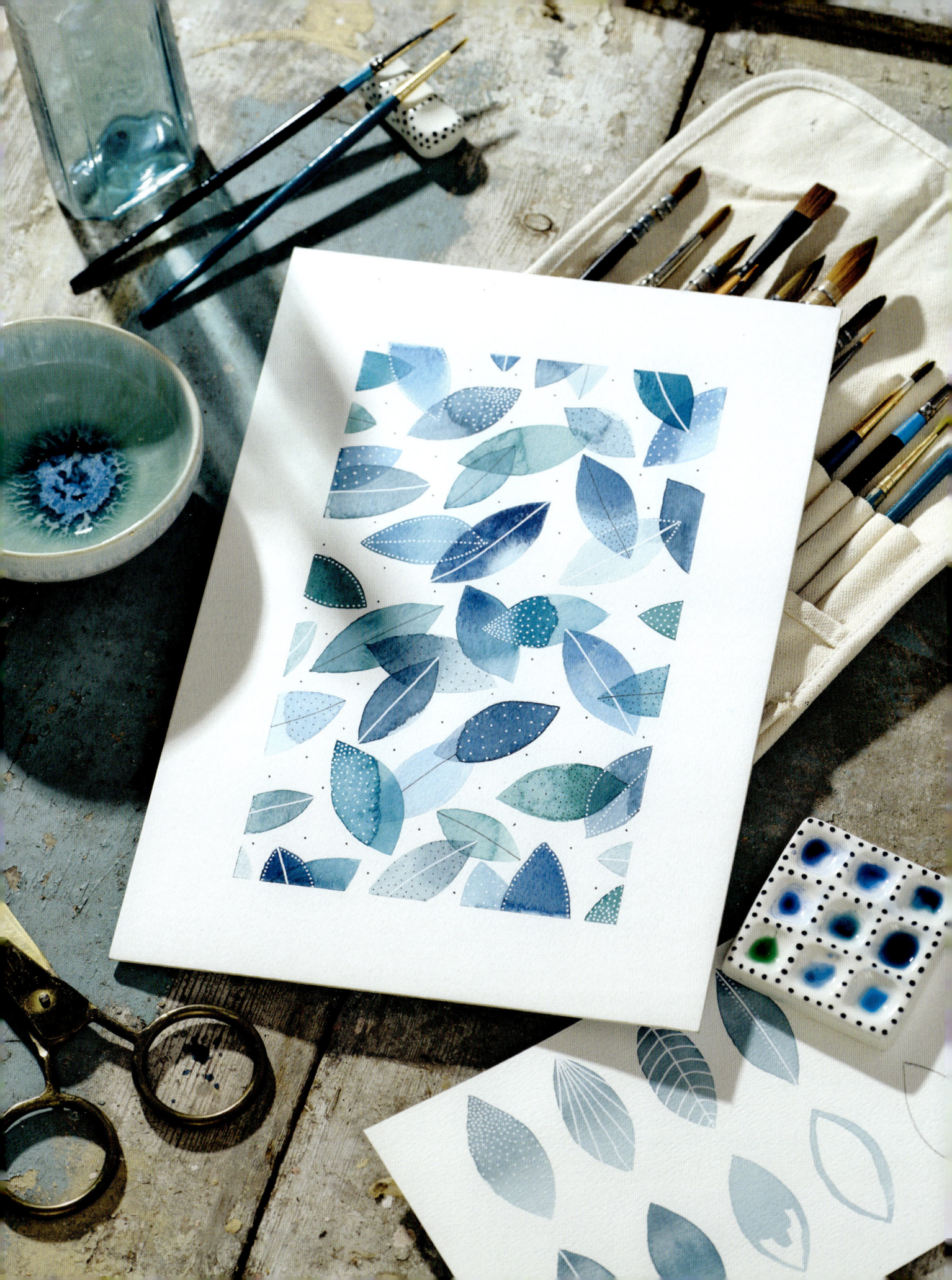

Step 1: WET PAINT

Start by masking your page (see Techniques: Masking Borders) to create a plain white border. This will give a lovely effect once the tape is removed. Start to paint simple leaf shapes in a mixture of three colors.

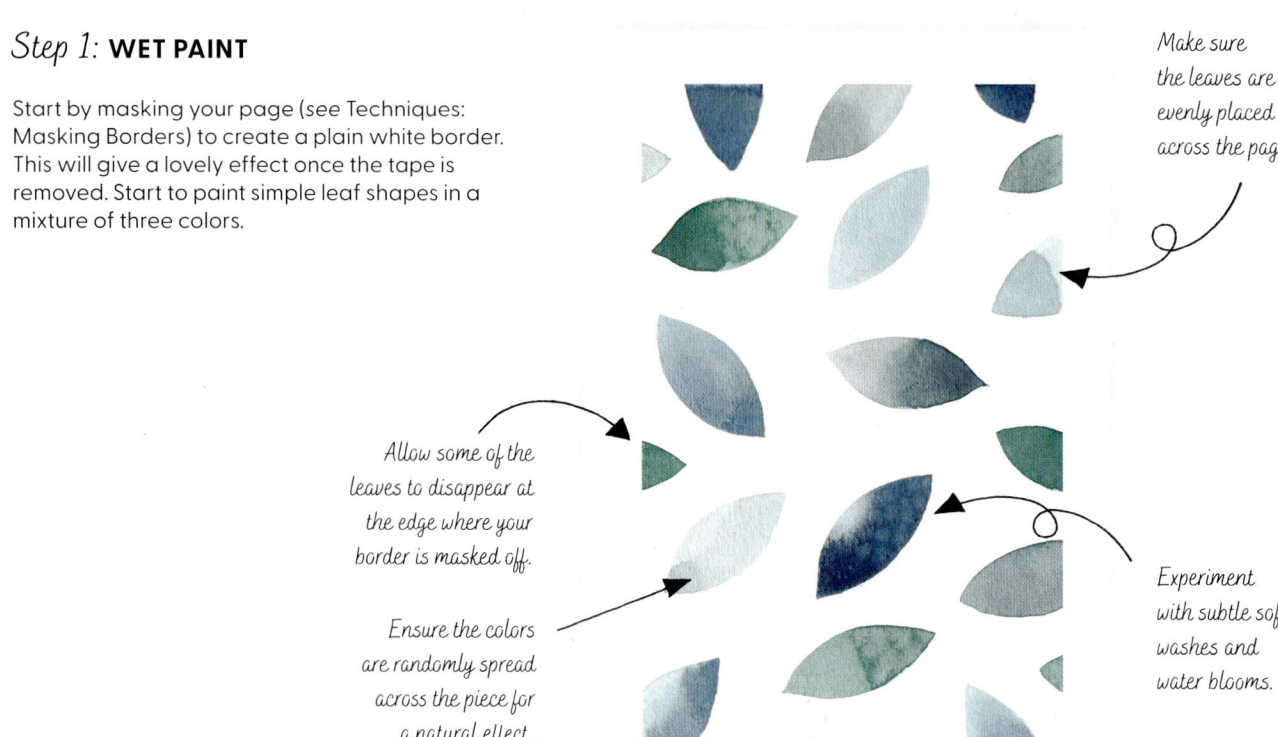

Make sure the leaves are evenly placed across the page.

Allow some of the leaves to disappear at the edge where your border is masked off.

Ensure the colors are randomly spread across the piece for a natural effect.

Experiment with subtle soft washes and water blooms.

Step 2: WET ON DRY

Once your initial layer of leaves has dried, start adding the second layer, filling any large gaps or white spaces. Allow your leaves to overlap.

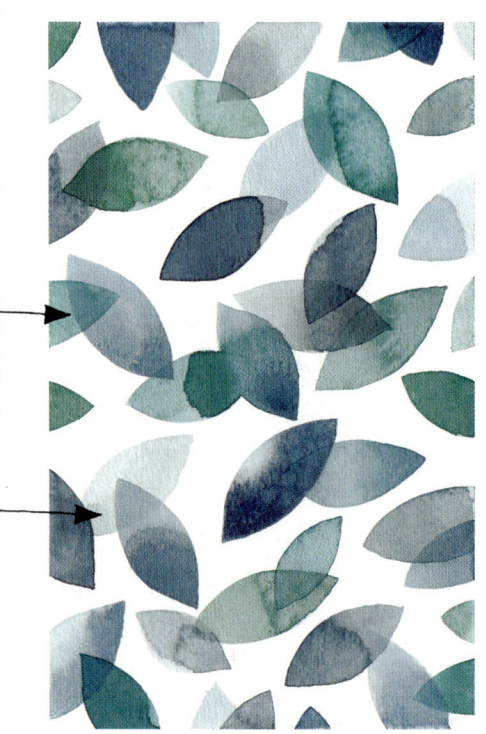

Paint overlapping leaves with a paler wash to let the dried leaves show through.

The sheer washes and contrast of dark and light build depth and movement.

Top tip: Some leaves are much darker at one end, achieved by "flooding" more paint into this area, which allows the pigment to pool and create a lovely, graduated color.

Step 3: **EMBELLISHMENTS**

These leave are a natural shape, but I still like to stylize the decorative elements – dots and lines – to add interest and variety (*see Techniques: Mark Making*). Again, keep the effect evenly scattered across the piece.

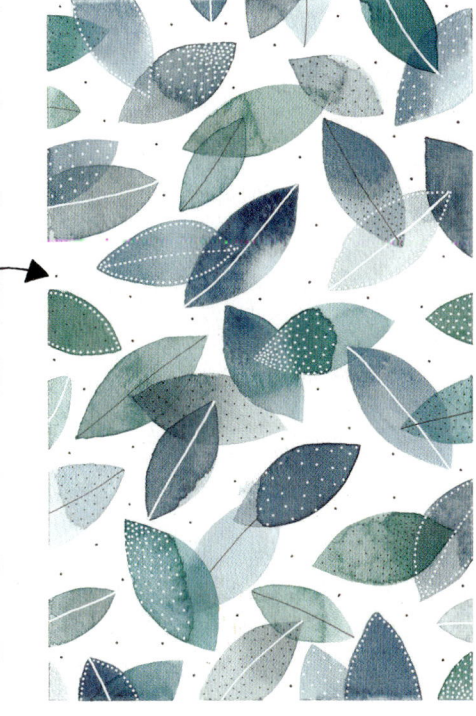

I've added simple black lines with black spots across lighter areas of the leaf.

Dots emphasize organic water blooms for a beautiful, intentional effect.

Simple white or black lines cut horizontally through some leaves, suggesting the central vein.

Marks help to showcase the transparency and layered effect.

Step 4: **EXTRA DETAILS**

Remove the tape and have a good look at your final piece – are you happy with it? Does it look balanced, or is there anything missing? Sometimes "less is more" and I'll be happy to stop. Other times I'll feel a little something extra is required! I've used a fineliner pen to fill the empty spaces with dots, but haven't gone too far as the piece could easily start looking too busy.

A nice alternative to these dots would be small gold circles, suggesting seed pods.

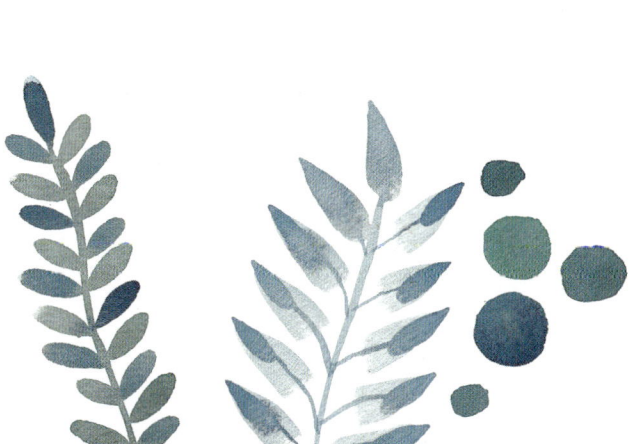

Striking Bloom

This slightly more challenging floral piece was inspired by art deco symmetry, pattern, and design. Although this isn't "true" abstract (you can see it's a representation of a flower), it's unlike any flower you would see in nature! The strict symmetry and floating petals are abstract in their design, featured purely for a pleasurable aesthetic rather than accuracy.

MATERIALS

- Winsor & Newton professional watercolors
- Daler Rowney Aquafine Artboard
- Jackson's quill brush – sizes 0 and 10/0
- Filbert and round brushes
- Uni-ball Signo pen – white, 1mm (Broad)
- Posca paint pen – white, 0.7mm (Ultra Fine)
- Staedtler pigment liner – black (in a variety of sizes/thicknesses)
- Sheet of tracing paper to fit over your flower design
- Ruler and pencil

COLOR CHOICES

I've kept things fresh and in keeping with art deco style by mixing soft pink, a deeper pink, and crisp, minty green. Most of these colors have been made using the base colors listed below, adding various amounts of white watercolor paint to create dreamy pastel hues. There are no strict rules or ratios when mixing your own colors, so go with your gut, experiment, and enjoy yourself!

WINSOR & NEWTON COLOR REFERENCES

- Alizarin Crimson
- Hooker's Green
- Permanent Rose
- White

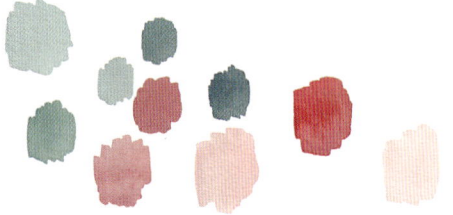

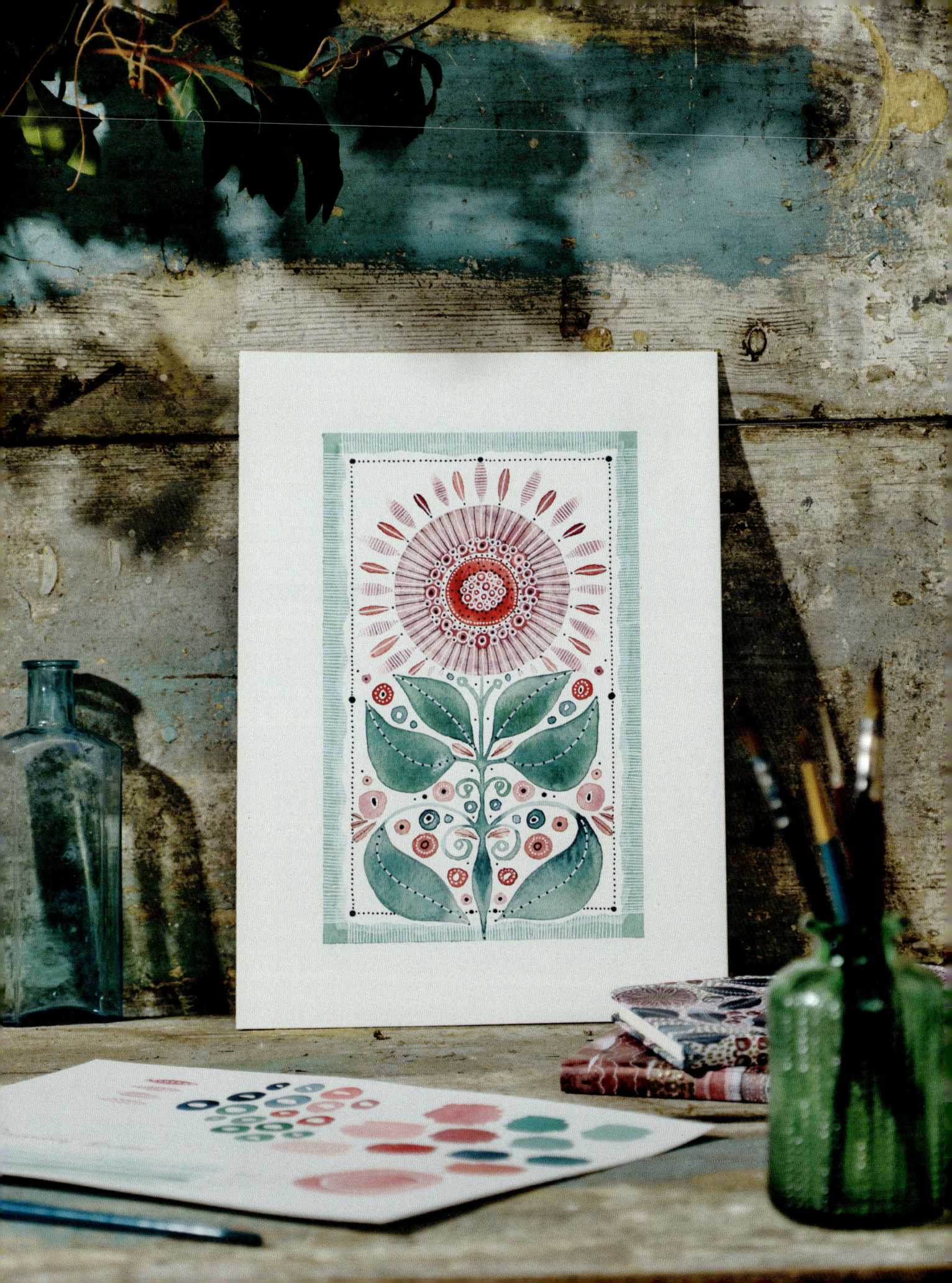

Step 1: PENCIL SKETCH

Start by masking your page (*see Techniques: Masking Borders*). I'm placing a decorative border *within* the masked frame, so mark this out in pencil and use the inner area for the design.

Next, sketch out your flower. I used a ruler to mark out a rough framework – this helped to keep my design central and symmetrical for a neat finish.

To ensure the leaves, stem, and tendrils are symmetrical, sketch your desired shape on to *one half of the paper only*. Trace the shape onto tracing paper, "flip" the paper, and use the pencil to draw back over the lines to leave an imprint on the opposite side of the paper.

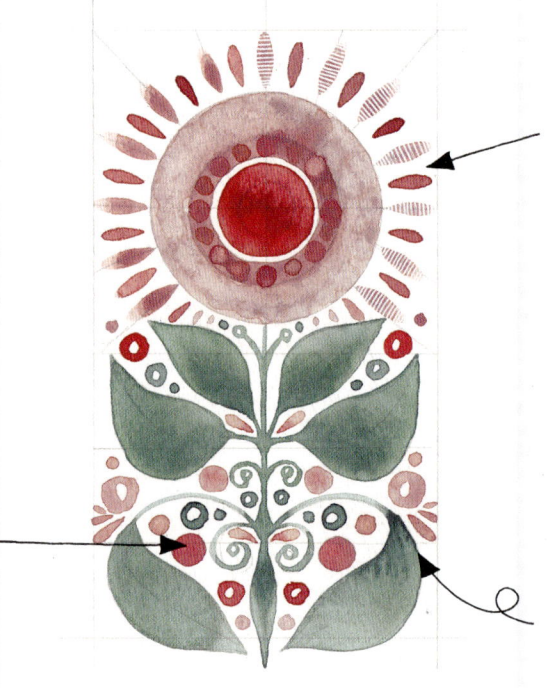

Two horizontal and two vertical lines mark out the decorative border, to be added later.

Use a ruler to place the vertical and horizontal guidelines needed to ensure symmetry.

Step 2: WET PAINT

With the basic design outlined, we can start to paint. I start at the top of the page and work down to minimize smudging!

Begin by painting "rings" of light and dark pink, and choose a color for the center of your flower. Refer to Techniques: Easy Organic Brushwork Shapes. Create the petal shapes (or leave the flower head plain for a more minimal look). Once you're happy with the final composition, leave the painting to dry completely.

Press the back of a quill brush gently around the head to create teardrop "petal" shapes.

Circular "berries" and loose watercolor circles add extra color and texture.

A darker shade added to one edge of a leaf creates depth and form.

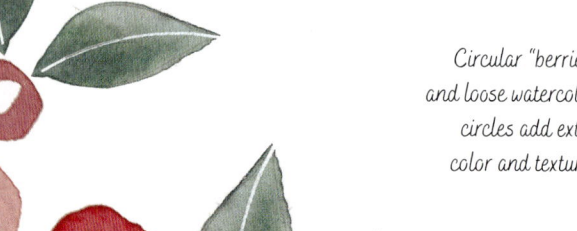

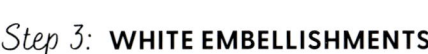

Step 3: WHITE EMBELLISHMENTS

Once your paint layer has dried completely, begin to embellish your piece. I've started with a white gel pen, working around the piece. Remember to keep your details abstract, rather than looking too literal or lifelike.

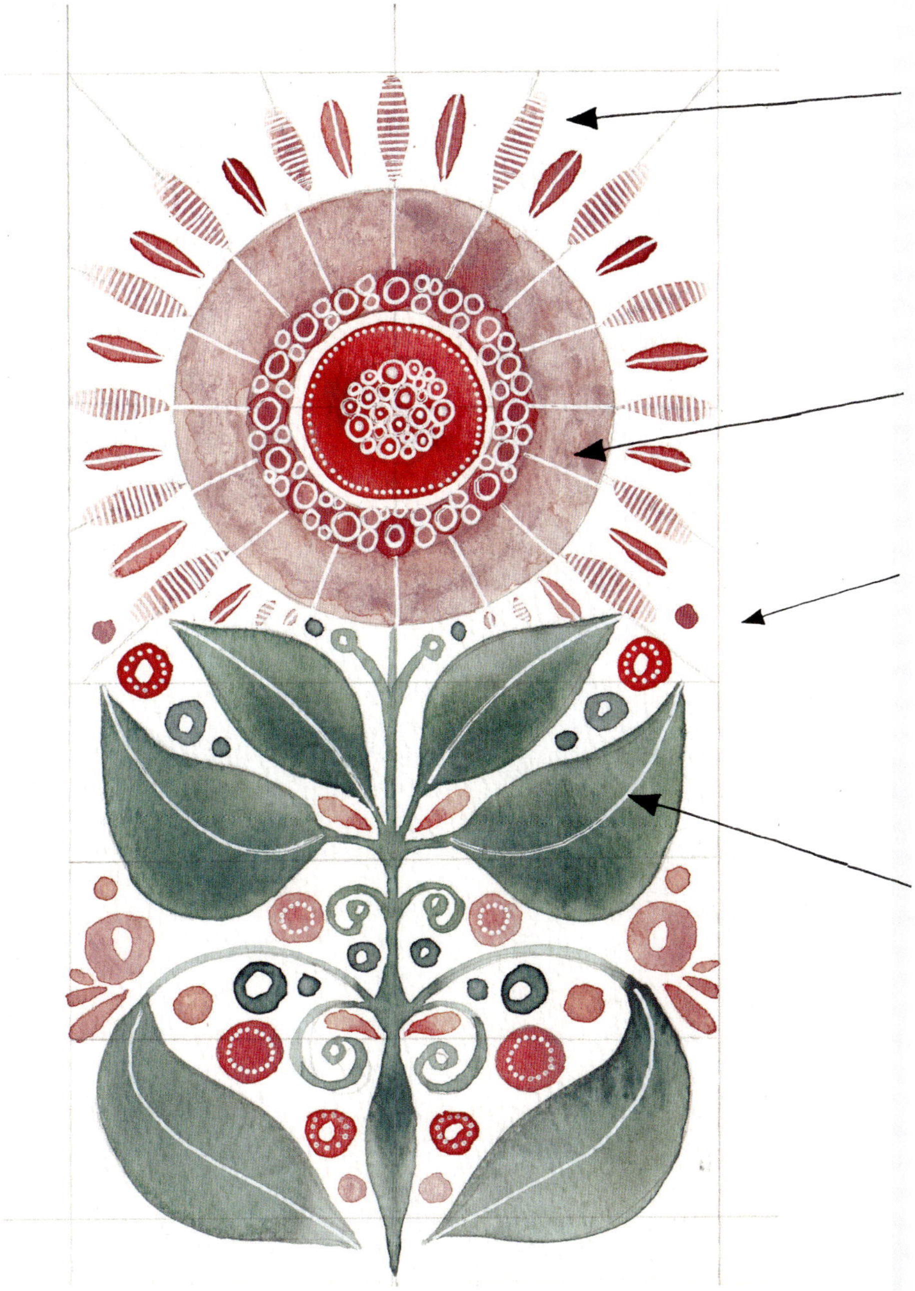

White lines add structured texture to the flower head.

Simple white circles in the bright center of the flower head suggest inner stamens.

The guidelines you drew in Step 1 are useful for keeping all the details beautifully aligned.

Curved white lines give the leaves subtle form and movement, but the strict symmetry reminds us that this is abstract.

Step 4: BLACK EMBELLISHMENTS

Now use your black fineliner pen to add additional details and create contrast. I felt the central circles still looked too plain with the black lines, so added some more white lines to balance the black and add interest.

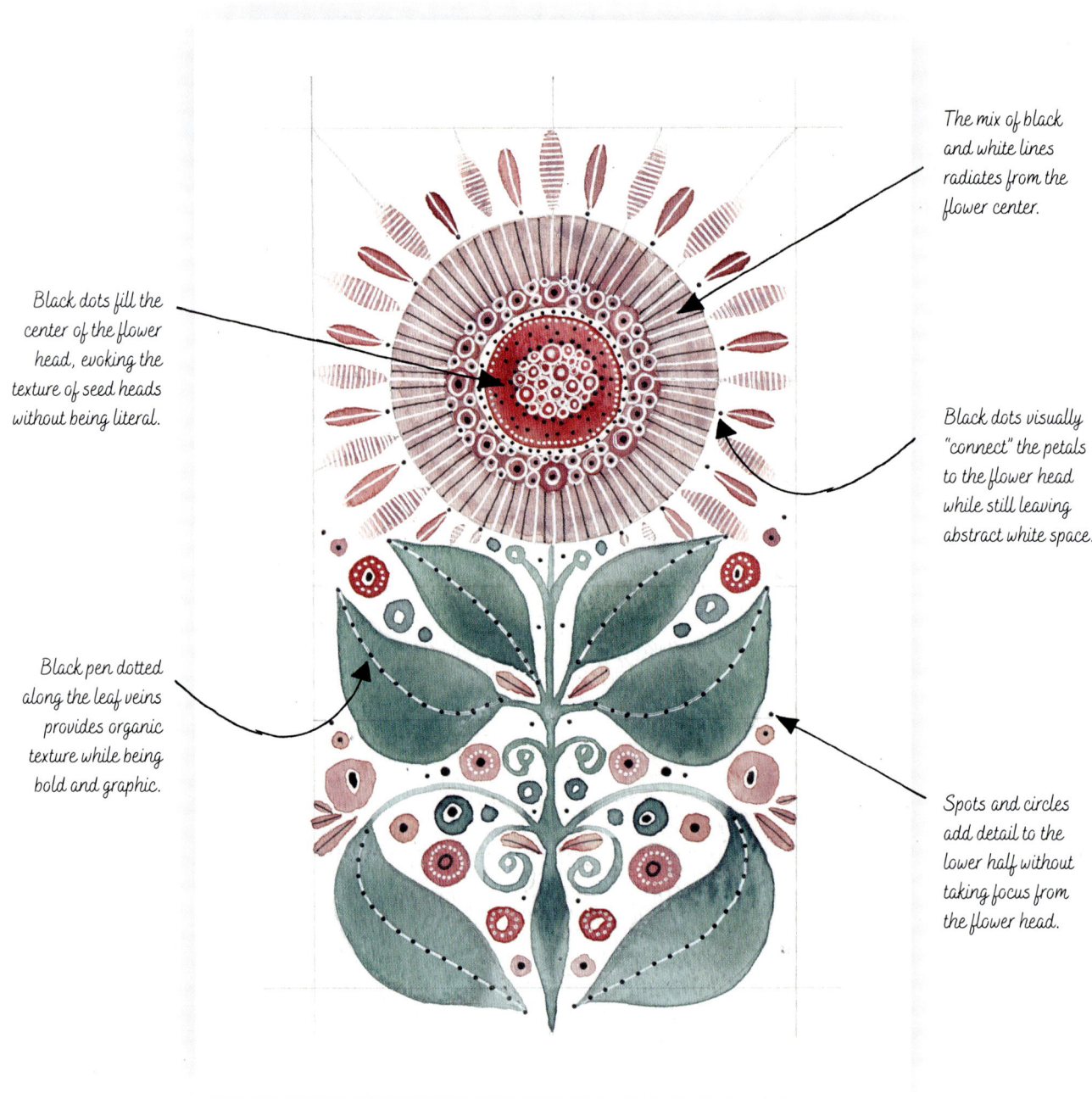

The mix of black and white lines radiates from the flower center.

Black dots fill the center of the flower head, evoking the texture of seed heads without being literal.

Black dots visually "connect" the petals to the flower head while still leaving abstract white space.

Black pen dotted along the leaf veins provides organic texture while being bold and graphic.

Spots and circles add detail to the lower half without taking focus from the flower head.

Step 5: BORDER

Once you're happy with your floral design, we can start adding the delicate watercolor border. I've broken the border down into its separate layers of paint for ease

Layer 1

With a wash of color, fill the space from the inside edge of the masking tape to two-thirds of the way to the pencil line. Leave the edge organic and wobbly (this looks better than too neat!). Repeat on all four sides.

Layer 2

When dry, repeat Step 1, but fill only about half of the border from the tape, using paint in a slightly darker shade.

Layer 3

When Layer 2 has dried, take your white gel pen and fill the whole painted border area with perpendicular stripes to add texture. The blank corners emphasize the graphic look.

Layer 4

With a black pen, add a neat row of dots along the pencil line. I've added a larger dot at each corner and center point of the sides. Remove the tape to reveal your finished piece!

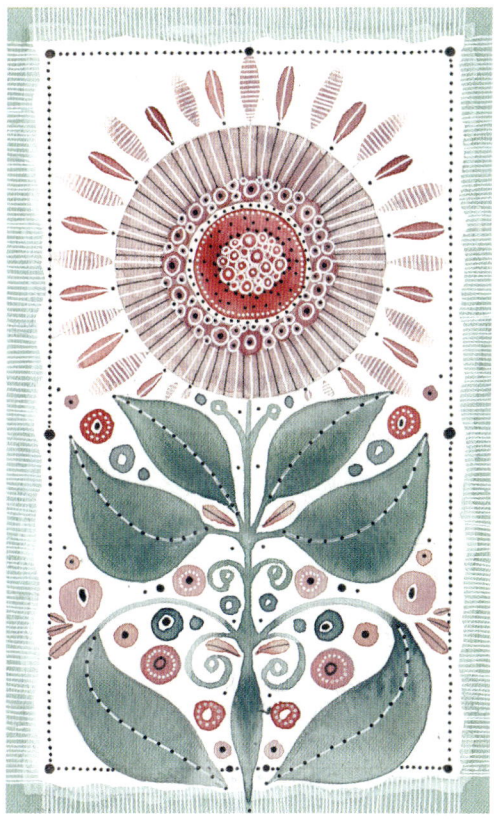

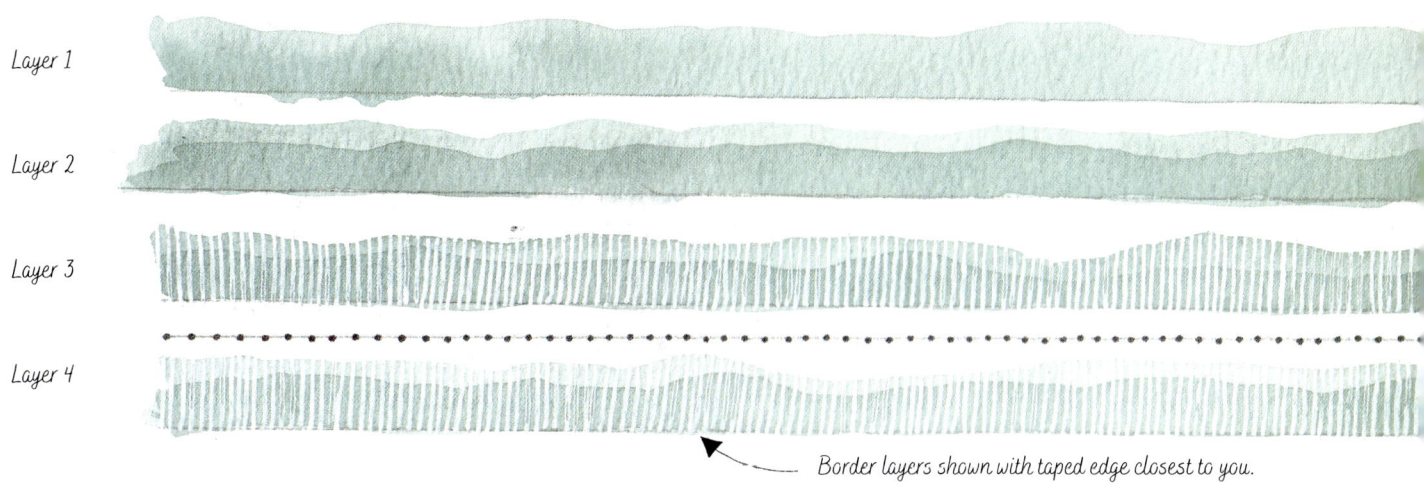

Layer 1

Layer 2

Layer 3

Layer 4

Border layers shown with taped edge closest to you.

Organic Trees

Nature is a constant source of inspiration, from its organic forms to seasonal colors. I like the random approach of this piece – it's not a literal painting of a forest, even if that's where the idea originated. This is a good introduction to using basic circles and oval shapes, but feel free to experiment with other shapes and watch your confidence (and forest!) grow.

MATERIALS

- Winsor & Newton professional watercolors
- Daler Rowney Aquafine Artboard
- Jackson's quill brush – sizes 0 and 10/0
- Filbert and round brushes
- Uni-ball Signo pen – white and gold, 1mm (Broad)
- Posca paint pen – white, 0.7mm (Ultra Fine)
- Staedtler pigment liner – black (in a variety of sizes/thicknesses)
- Winsor & Newton Drawing Ink – gold
- Ruler (optional) and pencil

COLOR CHOICES

I've stuck to a traditional color palette of greens, blue-greens, blue-grays, and browns for this piece. Try mixing together some of the colors below to create new and interesting mid-shades to add variety to your trees. This piece would also look great in autumnal hues of red, burnt orange, brown, and gold.

WINSOR & NEWTON COLOR REFERENCES

- Burnt Umber
- Hooker's Green
- Olive Green
- Payne's Gray
- Permanent Sap Green

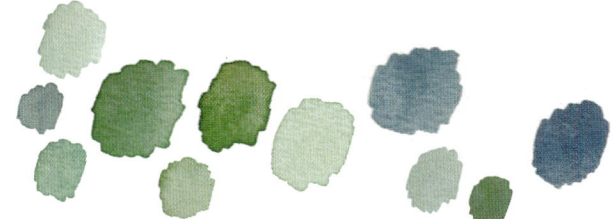

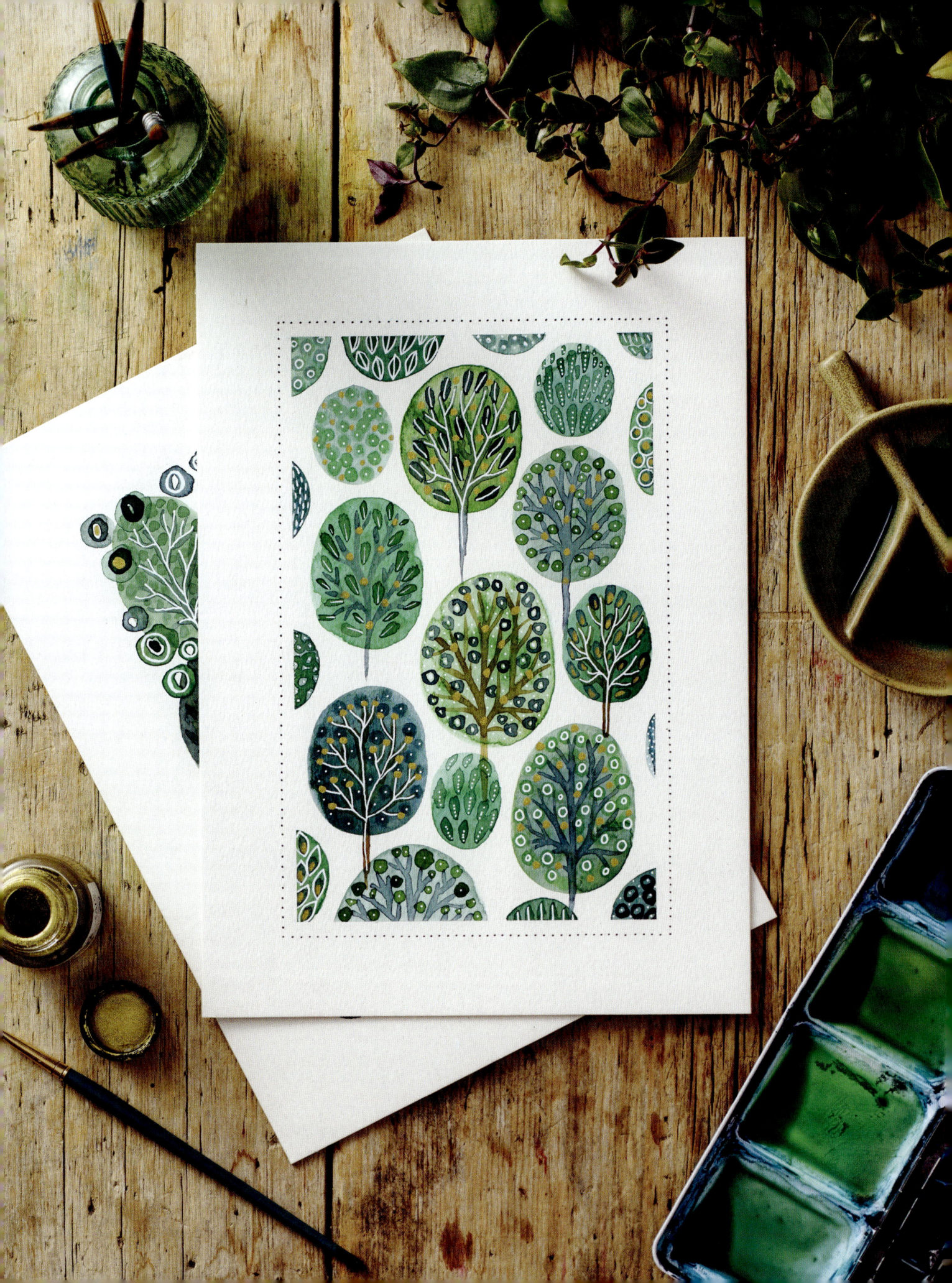

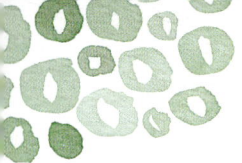

Step 1: **WET PAINT**

Start by masking your page (*see* Techniques: Masking Borders).

Cover your paper in a variety of soft circles and oval shapes. These should look natural, so don't worry about them being perfect – any lumps and bumps add perfectly to the design. Once you're happy with the number of trees, leave it to dry completely.

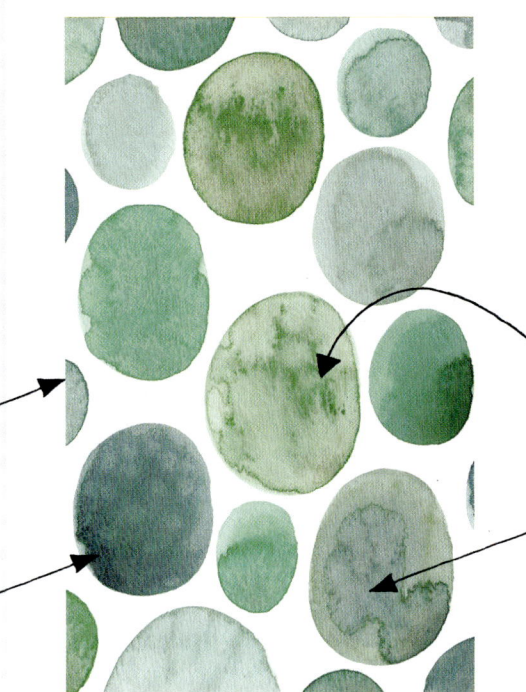

Mix your colors to create an assortment of blues, greens, and olives spread across your page.

Create organic texture by adding droplets of water to a light wash of paint.

Fault lines create interesting form and depth.

Lighter drops of paint have been added to this wash of mid-tone color.

Step 2: **WET ON DRY – BRANCHES**

With the base layer of paint dry, you can begin to turn some of your larger circles into trees by adding trunks and branches. The trunk of a tree should start slightly wider, then narrow as you add your larger and smaller branches. Leave to dry.

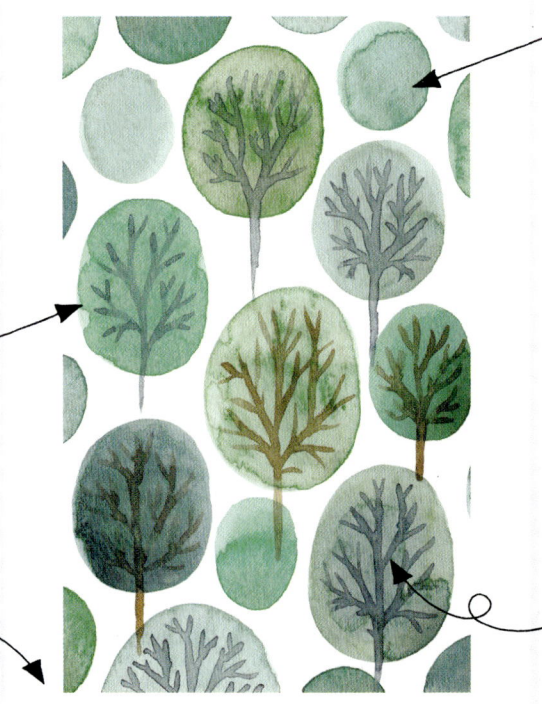

I haven't added branches and a trunk to every circle – some are left plain for now.

Paint some of the trunks and branches in Payne's Gray for a twist on the usual brown!

The translucent layers feel organic without losing the abstract effect.

Add some trees peeping in from the border to create a crisp edge.

Step 3: **WET ON DRY — LEAVES**

Once your branches and trunks are dry, begin adding leaves, foliage and fruit. Don't be too realistic when painting these, instead use different mark-making techniques to suggest different textures and varieties of tree.

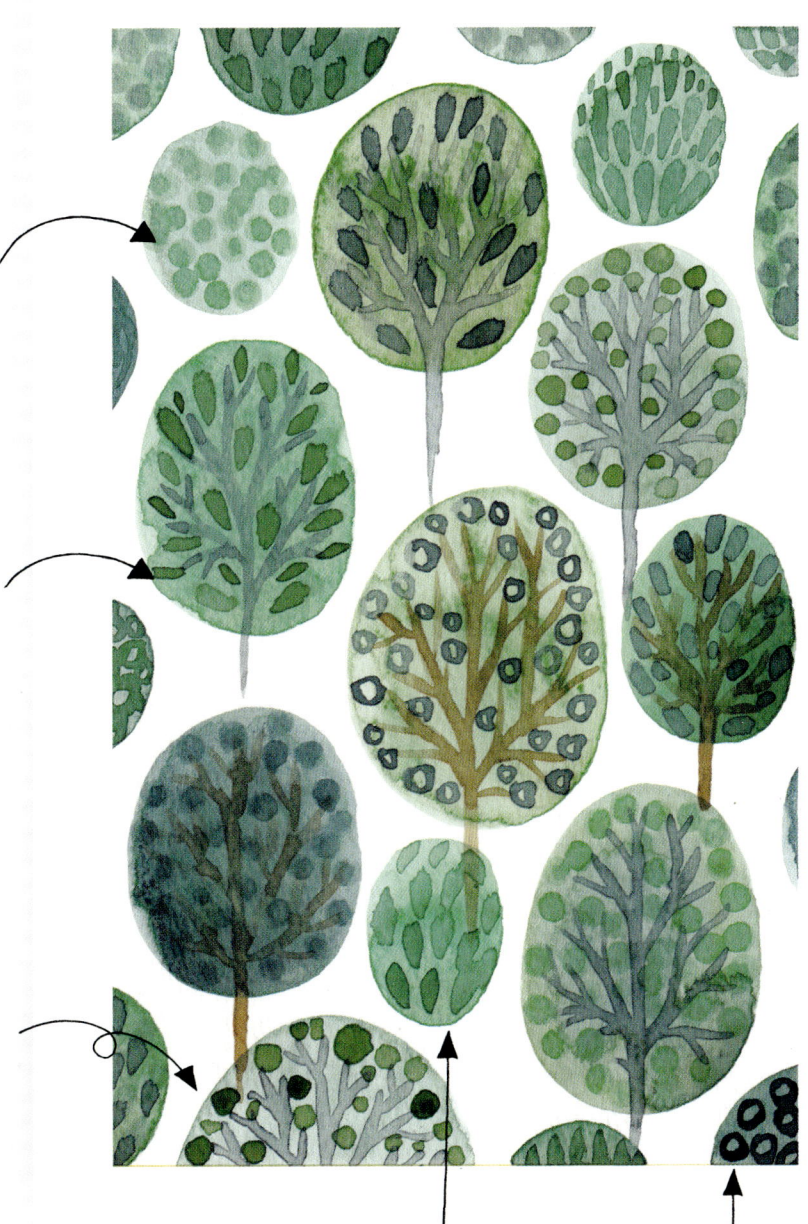

Small "fuzzy" spots are created using a cotton bud (Q-tip) dipped into paint and stamped on the dry base layer.

Use a quill brush to "stamp" leaf shapes (see Techniques: Easy Organic Brushwork Shapes).

Use more or less water to create a variegated leaf pattern.

The upward and rounded direction of these marks give form and dimension to the flat oval.

Loose watercolor circles create an airy feel with their open centers.

Top Tip: See Techniques: Spots and Circles for further ways to paint these shapes using brushes and other tools.

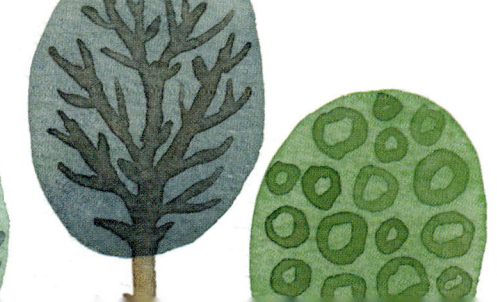

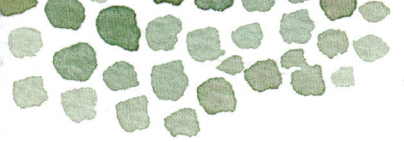

Step 4: **WHITE EMBELLISHMENTS**

Once the paint details are dry and you're happy with the overall composition and effect, you can move on to embellishment, starting with the white pen.

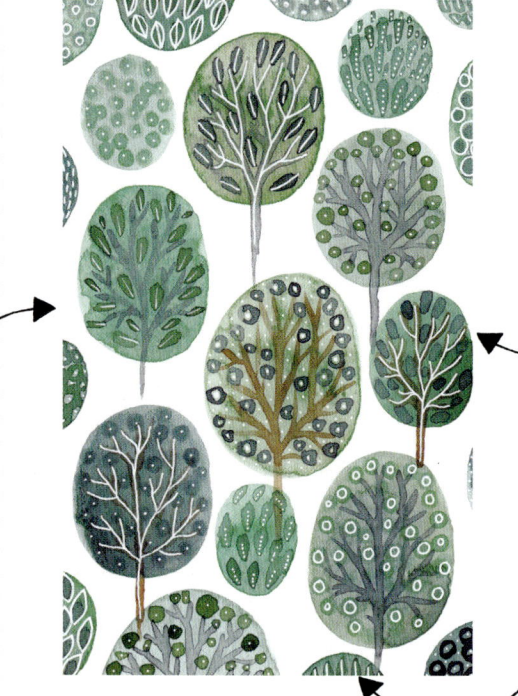

A variety of lines, circles, dots, and leaf shapes evoke the sensation of a forest filled with different species of tree.

White pen is a good way to add definition and interest, and lighten areas that look too dark.

Embellishment taken to the edge of the painting to meet the masking tape gives a polished look to the finished piece.

Step 5: **GOLD EMBELLISHMENTS**

Remove the masking tape slowly and carefully (*see* Techniques: Masking Borders). Stand back and decide if the piece is finished – does it need anything else? I felt gold highlights would really lift this painting, so added some details, let them dry, and reassessed it.

To finish, I decided the piece would benefit from a delicate border. I marked this in pencil 5mm (³⁄₁₆in) out from the edge of the trees, then created the small dots with a fineliner.

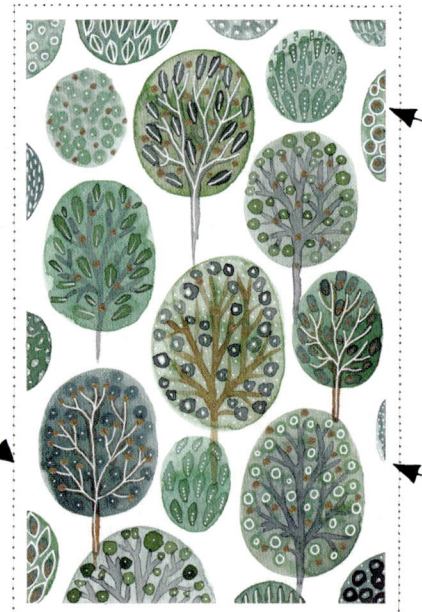

The gold ink gently catches the light, adding dimension and life to the trees.

Dots of metallic gold ink are added using a short, round brush.

Once the fineliner dots were dry, I could erase the pencil and the painting is complete.

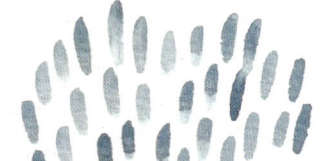

More inspiration

This piece uses the same basic techniques as the project, but I layered the trees to give a truly dense forest feel. To retain the distinctive outline of each tree and prevent them from merging into a single mass, I used different colors to keep them separate. For example, green against blue, or dark against light.

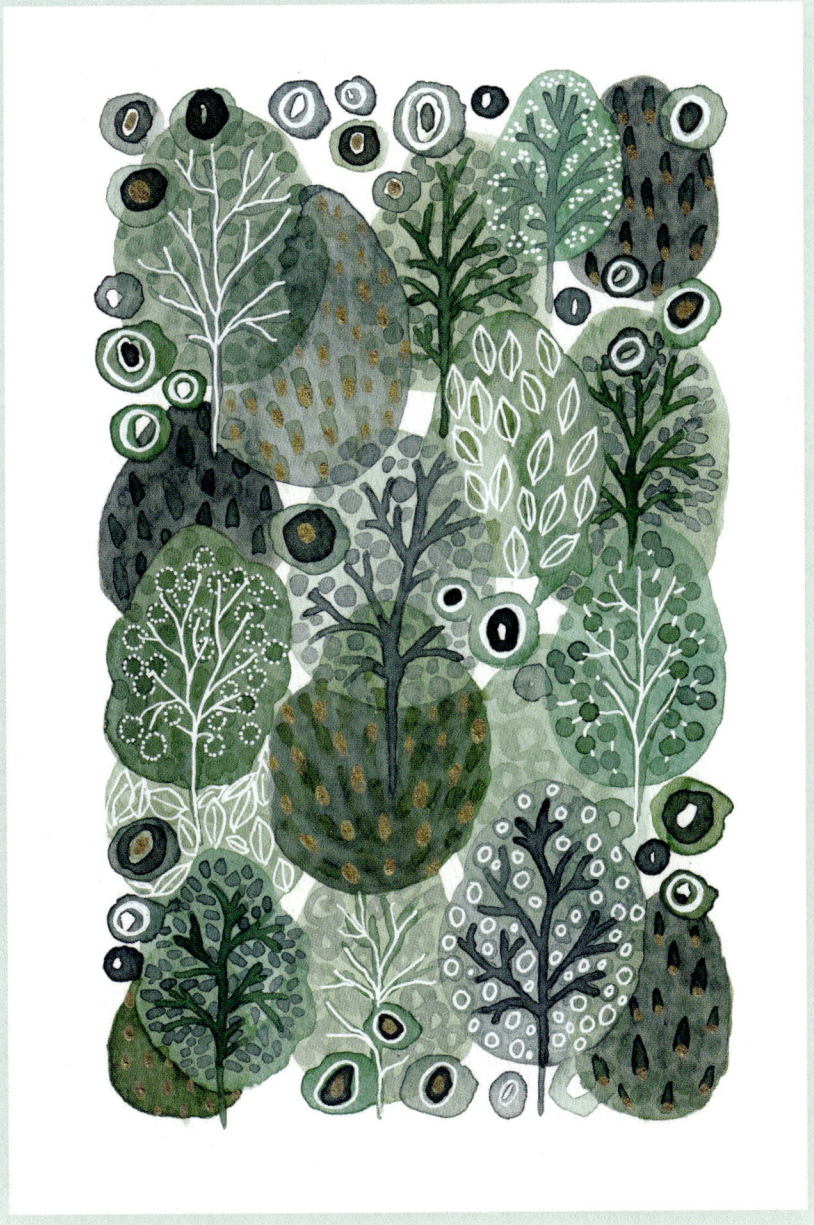

Botanical Pattern

You don't need to be too neat or precious with this fuss-free exercise in freestyle painting – just go with the flow and paint what feels right! The wet-on-wet technique, combined with the curving white lines, gives the simple leaf shapes form and movement – they're almost floating! I've painted a crocus, but you can choose any flower, real or imagined.

MATERIALS

- Winsor & Newton professional watercolors
- Daler Rowney Aquafine Artboard
- Jackson's quill brush – sizes 0 and 10/0
- Filbert and round brushes
- Uni-ball Signo pen – white, 1mm (Broad)
- Posca paint pen – white, 0.7mm (Ultra Fine)
- Staedtler pigment liner – black (in a variety of sizes/thicknesses)

COLOR CHOICES

A mix of light, bright and warm yellows give these flowers an authentic, springtime feel, but use whatever color appeals to you. The Payne's Gray of the leaves pairs beautifully with most other colors to create a minimal color palette that's soft yet eye-catching.

WINSOR & NEWTON COLOR REFERENCES

- Cadmium-Free Yellow
- Payne's Gray
- Winsor Lemon
- Winsor Yellow

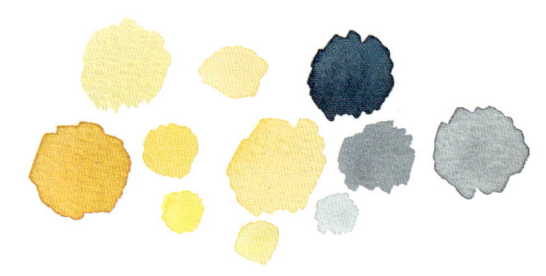

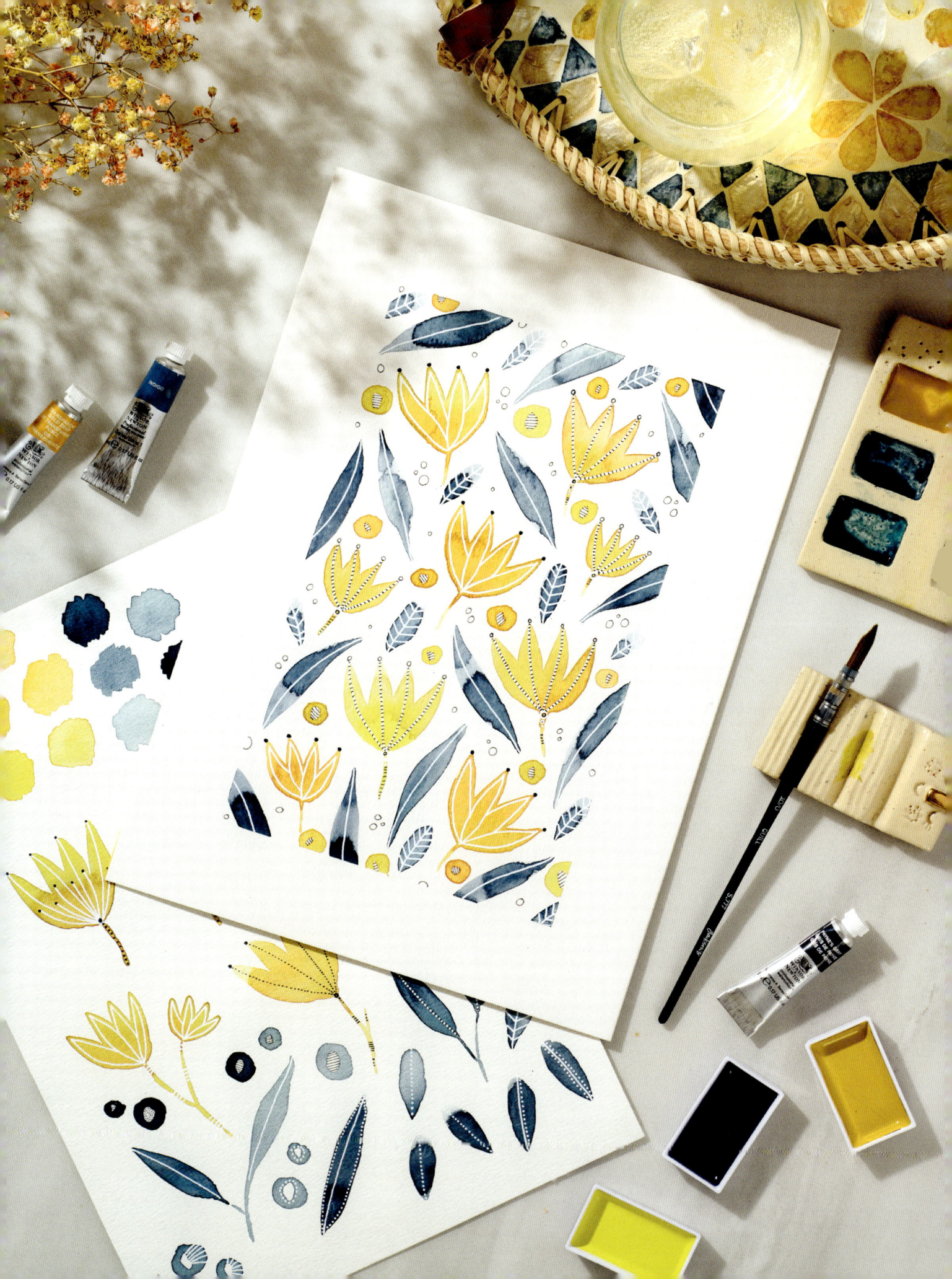

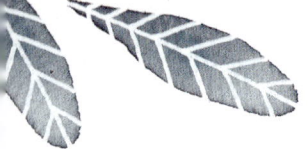

Step 1: WET PAINT

Start by masking your page (see Techniques: Masking Borders).

Mix up your colors – I've used a mix of warm and cool yellows to add variety and interest. I based these flower shapes on a spring crocus, but use whatever floral shape you like, or even a variety! I first painted the flowers, then the leaves, and finally the little circles. Add these until you are happy with the overall composition, using as many or as few details as feels right to you.

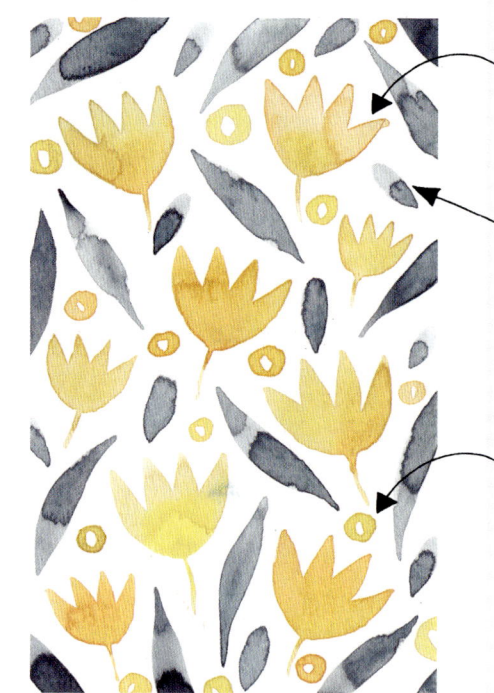

The flowers are painted first, positioned evenly across the sheet, making sure you allow space for leaves.

With the flowers painted, start to fill the gaps with large and small leaves.

Loose watercolor circles are added last, positioned in the small spaces remaining. These little circles remind me of seed pods!

Step 2: EMBELLISHMENTS

Once you're happy with your painted layer and it's completely dry, you can add embellishments. I added the white pen details first, then the black where I wanted more definition and contrast. Once I had decorated the painted elements, I used a very fine black pen to add small circles in the plainer areas of the piece.

Remove the masking tape carefully and admire your finished design – I bet it looks great!

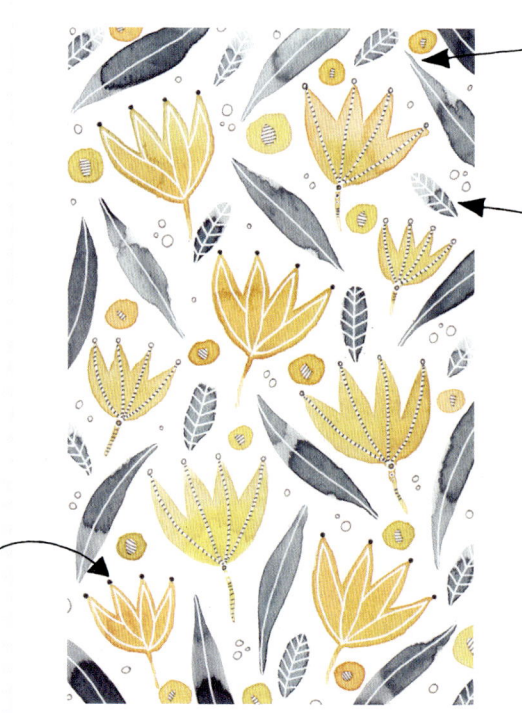

Fine black lines ground the seed pods.

I added a simple central line to the larger leaves, and a herringbone pattern to the smaller ones.

I experimented with a combination of black and white line work for the flowers themselves.

Top Tip: This design would make an amazing greeting card or gift tag!

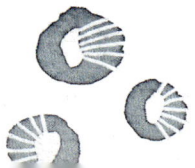

More inspiration

Here, I again mapped out flowers and leaves across the page, but this time connected them with a "vine" to create a flowing composition. The background details arose from a happy accident – I smudged wet paint on the clean white background, so created a busier background to cover it. I'm actually pleased I smudged the paint as the piece wouldn't have been as good without it!

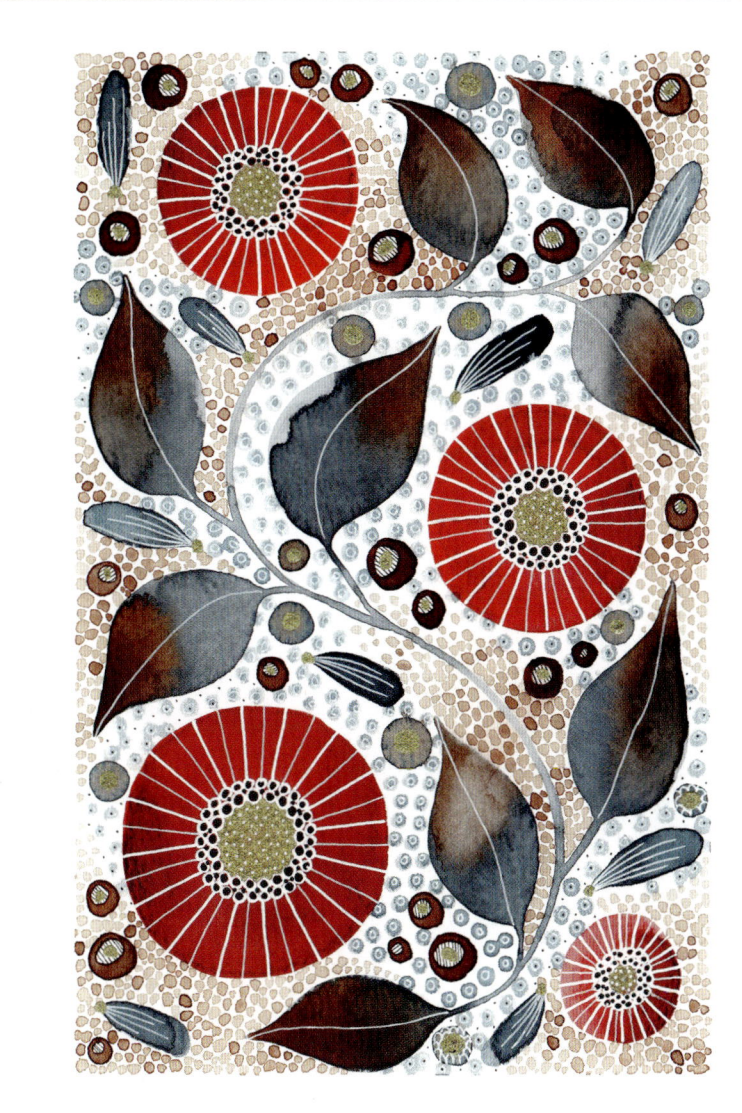

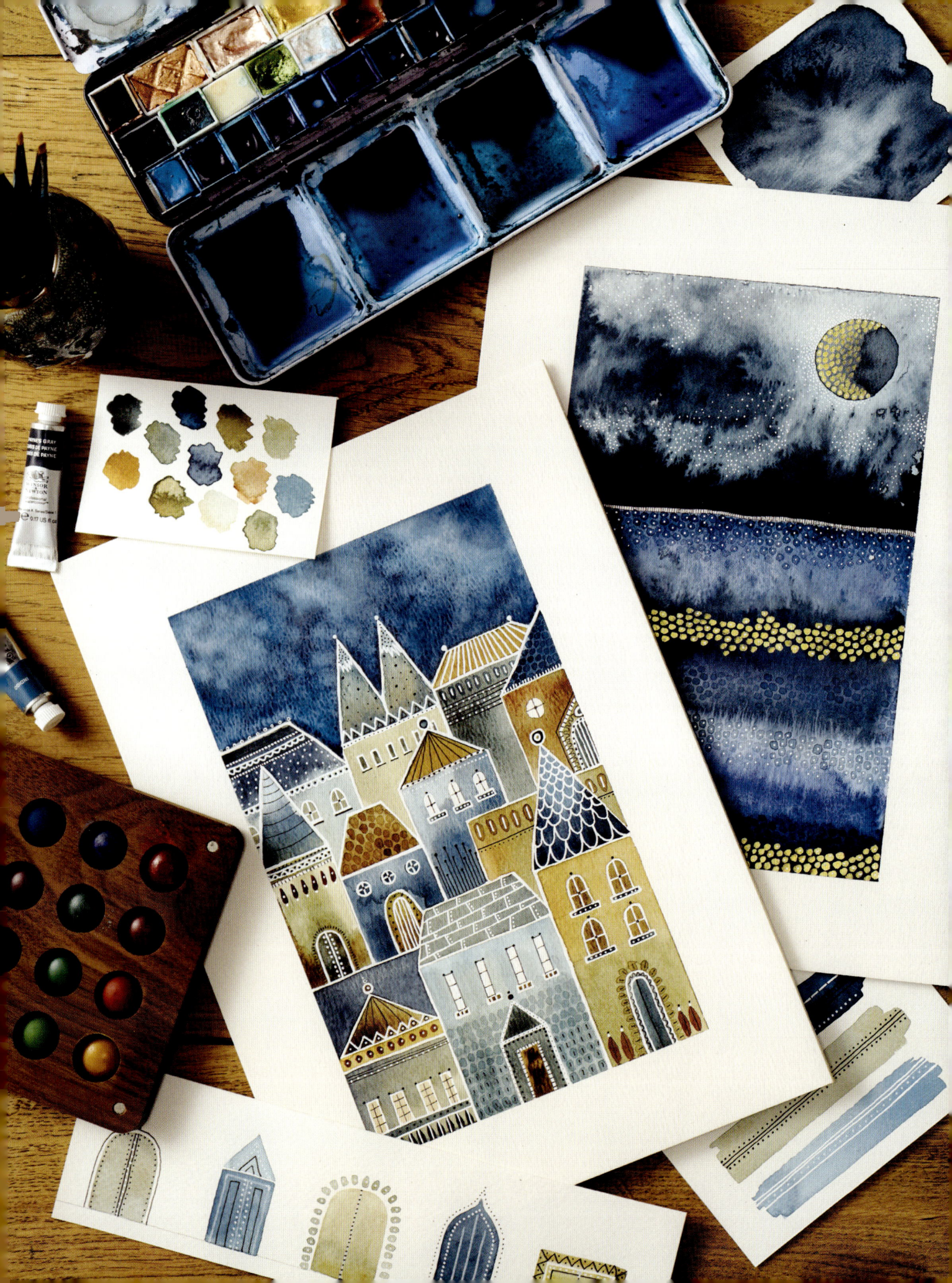

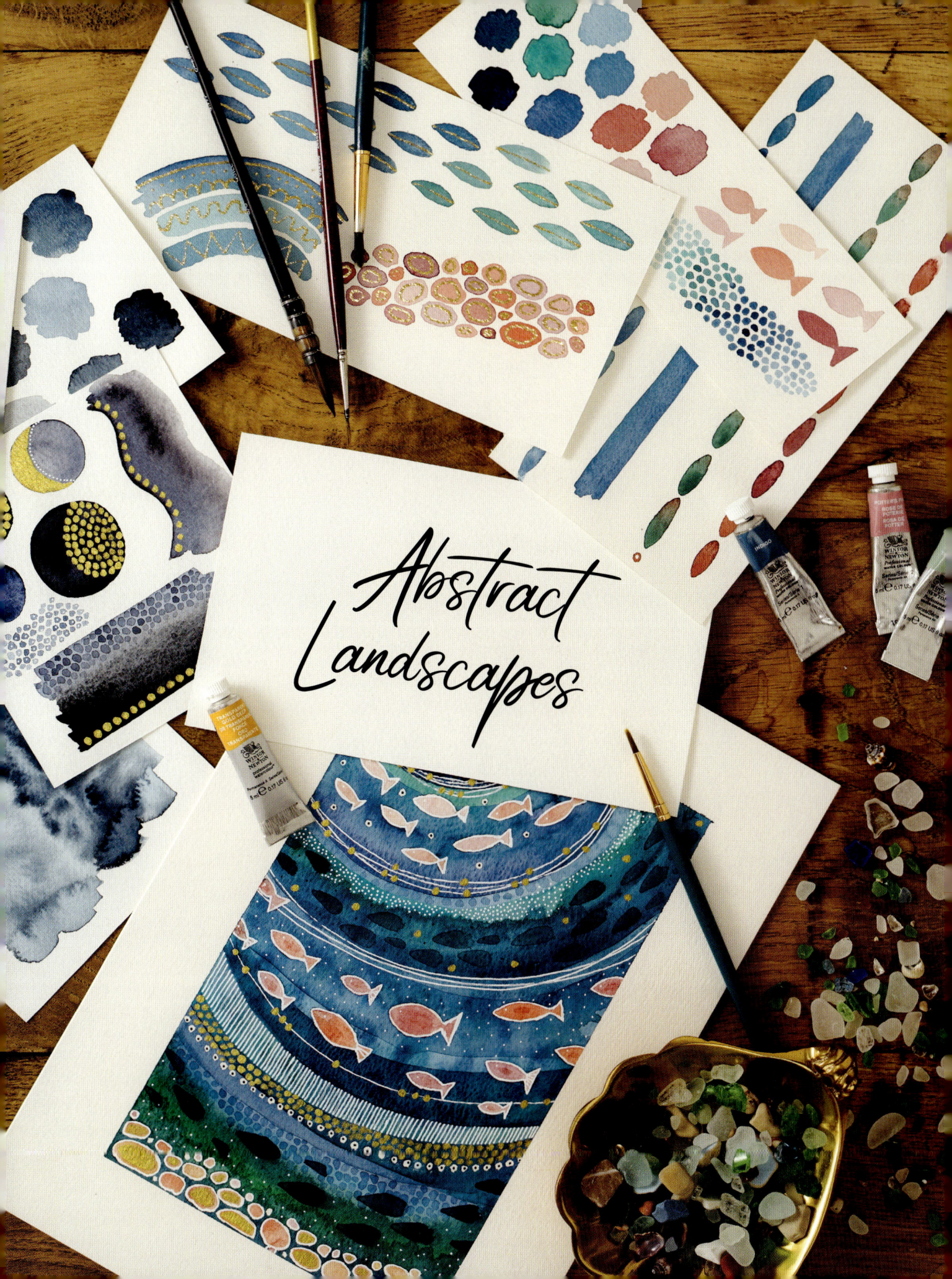

Abstract Landscapes

Striped Seascape

I love how these waves create a sense of calm and gentle movement. This is the first project in the book that uses masking fluid, in this case to mask off the pebbles and paint loose waves over that area. Retaining the white space allows the brighter, warmer pebble colors to pop through the vivid blues and greens of the sea.

MATERIALS

- Winsor & Newton professional watercolors
- Daler Rowney Aquafine Artboard
- Jackson's quill brush – sizes 0 and 10/0
- Filbert and round brushes
- Uni-ball Signo pen – white, 1mm (Broad)
- Posca paint pen – white, 0.7mm (Ultra Fine)
- Winsor & Newton Art Masking Fluid
- Kuretake Metallic Watercolors

COLOR CHOICES

I've used natural seascape colors – rich deep blues, aquas, and greens. It's fun choosing colors and marks for the pebbles – I've added contrast and warmth with rich golds, browns, reds, and ochres. This composition would also work as a true abstract by changing the colors – so reds, purples, or deep grays could look great. Even without the ocean-inspired colors, this would result in a truly pleasing composition.

WINSOR & NEWTON COLOR REFERENCES

- Aqua Green
- Burnt Sienna
- Indigo
- Payne's Gray
- Winsor Green (Blue Shade)

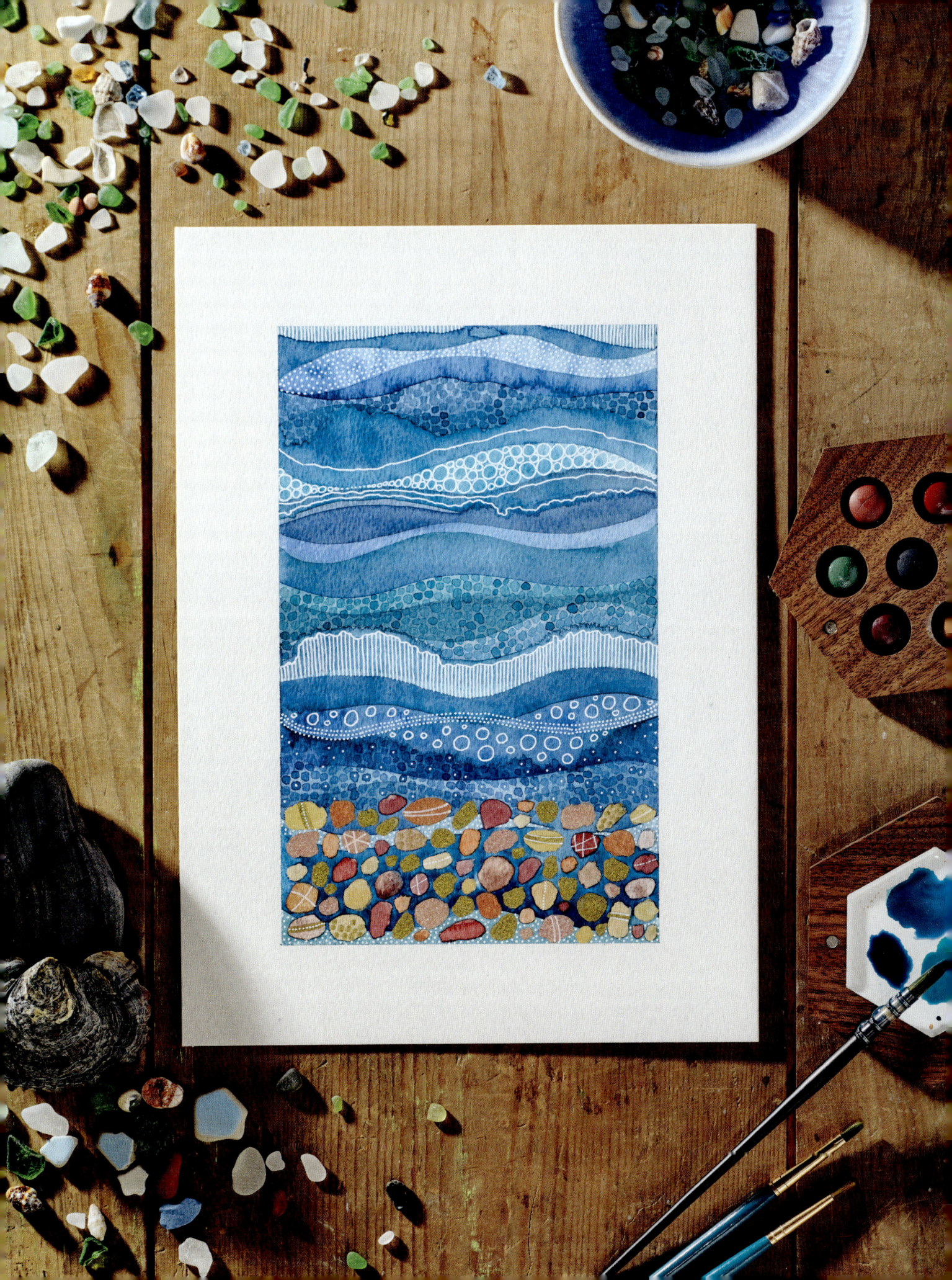

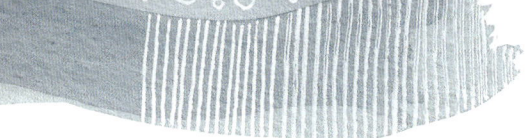

Step 1: SKETCH AND MASK

Start by masking your page (*see* Techniques: Masking Borders).

Sketch out your pebbles at the bottom of the page – I like to think of the proportions, filling a quarter to a third of the page with pebbles.

Once you're happy with your composition you can mask your pebbles. This simply means painting a thin layer of the masking fluid on top of your pebbles to protect the white paper underneath (*see* Techniques: Masking Shapes and Highlights).

Fill between one-quarter and one-third of the page with outlined pebbles.

Masking fluid protects the pebble shapes while painting the water.

Step 2: WET PAINT

Once your masking fluid is completely dry (it may still feel tacky even once dry – thirty minutes is usually enough drying time), you can start to paint your watercolor stripes. Using the techniques from the simple stripes project (*see* Abstract Shapes: Loose Stripes). Fill the page with waves.

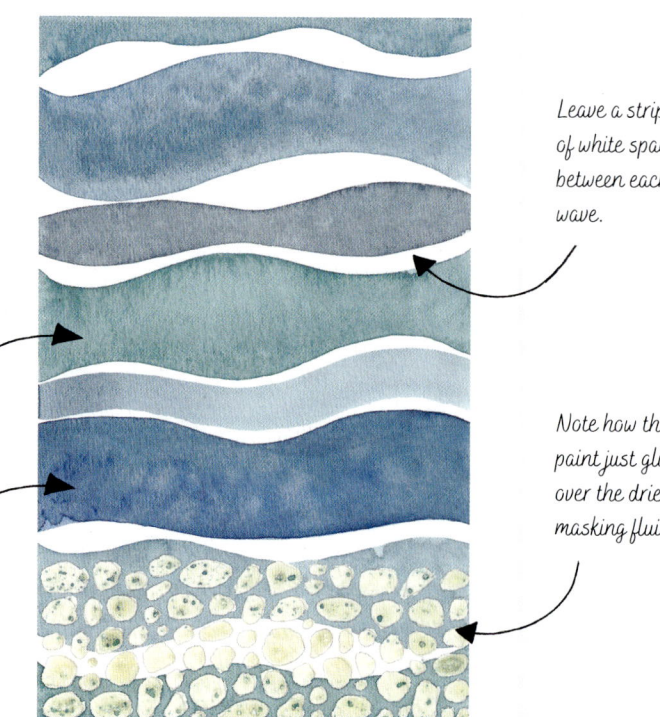

Use various shades of blue, green, and aqua.

The stripes of color should be wavy and soft to create the feeling of ocean waves and currents.

Leave a strip of white space between each wave.

Note how the paint just glides over the dried masking fluid!

Step 3: **WET ON DRY**

When your first layer of paint is dry, repeat the previous step, filling the rest of the space with new overlapping waves. You can achieve all kinds of effects with water blooms to add movements to the water (*see* Techniques: Water Blooms).

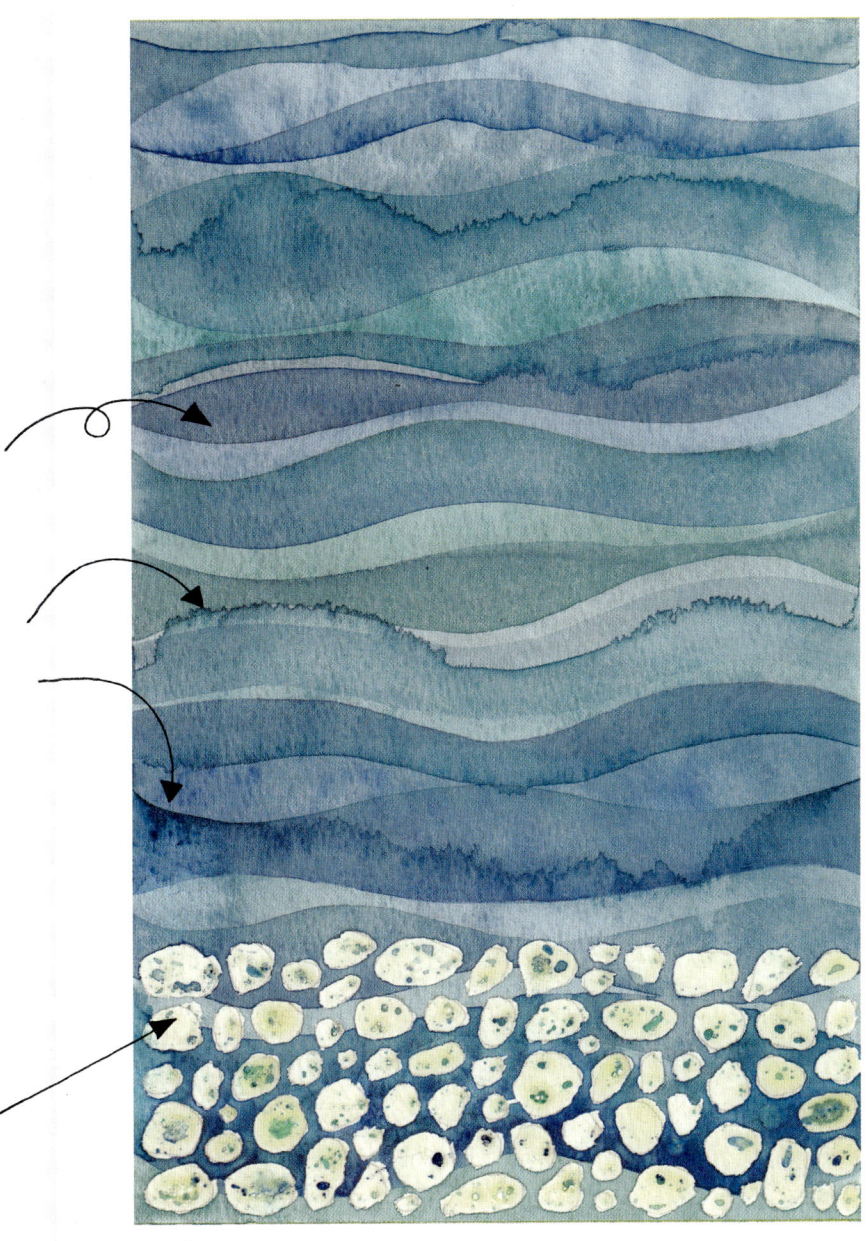

Overlap this set of waves with those you painted in Step 2 to create new colors and translucent effects.

Use plenty of water to allow the paint to move across the paper, resulting in interesting effects when dry.

Don't worry about blobs of paint attaching themselves to the masking fluid — it will all come off when you remove the fluid.

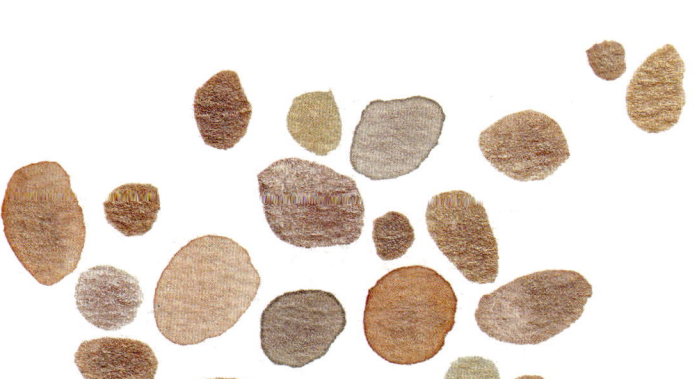

Top Tip: For this second layer of waves, use lighter tones painted in washes — the original waves remain visible, resulting in a sense of depth and perspective.

Step 4: REMOVE THE MASKING FLUID

Once the first two layers are completely dry, you can remove your masking fluid to reveal your lovely white pebbles under the layers of paint. You can do this with an eraser or simply by rubbing the edge of the shape with a clean finger and then peeling away the dried fluid from the paper (*see* Techniques: Masking Shapes and Highlights for guidance). Repeat to all of your pebbles.

With the paint dry, you can see water blooms and fault lines ready for details and embellishment.

It's always very satisfying to see the bright white paper that lies beneath the masking fluid!

Step 5: EXTRA DETAILS

If you wish, add extra paint details to your waves, creating texture and depth (*see* Techniques: Wet On Dry).

Now you can start painting in your pebbles. Because we've used the masking fluid to keep those areas white, you're free to use lighter and more transparent colors that will stand out from the deeper hues. I've also used metallic watercolors to add more depth to the pebbles.

Small "raindrop" spots added to three of the waves provide extra texture.

The values of the pebbles are similar to those of the water, creating a calming, cohesive color story.

Complementary colors allow the pebbles to "pop" from the blue without being too bold.

The pebbles are filled or just embellished with gold ink.

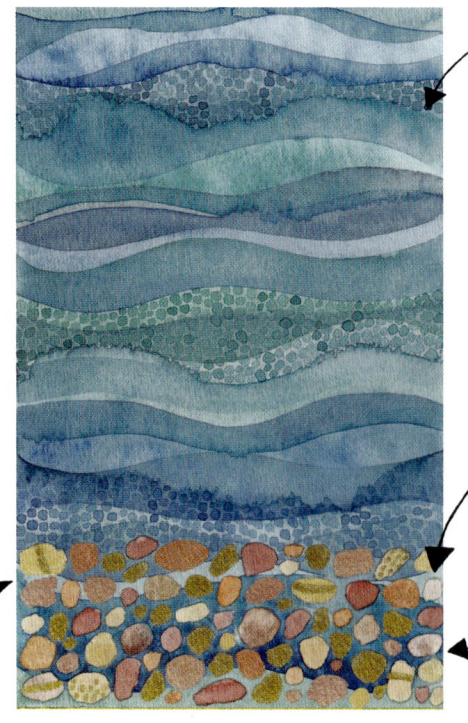

Step 6: EMBELLISHMENT

Your piece will be looking pretty good now, but there is always room for dots, spots, circles, and more! I've used a white pen for the embellishments, adding textures, details, and definition to the waves and pebbles (*see Techniques: Mark Making for some ideas to get you started!*).

Remove the masking tape carefully to reveal the border, stand back and admire your finished piece!

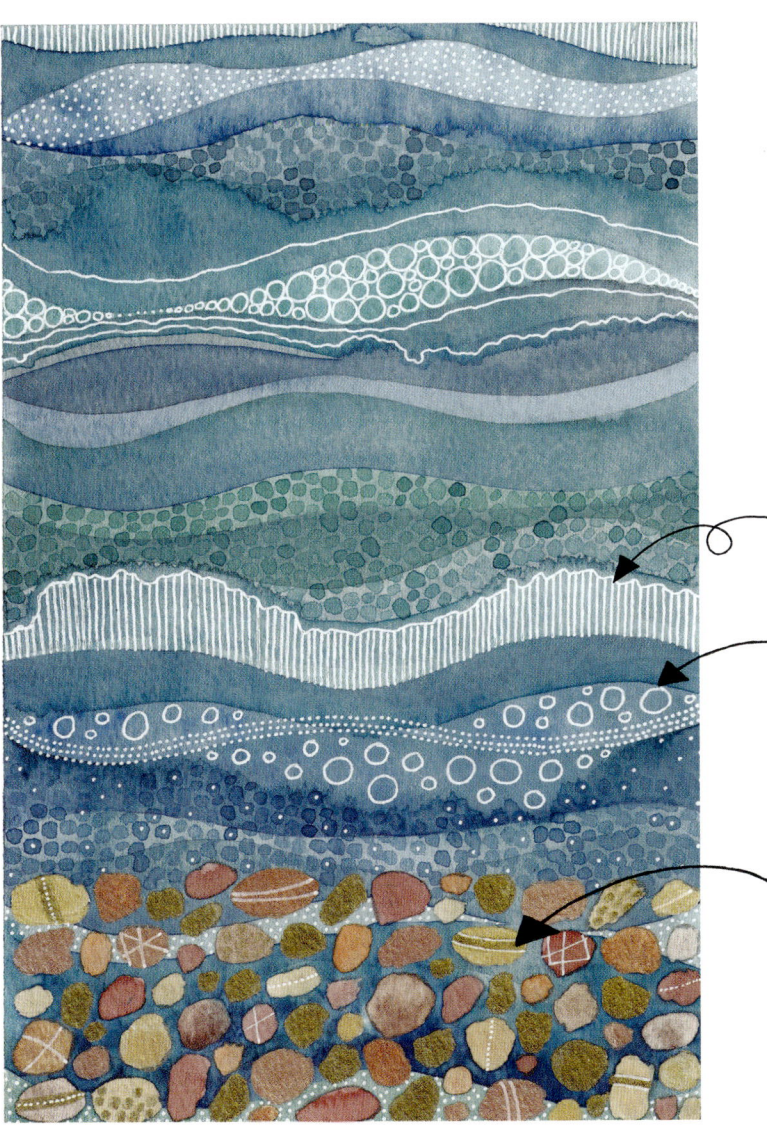

Wavy and straight lines echo the shape of this fault line.

"Bubbles" are a natural seascape embellishment, but their neatly grouped appearance creates an abstract element.

White pen adds pattern to the pebbles, even outlining some of the gold embellishments.

Top Tip: Embellishment is a good way to add contrast to waves that look too "samey". For example, if three waves are very similar, add bold white marks to the middle wave for variety.

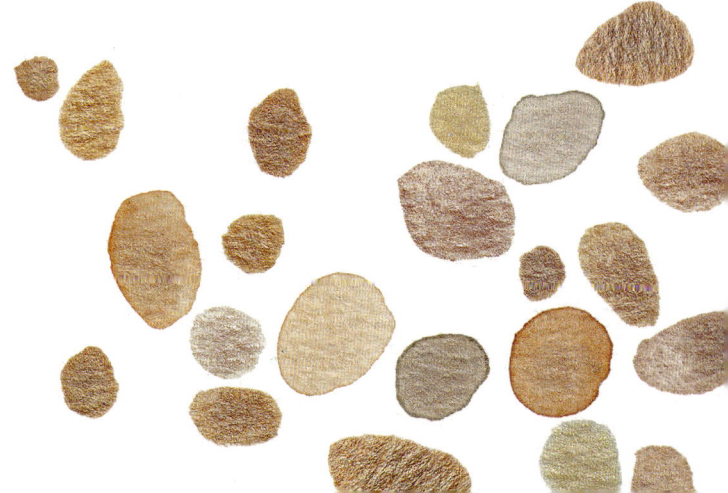

Underwater World

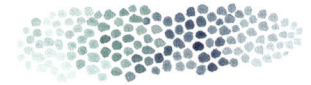

Using some of the techniques learnt in the Concentric Circles project, we're going to apply layers of paint to create dimension and give a glimpse into the depths of the ocean. Masking fluid allows the whirlpool of fish to retain its white and gold highlights under the layers of paint, so this project begins with a little simple planning.

MATERIALS

- Winsor & Newton professional watercolors
- Daler Rowney Aquafine Artboard
- Jackson's quill brush – sizes 0 and 10/0
- Filbert and round brushes
- Uni-ball Signo pen – white and gold, 1mm (Broad)
- Posca paint pen – white, 0.7mm (Ultra Fine)
- Staedtler pigment liner – black (in a variety of sizes/thicknesses)
- Winsor & Newton Drawing Ink – gold
- Winsor & Newton Art Masking Fluid
- Pencil

COLOR CHOICES

I've stuck to a fairly literal underwater color palette of blues, aquas, and greens, but this piece would look fantastic in a variety of color palettes. Substitute the fish motifs for flowers, birds, or simple abstract pebbles shapes to create a completely different scene.

WINSOR & NEWTON COLOR REFERENCES

- Aqua Green
- Cerulean Blue
- Indigo
- Viridian
- Winsor Green (Blue Shade)

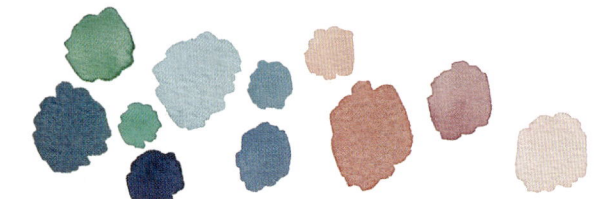

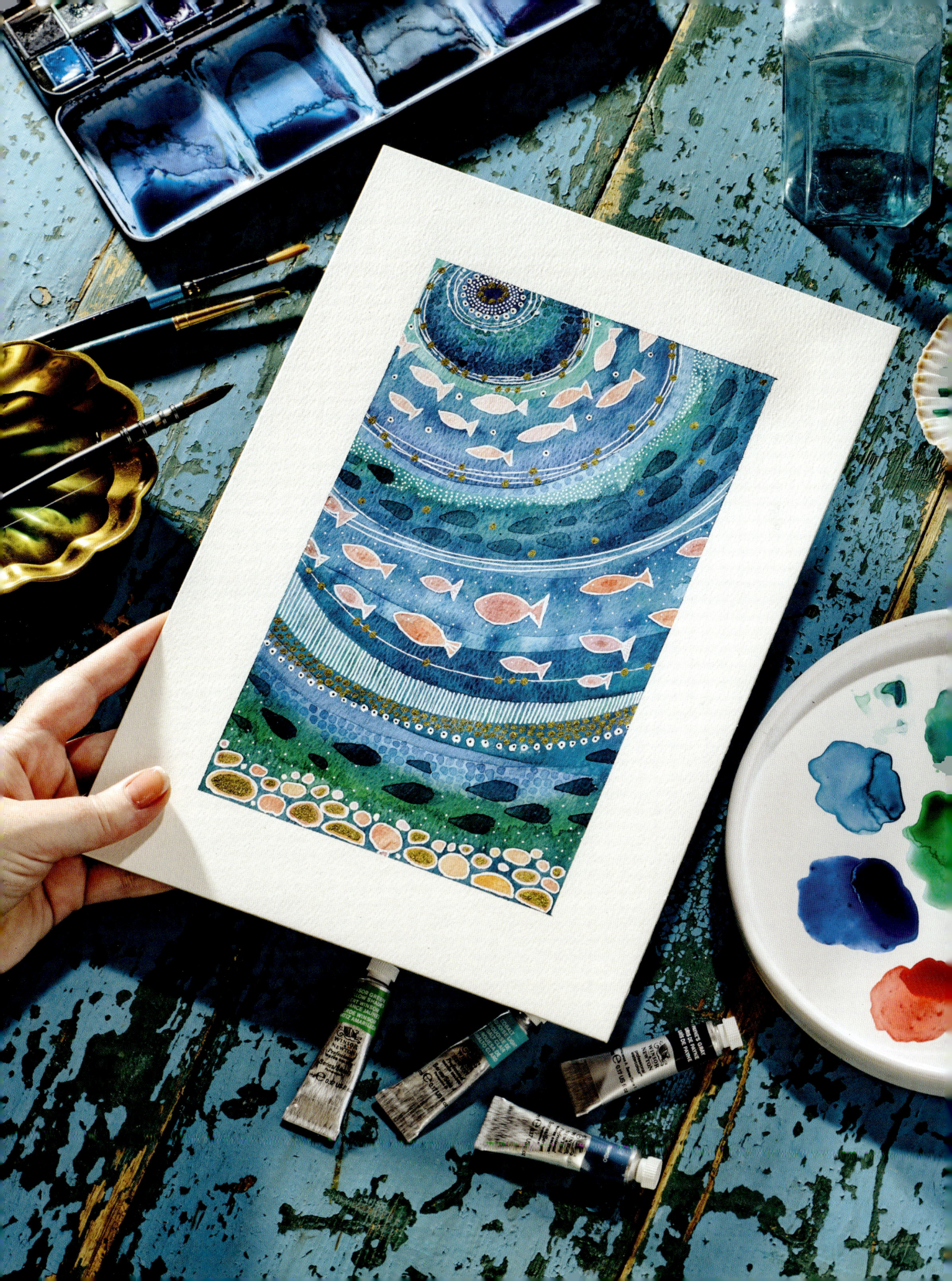

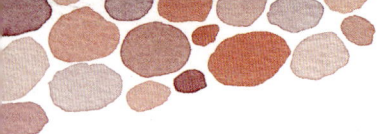

Step 1: SKETCH AND MASK

Start by masking your page (*see Techniques: Masking Borders*).

Sketch out your design, using my drawing as a reference. Use a pencil to draw irregular circles. Keep them small and close together at the top left, getting larger and more spaced out as you work down to the bottom of the page. This creates the optical illusion of looking into a whirlpool.

Once you're happy with your design, use masking fluid to paint in your fish, pebbles, and any areas of white space you would like to protect from the painted layers (*see Techniques: Masking Shapes and Highlights*). Let the masking fluid dry completely.

Mask a circle of dots at the top to help draw the viewer's eye through the whirlpool.

Create "stripes" of fish as shown, following the curve of your pencil lines.

Curved lines of spots add form.

Add pebbles to the bottom of the painting to ground the composition.

Step 2: WET ON WET

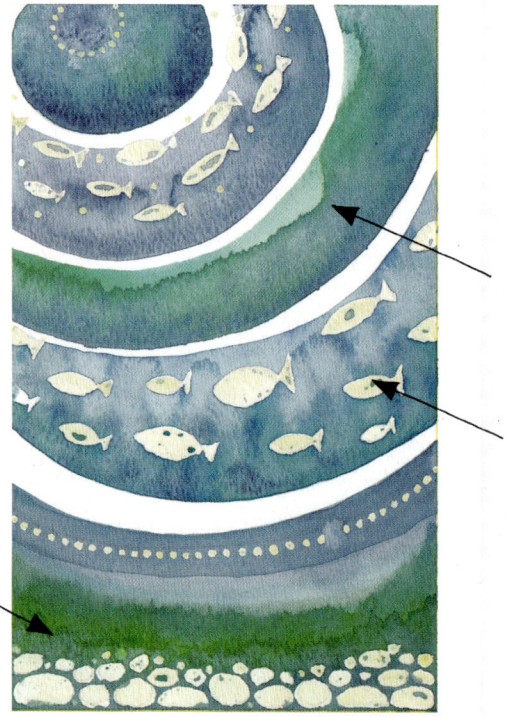

In your palette, mix your colors and start painting loose circles from the top of the page, working downward. As you go, alternate the colors to give you a pleasing mix of blue, green, and aqua tones. Leave some white space between the circles.

Water blooms add instant interest and begin to build detail.

You can already see how the masked areas will stand out from the water when painted.

Wet-on-wet techniques create seaweed or sea-moss textures.

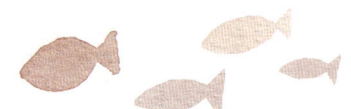

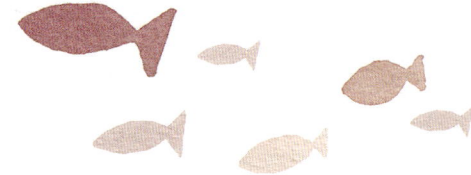

Step 3: WET ON DRY

Once your first layer of paint is dry, you can begin adding your next layer. Use this as an opportunity to overlap some of the circles to create new and different colors.

Don't overwork brush marks at this stage or your layers will become muddy and appear to merge together. Leave some areas plain, ready for embellishment in the next step.

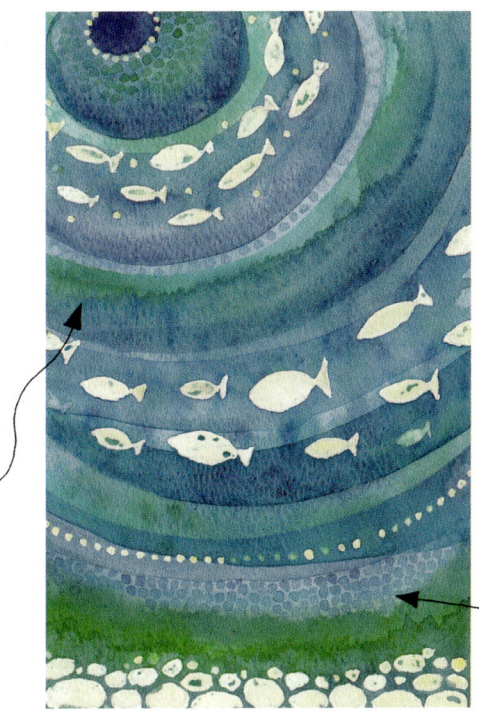

Overlapping layers of paint create contrast, depth, and movement.

Adding brush marks and deeper colors to this section adds further depth to the composition.

Raindrop spots add texture and interest.

Step 4: REMOVE THE MASKING FLUID

With the basic composition and color established, remove the masking fluid to reveal your fish and dotted details. Slowly rub the edge of the masking fluid with an eraser or clean finger – it should gently peel away to reveal the clean, white paper below (*see Techniques: Masking Shapes and Highlights*)

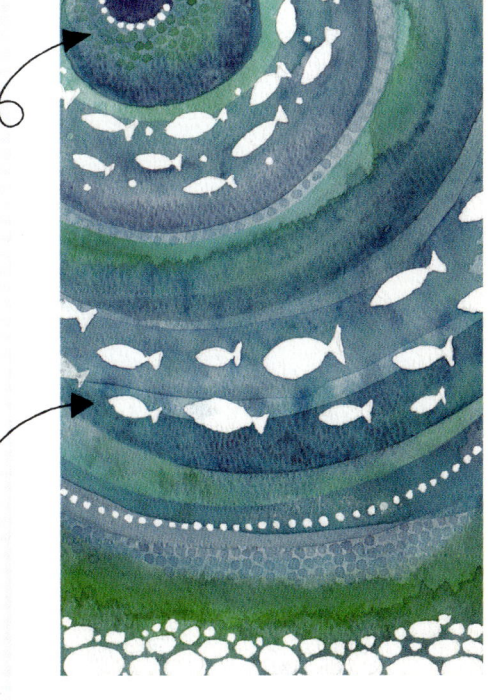

The masked ring around the deep blue allows you to create color contrast in this key focal point.

The outline of the fish is crisp and distinct – we want to retain that quality in the next step.

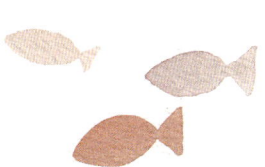
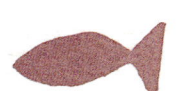

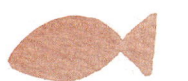

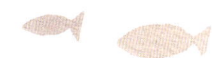

Step 5: FISH AND WHITE EMBELLISHMENTS

With the masking fluid removed, carefully paint in your fish, then decide if you want any further painted details. I added fish shadowed in the background to look like a faraway shoal in deeper water. To do this, I gently pressed the side of my quill brush against the page to leave a fish shaped imprint. I also added the white embellishments.

Top tip: If it's too fiddly to leave a border of white paper around the fish, it can be added with white pen later.

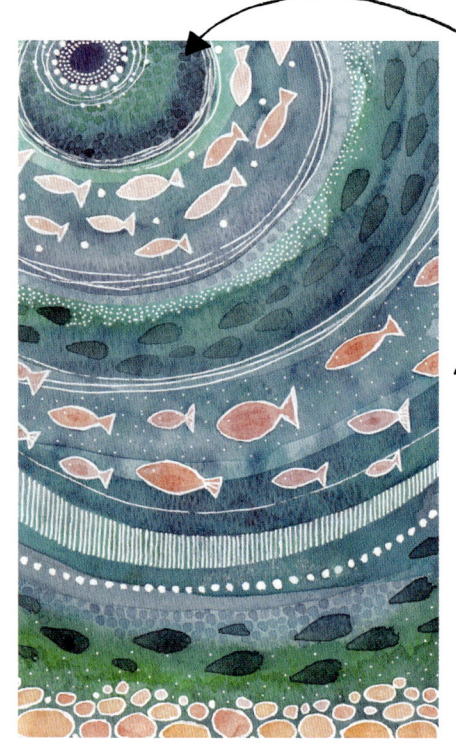

This focal point is where I concentrated my line work and dots.

To help them stand out, I left a border of white around each fish.

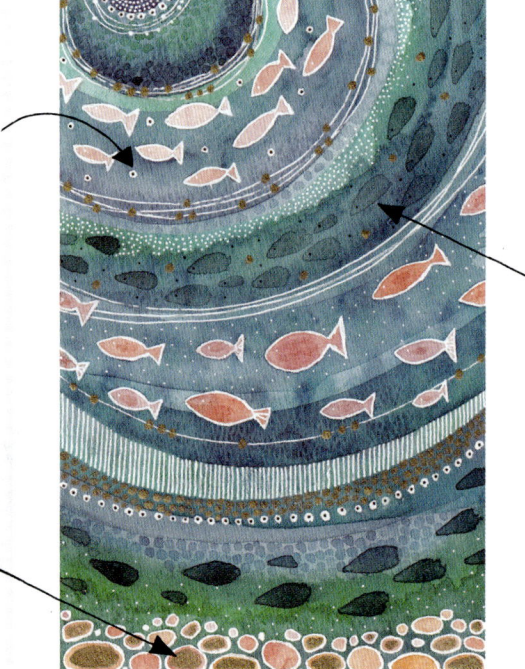

Adding black spots to the center of white dots provide depth and focal points.

Gold-embellished pebbles create texture.

Step 6: BLACK AND GOLD EMBELLISHMENTS

Once the fish and white details are dry, add further embellishment – this time in black and gold to add interest (and a bit of sparkle!). This includes dots, lines, spots, and stripes. Feel free to add whatever details feel right to you.

The distant fish have come to life thanks to the addition of a simple black dotted eye!

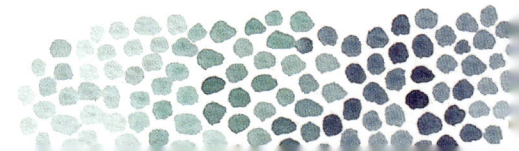

More inspiration

This is one of my favorite pieces due to the way the layers of watercolor build up to create such depth and texture. Multiple layers of background effects, foreground details, and layers of embellishment work together to create this final effect. I hope you like it as much as I do!

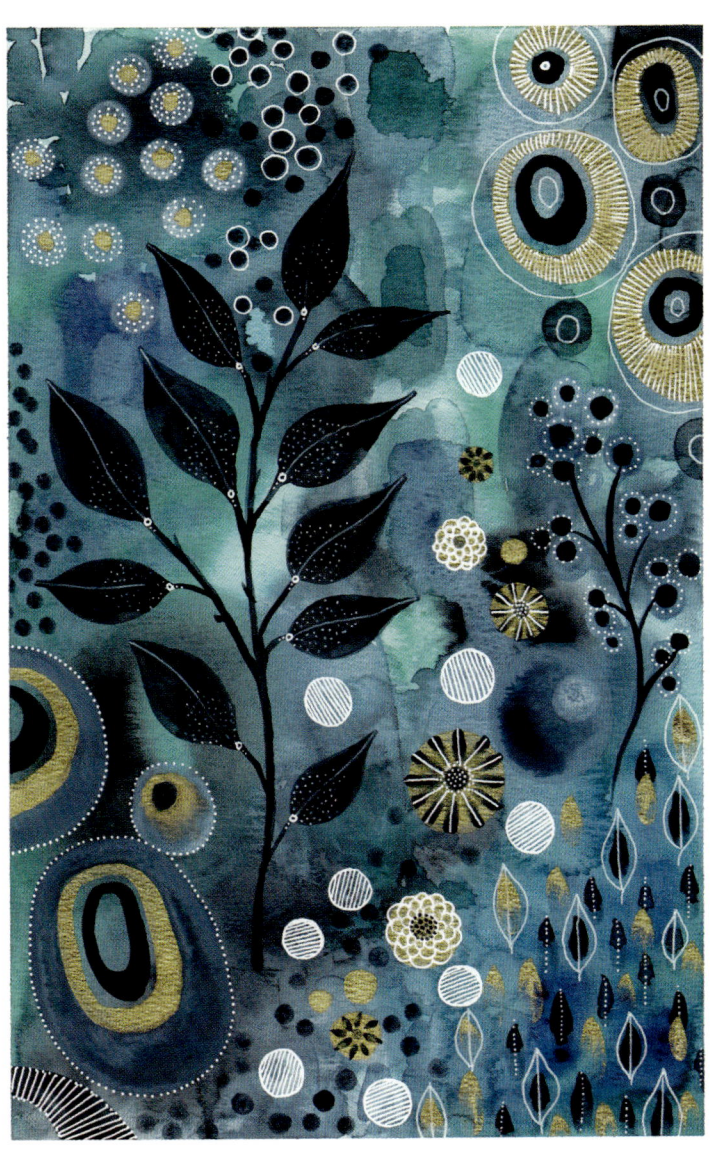

Little Houses

These town scenes crammed with lots of little houses may look complicated, but they're really quite easy. Simply break them down into the simple square shapes you painted previously in the Bold Blocks project. Add in pointed or domed roofs and decorate to create a little village so sweet that you'll want to visit!

MATERIALS

- Winsor & Newton professional watercolors
- Daler Rowney Aquafine Artboard
- Jackson's quill brush – sizes 0 and 10/0
- Filbert and round brushes
- Uni-ball Signo pen – white, 1mm (Broad)
- Posca paint pen – white, 0.7mm (Ultra Fine)
- Staedtler pigment liner – black (in a variety of sizes/thicknesses)
- Ruler (optional) and pencil

COLOR CHOICES

As you can see, I've gone with a muted color palette of blues and browns. I encourage you to get mixing in your palette – by blending these shades, I've created stunning new hues of greens, grays, and taupes. Cleverly, these colors never look dull or drab thanks to the crisp white outlines and delicate black details.

WINSOR & NEWTON COLOR REFERENCES

- Burnt Sienna
- Burnt Umber
- Indigo
- Payne's Gray
- Yellow Ochre

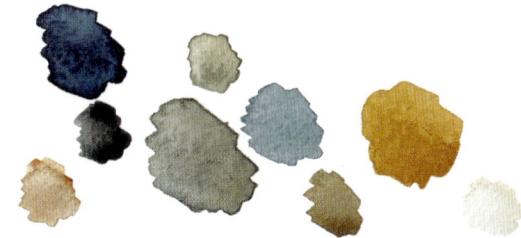

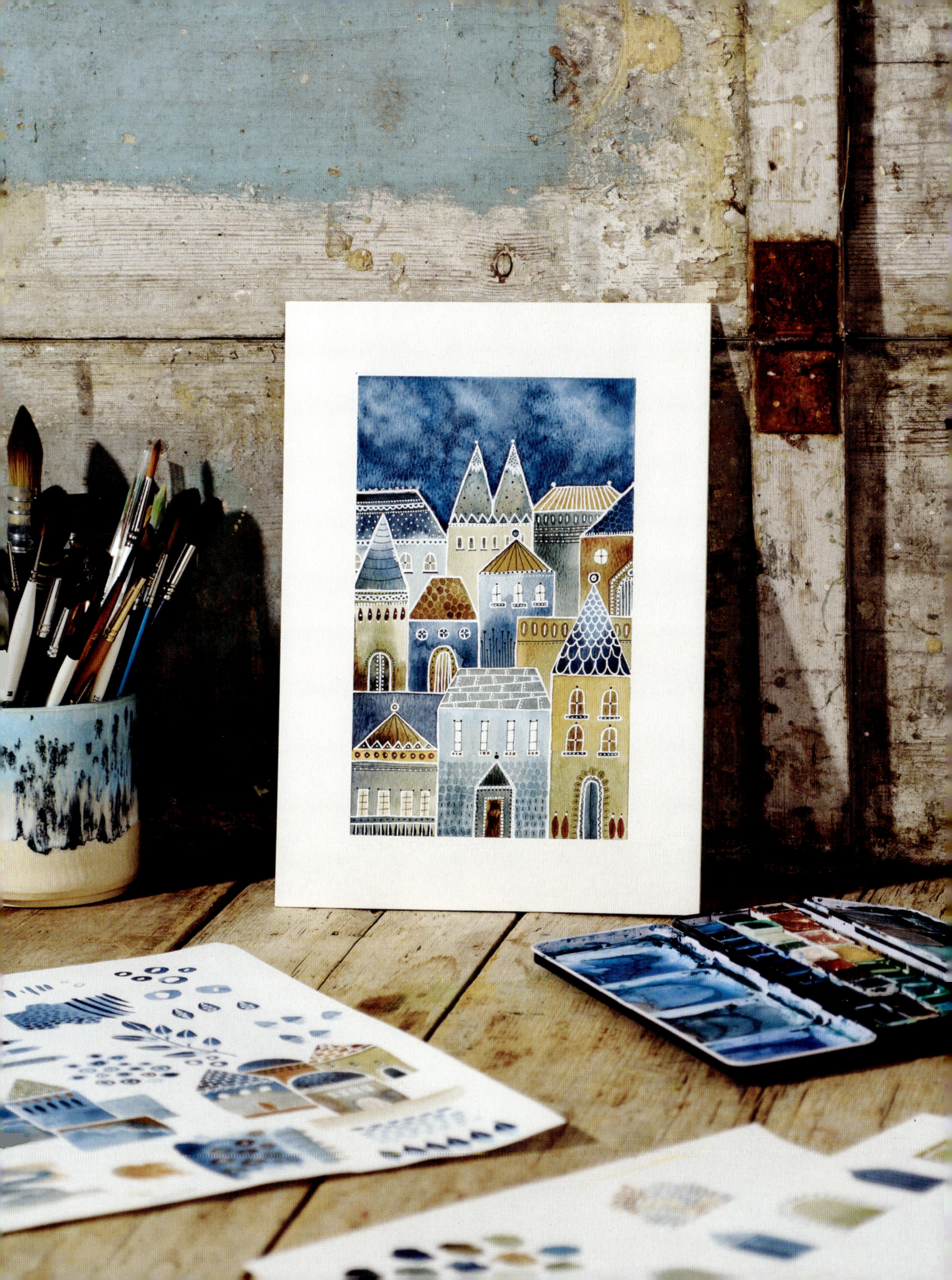

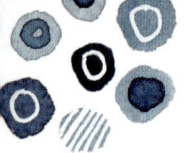

Step 1: SKETCH AND MASK

Start by masking your page (*see* Techniques: Masking Borders).

Take a pencil and lightly sketch out your chosen design. There is no hard-and-fast rule for the layout of the houses, but I would just be mindful of not drawing anything too neat or symmetrical. You don't want even rows of houses, but instead houses and rooftops peeping out from behind each other. Think mismatched and quirky rather than neat and tidy!

I make each row of houses a touch smaller than the last to add perspective.

Make sure the heights and widths of the houses are varied.

A ruler can help when planning, but still keep the composition loose!

Step 2: WET PAINT

With the pencil outline in place, start painting in your square, rectangle, and triangle shapes. You can keep these quite blocky and plain, and add details like windows and doors afterwards if that's easier. Let your first layer of paint dry completely.

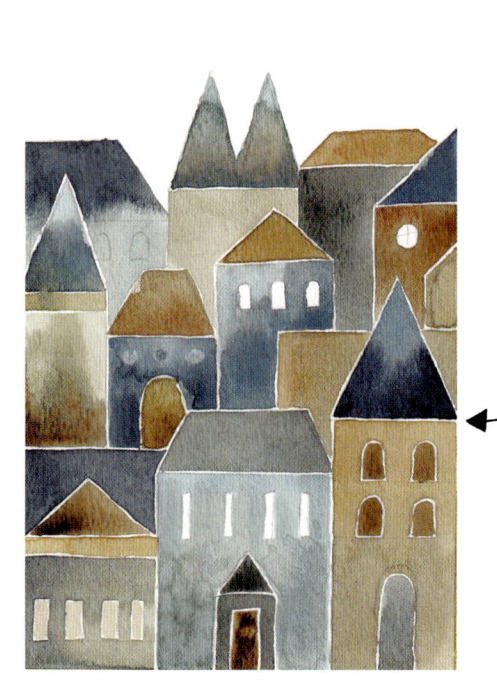

Leave a thin line of white paper between the blocks to help each house stand out.

Top Tip: Don't be afraid to mix and match colors on the page or in the palette. For example, paint a pale brown house and add dark blue along one edge. The colors will merge to create striking textures and colorways.

Step 3: **WET ON DRY**

You can now start to add details with a layer of wet paint. I've started adding doors, windows, and decorative elements like windowsills and roof tiles. I like to use the raindrop spot techniques (small dabs of very watery paint) to add definition and texture to the houses – they're perfect for embellishing in our next step. Once again, let this layer dry completely before moving on.

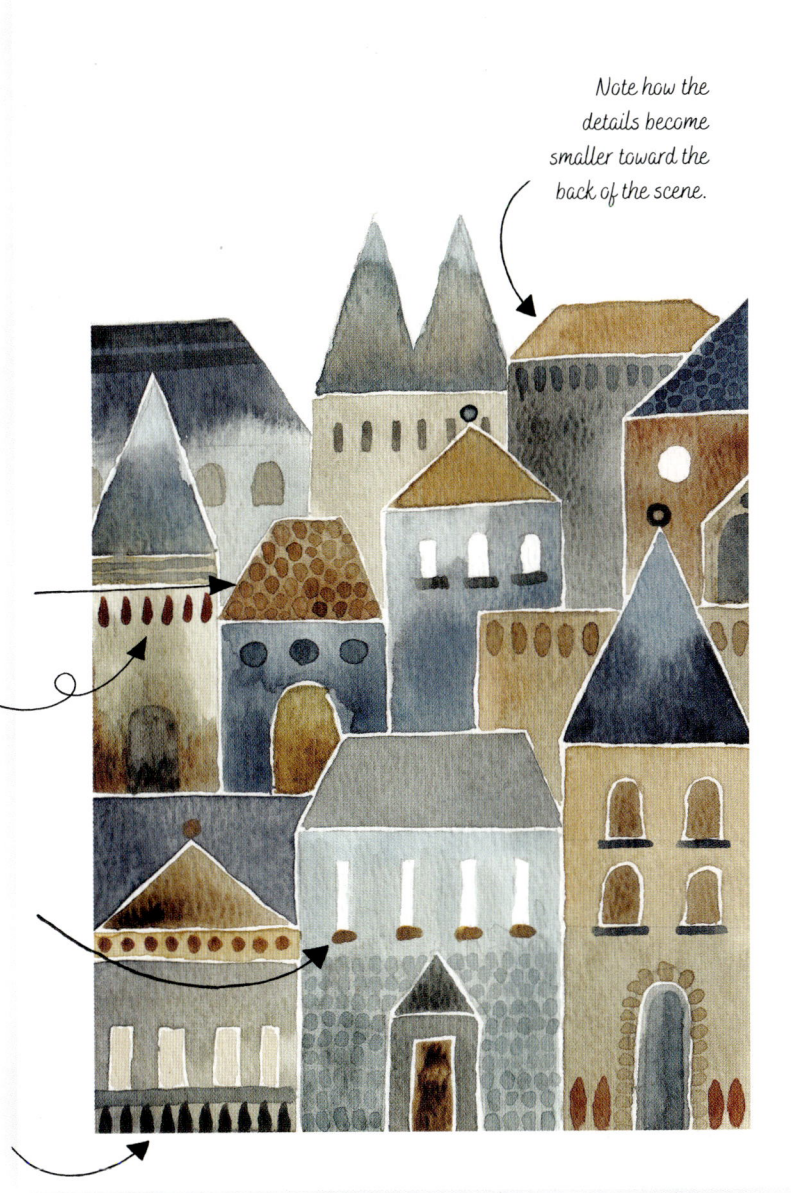

Note how the details become smaller toward the back of the scene.

Raindrop spots are perfect for creating roof tiles.

Leaf shapes created decorated eves under this roof.

Windows are a great focus for design details.

At the front of the scene you can have lots of fun with decorative walls, doors, and fences.

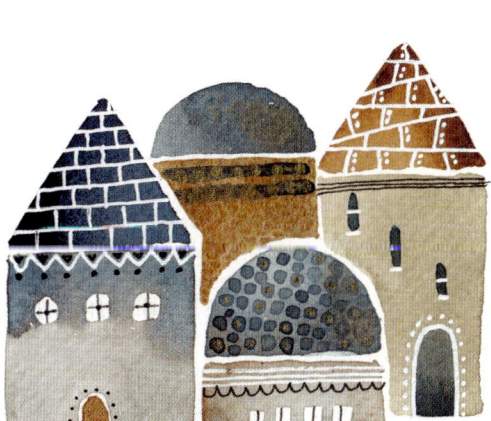

Top Tip: Try using contrasting colors when painting your second wet-on-dry details. On a pale blue house, why not add brown details? Alternatively, if using a single color, try painting a beige roof one shade darker – the textured result works well for roof tiles and other features.

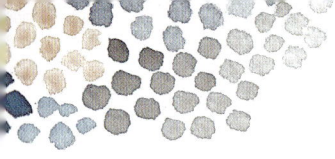

Step 4: **WHITE EMBELLISHMENTS**

Once your first two layers of paint have dried, you can begin working with a white paint pen. My first job is always to "clean up" any white lines that are uneven, or where the colors have touched and broken the line. This helps to keep everything sharp and crisp looking.

Once done, I use the same pen to begin adding details and embellishment. Don't fill every available space – you have black details to add in the next step (you can always add more white later).

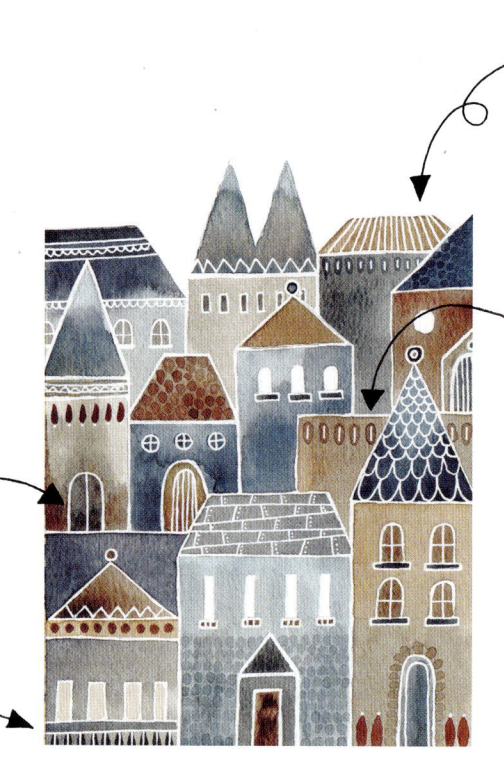

Use lines and dots to add character to each house.

The white paint pen is ideal for tidying the white gaps between blocks of color.

Add windows, doors, roof tiles, railings, and other decorative elements.

Step 5: **BLACK EMBELLISHMENTS**

Once you are happy with the white decoration, it's time to start adding dark contrasting marks with your black pen.

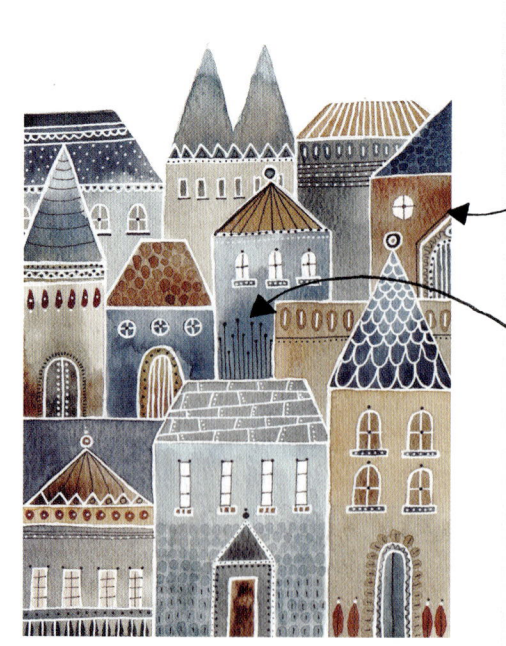

Outlining the white lines with black adds further definition.

Black lines can create tiny details that viewers will love spotting!

Top Tip: Use the white pen on darker houses to add brightening highlights, and the black pen on the lighter shades. This ensures your design details really stand out.

Step 6: ADD THE SKY

Now that you are happy with the town, you can fill in the sky. Depending on how dark or light you've painted your houses, you may want a contrasting sky. My town has some lighter houses toward the back so I've opted for a dark, stormy looking sky.

To create this, I painted the whole space with a dark indigo wash, leaving a white edge around each roof. Once this wash had settled on the page but was still wet (after a minute or so), I dipped my brush into clean water and added drops to the sky. This "bleached out" areas to create the marbled effect.

Leave this to dry completely before attempting to remove your masking tape (you don't want to smudge any paint that might still be slightly wet). Your piece is now finished!.

The town scene stands out beautifully against the dark and dramatic sky.

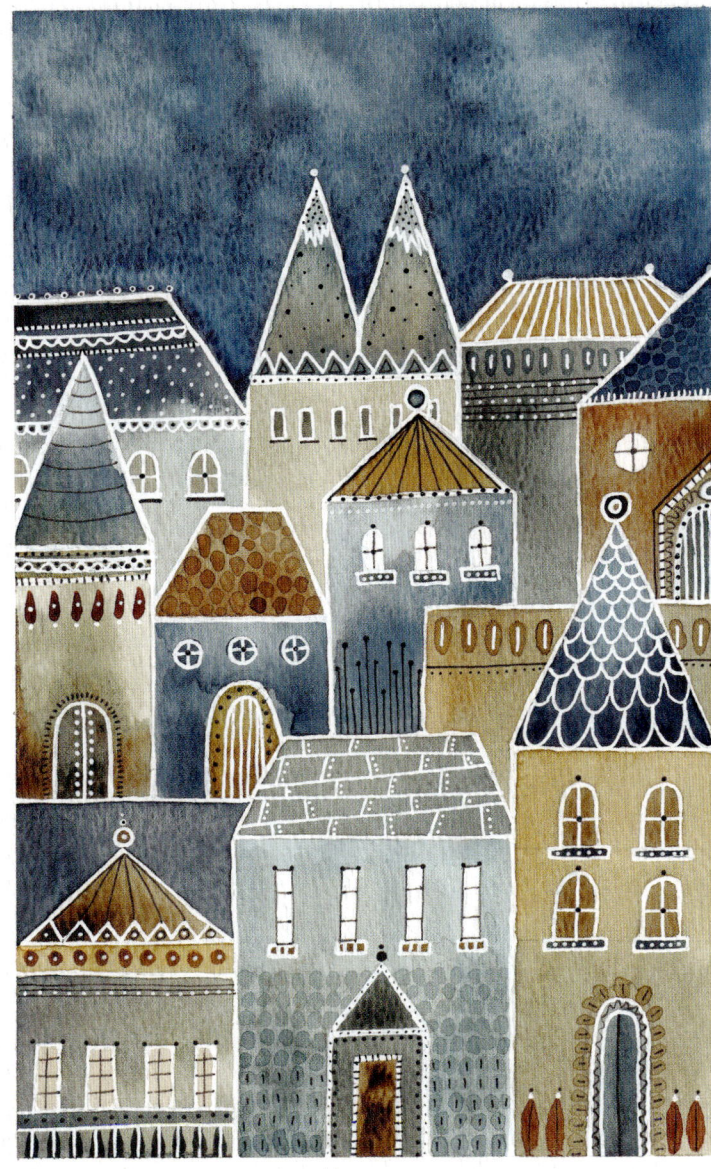

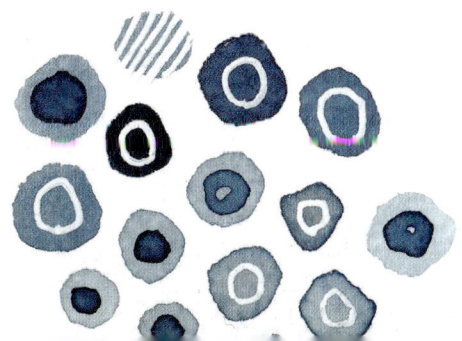

Top Tip: Remove the tape slowly, pulling it toward you at a low angle to prevent the paper tearing away from the board.

Moonlight Seascape

This moonlit landscape is darker than my normal pieces, but it's filled with atmosphere and subtle details that can be explored by the viewer. The deep, inky night-time color palette is accentuated only by the delicate white highlights, so the gold highlights on the sea and crescent moon stand out with extra sparkle.

MATERIALS

- Winsor & Newton professional watercolors
- Daler Rowney Aquafine Artboard
- Jackson's quill brush – sizes 0 and 10/0
- Filbert and round brushes
- Uni-ball Signo pen – white, 1mm (Broad)
- Posca paint pen – white, 0.7mm (Ultra Fine)
- Winsor & Newton Drawing Ink – gold
- Pencil (optional)

COLOR CHOICES

As one of my more literal, less abstract pieces, the natural color palette was a rich blend of deep blues, indigo, and black. But this would also be beautiful as a sunlit seascape, using a lighter, brighter palette of blues and sea green, with a sun-dappled sky. The yellow-gold of the sun would look striking against water-bloom clouds in the sky.

WINSOR & NEWTON COLOR REFERENCES

- Indanthrene Blue
- Indigo
- Ivory Black
- Payne's Gray

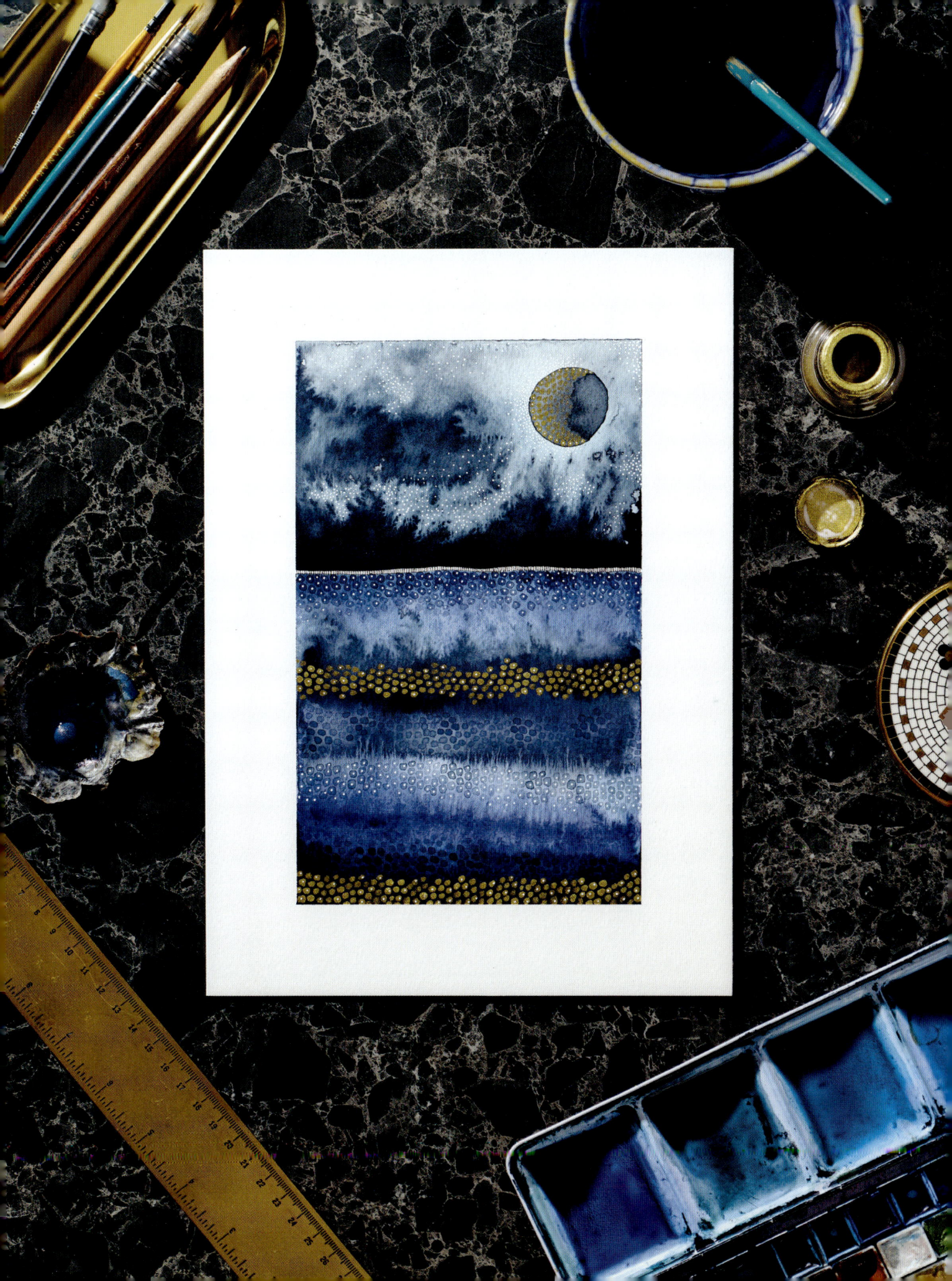

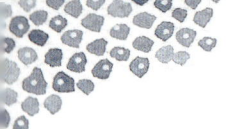

Step 1: WET PAINT

Start by masking your page. This piece uses lots of very wet paint, so ensure the edges are well stuck down (*see Techniques: Masking Borders*).

The proportions of sky to sea is about one-third to two-thirds. If helpful, add a pencil mark, then brush a very wet wash of diluted Payne's Gray across the whole page. This is the wet base to which you'll start adding extra color.

The sky

Create a deeper mix of Payne's Gray and Indigo and brush this along the waterline, working up the page about 2–3cm (¾–1¼in). Add this same mix to the top-left corner of the page, leaving white space to begin forming clouds.

Once you're happy with the color distribution, let this begin to dry for a minute or so. Dip a brush in clean water and start adding drops onto your "white" space. This will create mini blooms that will dry to create cloud shapes. This will all still be quite wet but don't worry – the drying of all this paint and water is what will create your textured sky.

The sea

Begin with a wash of color under the sky, taking care to leave a small line of white paper to divide the two areas and stop the colors merging. Work down the page, adding stripes of Indanthrene Blue, Payne's Gray, and Indigo to create waves. Alternate heavy washes with lighter ones to add contrast. Let the paper dry completely.

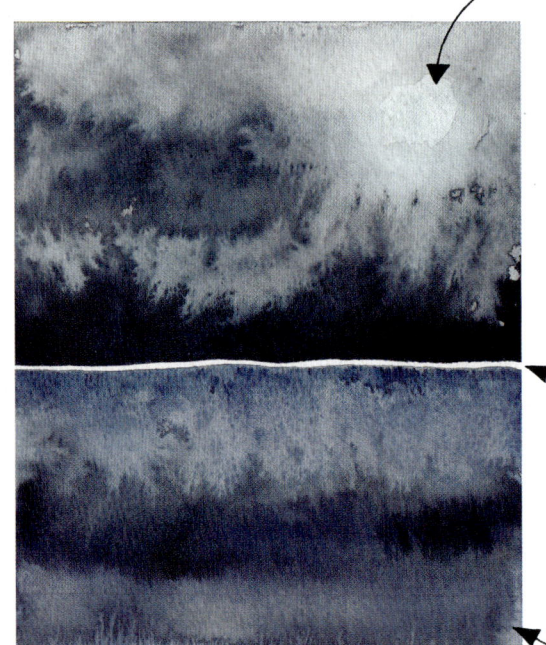

The top-right corner has been left the lightest in preparation for Step 2.

If it helps, mark the position of the waterline before you begin. Leave this strip unpainted.

Alternating light and heavy washes creates contrast and depth.

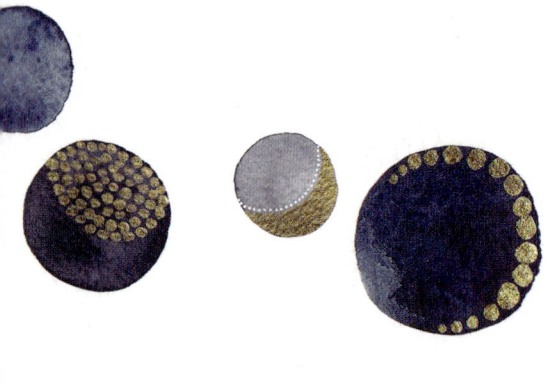

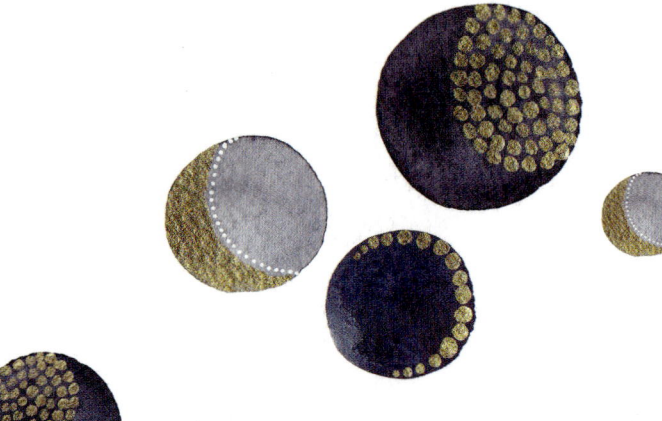

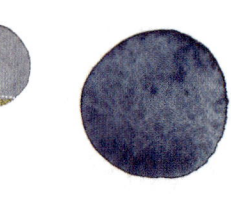

Step 2: WET ON DRY

With the first layer of paint fully dry, start adding texture with a layer of wet paint on top.

The sea

I love to see the natural shapes formed by the paint, so I sparingly added rows of raindrop spots across some of the lighter areas to create texture. Make as many of these as you like and leave to dry completely.

The sky

Take a careful look at the composition and decide where to add the moon. I chose the top right-hand corner where I left the lightest areas of paint. This will ensure the moon stands out – I've planned a full moon but you can also paint a crescent.

I used a black pen to add tiny vertical lines across the white central border between the sea and sky.

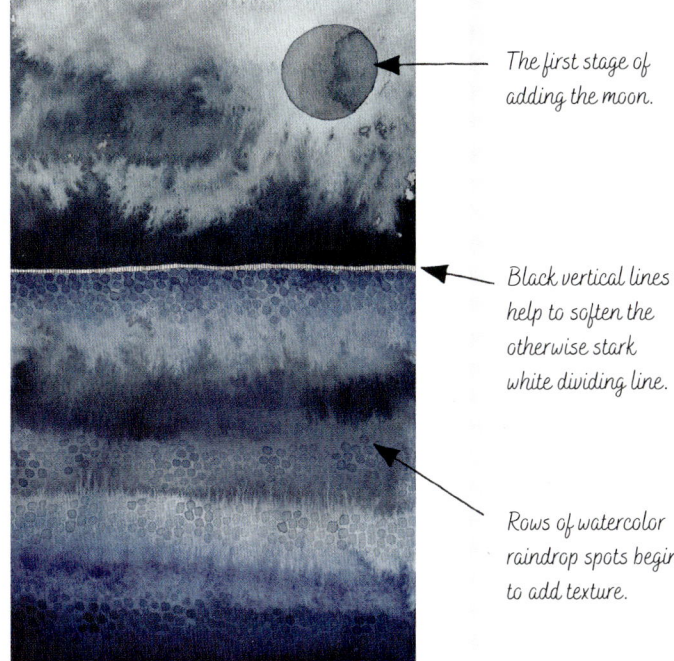

The first stage of adding the moon.

Black vertical lines help to soften the otherwise stark white dividing line.

Rows of watercolor raindrop spots begin to add texture.

Step 3: WHITE EMBELLISHMENTS

It's time to add white details and highlights. These are helpful as this piece is dark, so using touches of white add areas of interest, or lighten up areas that feel too dark or look muddy. I've stuck to white around the moon and in the clouds to brighten things up. I've also added white dots across the top of some waves to give the impression of the crest of waves and sea foam.

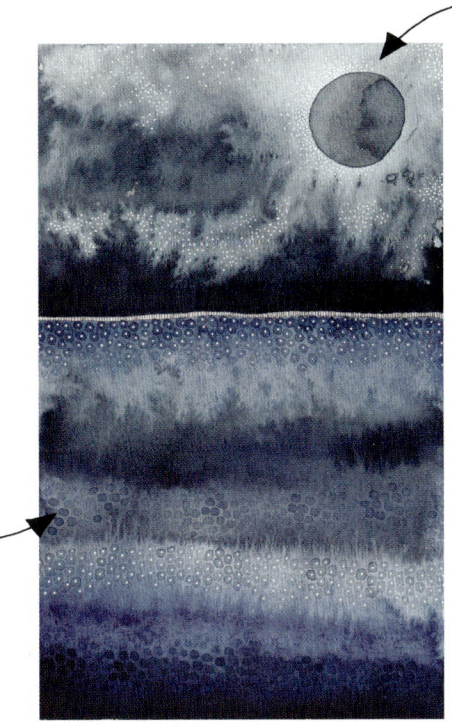

I added scattered white dots in various densities, with them being "brightest" around the moon.

Dots scattered loosely across the waves give a sense of movement and depth.

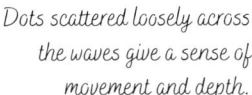

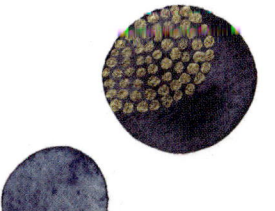

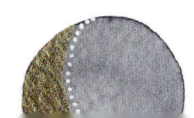

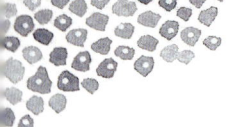

Step 4: GOLD EMBELLISHMENTS

Now for the fun part – adding the gold highlights! As mentioned in the introduction, gold adds drama and sparkles to the deep richness of the colors in the piece.

I've used gold to add contrast to two of the darkest waves and highlight the crescent of the full moon. You could add gold stars in the sky if you like – just go with what feels right to you. I would encourage you to stand back and look at your piece before adding too much gold though, sometime less is more (and it's easier to add than remove!).

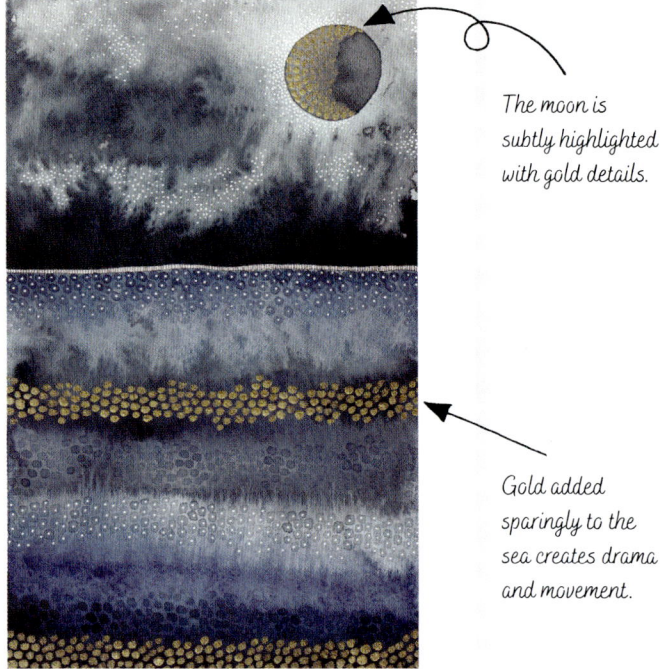

The moon is subtly highlighted with gold details.

Gold added sparingly to the sea creates drama and movement.

Step 5: FINAL TOUCHES

Step back to look at the painting again and add a few more white dots if needed. Then your painting is complete!

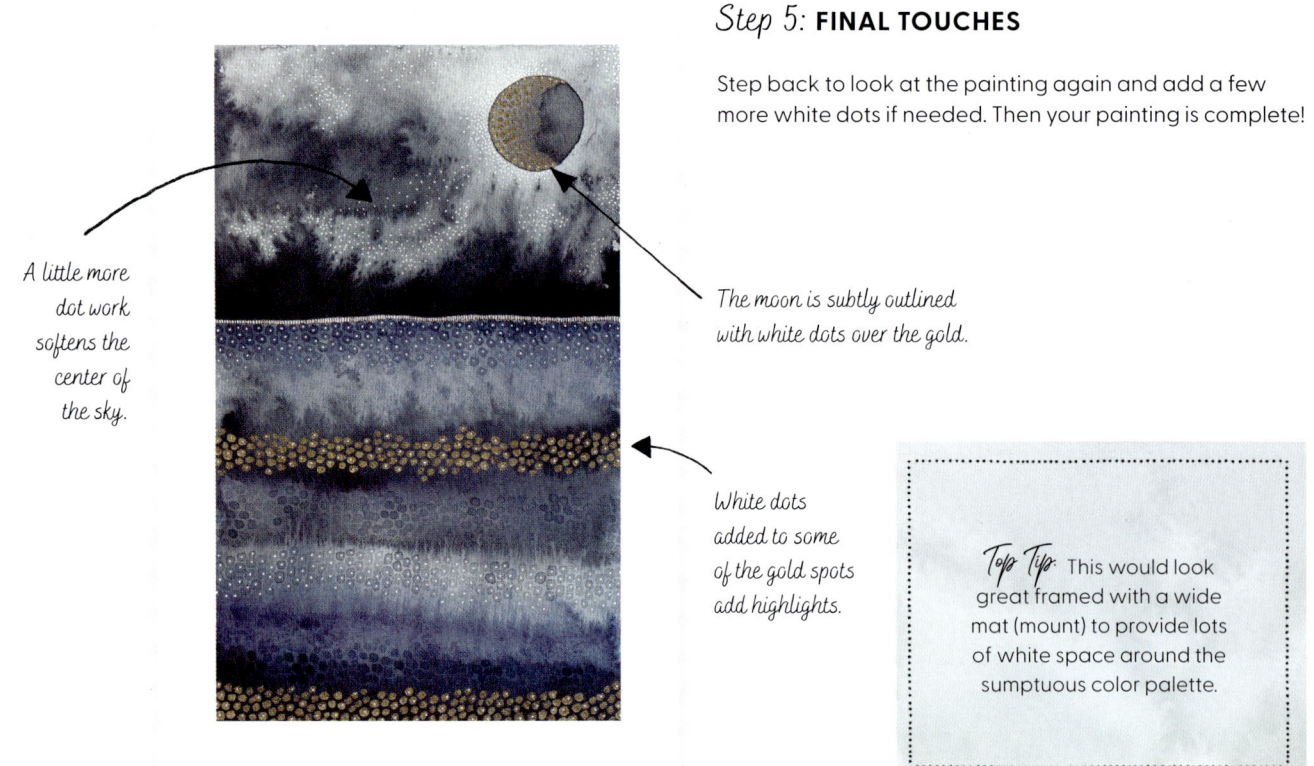

A little more dot work softens the center of the sky.

The moon is subtly outlined with white dots over the gold.

White dots added to some of the gold spots add highlights.

Top Tip: This would look great framed with a wide mat (mount) to provide lots of white space around the sumptuous color palette.

More inspiration

This piece is "day" to the main project's "night". Using the same basic techniques, I changed the color palette to softer, paler blues. Instead of a moody night sky, an abstract sun sits in a sky awash with wispy clouds. These paintings would look lovely displayed as a pair, framed and placed side by side.

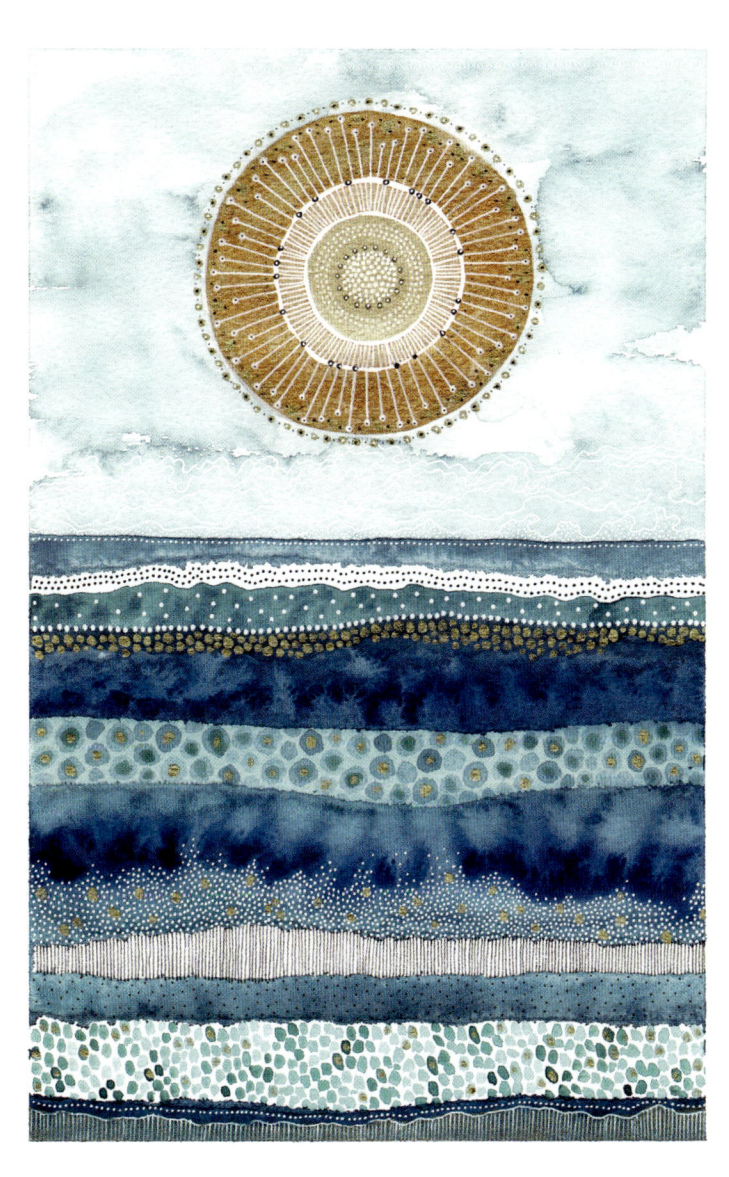

About the Author

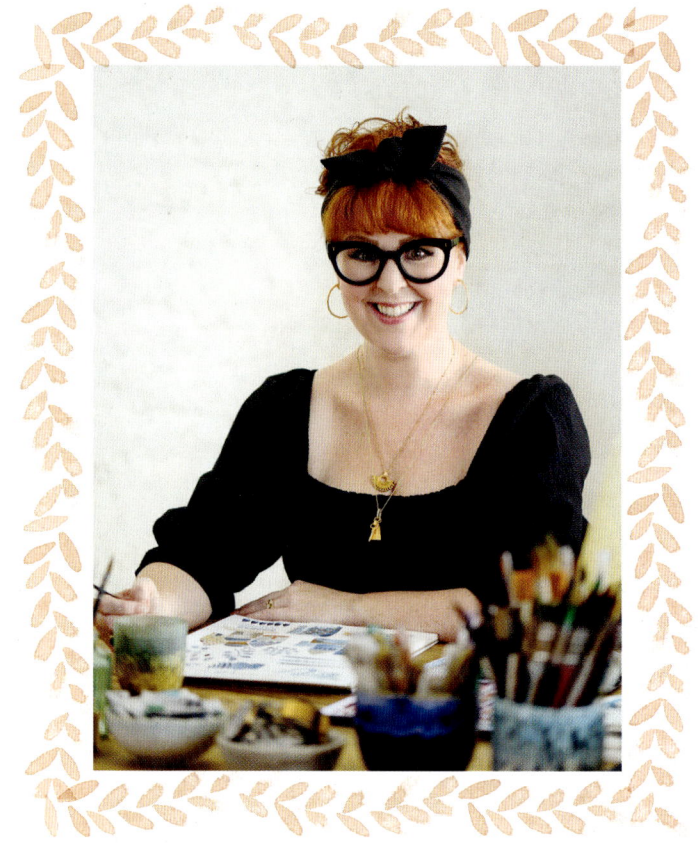

Kate Rebecca Leach is an artist, illustrator and tutor based in Hertfordshire, UK.

She founded her brand, Essoldo Design, in 2020 and since then has been lucky enough to have built a community of over 100,000 Instagram followers, sold her work in more 35 countries worldwide, and licensed products across the UK, Europe, and the USA. *Creative Abstract Watercolor* is Kate's first book.

Kate would love to see how you're using the book and your experiments with abstract watercolors. Share your photos on social media using the hashtag **#EssoldoAbstractWatercolor** for your chance to feature on her social media channels! You can find out more about Kate and her art here:

Instagram + Facebook: @essoldodesign

Website: essoldodesign.com

Acknowledgments

This book wouldn't have been possible without the love and support of those closest to me.

To my brilliant partner Anthony – you've encouraged me from the start of my art journey, and without you here cheering me on, I don't know where I'd be! Your love and support (not to mention graphic design prowess!) has helped shape the experience – thank you.

To my parents and brother for their unwavering faith in me. You've always been there, from childhood trips to Kew Gardens to study the flowers, to my arty student days and beyond – thanks for nurturing my creativity.

This book wouldn't have been possible without Ame, Jenny, and the team at David & Charles for making my dream of becoming a published author a reality. Your guidance every step of the way has made the (slightly terrifying) prospect of writing a book an absolute joy. I hope you're as pleased with the result as I am.

Finally, a huge thanks to my supportive Instagram family. Without your daily kind words, feedback and positive energy, I wouldn't be where I am today. This book is for you!

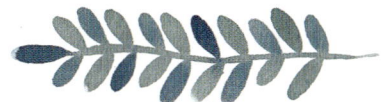

Recommended Brands

These are the brands I use in my own work, and throughout the book:

Paints
- Daler Rowney
- Kuretake
- Skrim Watercolors
- The Art of Soil
- Winsor & Newton

Paper
- Arches
- Canson
- Daler Rowney
- St Cuthberts Mill

Brushes
- Daler Rowney
- Jackson's Art
- Panart

Inks
- Winsor & Newton Drawing Ink

Pens
- Posca
- Staedtler fineliners
- Uni-ball Signo

Masking fluid
- Winsor & Newton Art Masking Fluid

Masking tape
- Frog Tape Delicate Surface Painter's Tape – Yellow

Ceramic palettes
- Muddy Ceramic
- Mud Made Ceramics

Brush pots
- The Love of Pots

Index

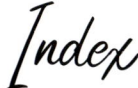

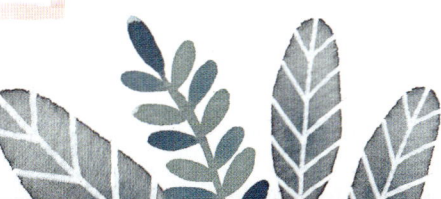

A DAVID AND CHARLES BOOK
© David and Charles, Ltd 2024

David and Charles is an imprint of David and Charles, Ltd
Suite A, Tourism House, Pynes Hill, Exeter, EX2 5WS

EU GPSR Authorised Representative:
Logos Europe, 9 rue Nicolas Poussin,
17000, La Rochelle, France
Email: contact@logoseurope.eu

Text and Designs © Kate Rebecca Leach 2024
Layout and Photography © David and Charles, Ltd 2024

First published in the UK and USA in 2024

ISBN-13: 9781446310564 paperback
ISBN-13: 9781446311936 EPUB
ISBN-13: 9781446311912 PDF

This book has been printed on paper from approved
suppliers and made from pulp from sustainable sources.

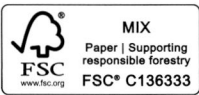

Printed in China through Asia Pacific Offset for:
David and Charles, Ltd
Suite A, Tourism House, Pynes Hill, Exeter, EX2 5WS

10 9

Publishing Director: Ame Verso
Managing Editor: Jeni Chown
Project Editor: Jenny Fox-Proverbs
Head of Design: Anna Wade
Designers: Sam Staddon and Lee-May Lim
Pre-press Designer: Susan Reansbury
Photography and Art Direction: Tom Hargreaves
Production Manager: Beverley Richardson

David and Charles publishes high-quality books on a
wide range of subjects. For more information visit www.
davidandcharles.com.

Share your makes with us on social media using
#dandcbooks and follow us on Facebook and Instagram
by searching for @dandcbooks.

Layout of the digital edition of this book may vary
depending on reader hardware and display settings.